Run!

From Civil War to the NFL

The Jehuu Caulcrick Story

The Bullet Doesn't Pick and Choose

By Bill Burk

RUN! From Civil War to the NFL
The Jehuu Caulcrick Story
The Bullet Doesn't Pick and Choose

Published Through William Burk

Copyright © 2023 by William Burk
Cover art copyright © 2023 by Nina Romeo

ISBN: 979-8-9884092-0-5 (Paperback Edition)
ISBN: 979-8-9884092-1-2 (eBook Edition)

All Hail, Liberia, Hail!
All hail, Liberia, hail! (All hail!)
All hail, Liberia, hail! (All hail!)
This glorious land of liberty, Shall long be ours.
Though new her name, Great be her fame,
And mighty be her powers, And mighty be her powers.
Long live Liberia, happy land!
A home of glorious liberty, By God's command!
                    Liberian National Anthem (Part 1)

All Hail, Liberia, Hail!
All hail, Liberia, hail! (All hail!)
All hail, Liberia, hail! (All hail!)
This glorious land of liberty, Shall long be ours.
Though new her name, Great be her fame,
And mighty be her powers, And mighty be her powers.
Long live Liberia, happy land!
A home of glorious liberty, By God's command!
Liberian National Anthem (Part 1)

Table of Contents

Dedication

"JEHUU, YOU BETTER get that sheepskin."

Although Jehuu led Clymer to great success on the field and eventually star at Michigan State, Coach Mac would always emphasize to him the importance of getting a degree. He took a genuine interest in guiding all athletes throughout their journey in high school and well beyond.

That is why high school sports matter! Lessons learned on fields, courts, and track leave a lasting impact and help shape future successes. Coach Mac was a firm believer in this. Throughout Jehuu's career as a football player at Clymer he scored countless touchdowns. He once asked Coach Mac if he could do a touchdown dance after scoring. Coach let him know while he was free to do his dance, it would be his last for a longtime. Winning and losing with grace and humility were two important lessons to be instilled upon Pirate teams.

Putting the team first was another valuable lesson to be taught. With Coach Mac, the needs of the team always came first. Jehuu and his backfield mate, AJ Maleki experienced much success because of a great offensive line opening up holes and winning the battle at the line of scrimmage. Everyone doing their job so the team could succeed.

While Jehuu would be a part of championship football teams, win a state championship as a shot putter, and become a team captain at Michigan State, Coach Mac would most definitely say his greatest accomplishment was getting his college degree. He was always working to help athletes grow and develop in ways that would benefit them well beyond their playing days. If you talk with Coach Mac you quickly understand he was always more interested in a young person's development more than any wins, championships or accolades.

A leader needs to be a great role model for others. Coach Mac would be the first to tell you that the most important person in his life was his wife Sally. She was always there to love and support him. Pirate teams will remember her famous BBQ ham season-ending dinners.

High school sports matter and make a difference in the lives of young people. Coach Mac dedicated his life to making a difference in those he worked with. As he is fond of saying, "the lesson is more important than the result." To Coach Mac it was never about the championships or accolades, although there were many. It was always about the relationships and the lessons to be taught.

Mike McMullin 2022

Introduction

THIS IS A story about boys.

The first boy, the real one, was Jerome Blomo, a child of Liberia, Africa. He lived in a carefree world surrounded by people who cherished and nurtured him. He loved football (soccer), played with cousins and friends and neighbors in a suburb of a big capital city. He lived in a fine apartment then a resort plantation, then in a big house. His mother was a nursing student, then a resort manager. His father was head of security for a famous Liberian General. His grandparents were government workers and owned a large farm. He was a happy, spoiled child of Liberia.

And then civil war came to his doorstep.

After that he became Jehuu Caulcrick (Jayyou Call-crick). A different boy, one who wandered the country as a refugee, wondering where his next meal would come from, when he'd drink again, where he'd sleep. This boy was forced to survive the viscous world of murder and torture that was The Second Liberian Civil War.

This boy is real. You could find him today and shake his hand.

. . . .

I met Jehuu when he coached my son in high school football. I knew of him before that, of course, everyone in western New York did. His skills on a football field (on the track and basketball courts as well) made him one of those athletic prodigies that pass through all sorts of small towns, decade after decade; the ones trapped in perpetual motion on the field and courts by bloated memories,

xv

barroom arguments, faded sports pages, and hyperbolic legend. Everyone who knew Jehuu as a football player also knew some version of his past, innuendo passed down and filtered through small town rumor mills. His story wasn't without controversy.

"He came from Africa. How did he end up in Clymer, of all places?"

"He's 25 years old."

"He's on steroids. Nobody could be that big without steroids."

"He was in a civil war."

Some were true, most were bullshit, embellishment of imagination.

My own uninformed opinion, before I met the man, was like most, that Jehuu was so much older than the boys he ground up on the high school fields of small-school Western, New York. That he was physically mature beyond a reasonable competitive advantage, that he was patently unfair.

Then he went to Michigan State University on a full ride scholarship. Then he started at running back for a Big 10 college, then he broke records, was a team captain. That's when I knew he was the real deal. So I transformed from skeptic to fan, and I looked closer. Every ex-athlete (like me) is a cynic when it comes to later generations. Until they're not. Then comes the respect.

So, I embraced other rumors and stories. The ones that described his journey to Findley Lake, New York (his home), to Clymer High School, the building lore of his athletic achievement while there, to Michigan State and beyond to the National Football League. I studied up.

What I learned was fascinating. So fascinating, in fact, that I wrote a book. Something I'd never done before.

· · · ·

There's another boy.

His name was Hope, and he was forced through the eye of a different needle than Jehuu.

He came out a *Ghost*.

Ghost is imagined. He's a blend of true stories about boys who didn't escape Liberian civil war, like Jehuu. He's a synthesis of experiences that Jehuu missed by just that much, by fickle fate, by oblivious randomness, turning left at a crossroad instead of right. *Ghost* represents my fascination with the child soldiers of Africa, how they came to be, and, importantly, how Jehuu and his family avoided the fate of so many other Liberian refugees.

This boy is out there, in my imagination, no less real for the fact that he never existed.

He is a child soldier.

. . . .

There are women as well.

Bonita Caulcrick is Jehuu's mother. She is real, lived through her own version of the war. I've shared her memories word-for-word, the best way to understand her part of this adventure. She's one of the rocks that Jehuu bases his life on, his brilliant inspiration. If Bonita's name is attached to it, she said it.

Other women weave Jehuu's story. Joann is his grandmother and what Liberians call the Big Jue. Her talent and resourcefulness, not to mention her religious piety -along with her husband and Jehuu's grandfather David- helped shepherd her family from fairly certain catastrophe to a life outside of Liberia.

And Mardea, Jehuu's sister. The amazing story of her time in Liberia, and her escape mirrors Jehuu's experience. You could easily exchange their names and not be too far from the truth of their mutual existence during their two years as Liberian refugees.

. . . .

Last, and least important, is me.

I won't go to Liberia.

I might have, when I was young, more daring, more agile. Maybe when I was brave, when I cared to say I've done something important and daring.

Maybe before I soaked myself in craft beer, and white-suburban-privilege. Before 401ks, USGA handicap, a yard to mow, sun-screen to consider. Maybe before I got comfortable with ambiguity, and an average life to jealously guard. Maybe when I was able to get out of my own way, and the world was less capable of cutting my throat.

No, I'll do better to look at the place from a distance, across an ocean. I'll nurse my sorrow for those poor, abused Liberians who suffered at the hands of horrible men. I'll try to express my moral outrage at their assault on civility and humanity.

I don't know journalism and biography, I don't know the expected or required commitment of the discipline, or the unspoken rules of the craft. I don't know if that makes me a hypocrite as a writer or intellectually lazy. But I'm not going to Liberia.

I don't want to die. Not yet.

. . . .

When I least expected it, I lost my way. I wandered in a haze of rote daily activity, treading in self-doubt and depression. Depression presented to me as endless hopelessness. Minor setbacks were event horizons. The wrong song on the radio, a stop-light that didn't co-operate, weather that didn't oblige my will…all part of a conspiracy to end my days. That's the thing with depression, it feels like the end, all the time. I was kept afloat, out of an abyss, out of the well of suck, by desperately putting one foot in front of the other, over and over again, by my kids and my job, doing what you're supposed to do, holding at arms-length abject misery mitigated only by panic and despondency. I lost rage, my tool for coping. I lost grit and determination, instilled into me by my parents. I was a television character with amnesia, in a drug fog. I hadn't the ability to complete the serenity prayer; I did not know the difference between the things I could control and everything else in the world.

Mark Twain said, "The difference between the right word and the almost right word is the difference between lightening and a lightening bug." Find the almost right word and you can be illuminated. Find the right word and you are struck. Writing became a salve for me, something I could control. I could command the light to turn green, the sun to shine, the plane to be on time.

So I had to write this story, for Jehuu, for his family, and for me.

. . . .

I am here to tell a story, for a couple of reasons. The first is it's compelling. You need to hear it. It's inspirational. It's bleak. It's redemptive. It's rough and it's brutal. It's a healthy dose of perspective in a world where people believe life is hard when their cell phone shows one bar instead of four; when their flight is delayed, when gas prices go up. I've done that, fell for the idea that my inconvenience is the end of the world.

It's a good story about a good family who miraculously found a good life.

It's Jehuu Caulcrick's story. How he went from a seven-year old running around Liberia during a war he couldn't possibly understand, to running around football fields in the United States. It's the story of his escape from there, and his life in one of the most entitled kingdoms there is, the National Football League.

It's a story about his mother, Bonita, who left Liberia to carve out a different life for her children, only to find out that a war would separate them for more than two years.

It's a story about people in a far-away place who built their own version of Hell, then dragged a bunch of people around it; the warlords and politicians and diabolical African men who perpetrated death and murder and rape on their country.

It's the story about Liberian kids who didn't make it out. A story of child soldiers who died by the thousands. The story of what might have become of the Caulcrick children, Jehuu and Mardea, had they not threaded a needle of survival that's as improbable as it is satisfying.

It's a story of Liberia's lost generation, and I have to tell it, I'll feel better if I do.

It's Jehuu's story, but in a way, it's my story.

Author's Note: RUN! is told in three "Books" using three "voices". Chapters titled "Jehuu" are first person from his perspective as told to the author (a biography, if you will) to the best of his memory. Some dialogue is an interpretation of those memories for the sake of a good read. Chapters titled "Bonita" are directly quoted from interviews. Chapters titled "A Child Soldier" are historical-fictional narrative based on real accounts of child soldiers of Liberia. All other chapters are the voice of the author.

BOOK 1

TWO BOYS IN LIBERIA

Prologue

A YOUNG BOY from Liberia, let's call him Jehuu, hurries through the front doors of a large (intact) brick building.

His new backpack bounces across his broad back (the old pack, the one he hauled around for two years, was discarded in the African bush months ago). He blinks up at the lights, down at the polished floor, grinning at the bright white sneakers at the bottom of his thick legs. He holds one shoe out to admire it, balances on the other, and thinks, *New shoes. New clothes.*

A hundred other children rush around inside the building, a beehive of energy. Adults, wearing important clothes, carrying important papers, are sprinkled among the children. They move to important parts of the building to do important things. The cacophony is confusing but engaging. A door slams down a deep hallway echoing off the tiled floor and antiseptic walls. He winces involuntarily, those hefty legs twitch, his hands drop to the side, a sprinter's initiate. He doesn't run…this time. Instead he relaxes his clenched shoulders, smiles, and moves down the hall to his classroom.

. . . .

That same boy of Liberia finds himself on a football field. He's grown now, almost a man. For high schools in New York state, it's a week of conditioning before the players are allowed to hit in full pads. A week of sweating in late August heat, running sprints, up and down hills, stretching and pushing a blocking sled around.

Finally, the first day of real blocking and tackling comes–time to hit someone, to get hit back. This day the sun is blazing already, hazy and heavy.

Teenage football players gear-up in the locker room half asleep, sweating before they get to the field, staining uniforms already yellowed from years of handing-down, seniors to juniors, juniors to sophomores, on down the line.

White is a bad color for warriors anyways.

"Let's go! On the field in fifteen!"

To get to the field, they walk out the locker room door, across the hot asphalt parking lot, a staggered line of boys, cleats clicking dully. A twist of the mouth tells them coach wants to smile but won't. He's seen more than a few first day in pads.

"Let's go Pirates! Summer break's over. This is football!"

The muggy morning lays a blanket of dew over the field. Steam rises where the sun touches it. The air bakes the practice field, armors the team in sweat.

This is the boy of Liberia's fifth first day in pads. He is a senior in high school in the United States of America. Improbably. This field has become his home, since the day he stepped on it as an eighth grader with big legs, a big smile, and no clue about the sport of football. That day, the first of his football career, he grabbed the football and ran to his destiny, across the field and into the end zone, the very first time he touched the ball. It was easy. He didn't exactly know what to do with the ball, so he dropped it and walked back to where the play started, fifty-seven yards away.

Today, he breathes in the grass, the churned-up turf. He smiles inside his helmet, leans against a teammate who struggles for balance against his weight. He adjusts kneepads, and socks. He's ready to hit, to be hit.

Bang bang pop pop pop. Sounds of summer maintenance on the school ring in the heavy air from across the parking lot. Roofers, painters, masons crawl over the square block building, wielding power tools and working-men curses. "Watch that compressor line!" "Slower on the winch." "Pour the asphalt faster, dammit!" A drill whirrs, a nail-gun pops, compressors bang and wheeze, molten tar hisses.

On the field, the team stretches in short, straight lines. Thick, tired blood wakes and flows along with sweat. Coach sees the boys glance at the sounds from the school, the hard labor. "You want to go over there? Do some real work?" Nobody answers.

Line up! A hundred times the boy has done this drill. Since eighth grade. It's a running-backs drill, a warm up. High-step, lift your knees, cleats clear the practice dummies, pump your arms, keep your head up, cover the nose of the ball with your dominant hand. Nothing to it. The mind wanders between reps. He looks at guys bent over, hands on knees, heads bowed, sucking air. The ones who didn't prepare. The ones getting a wake-up call a little too late. When it's his turn, he takes the ball and starts down the line. He makes it look easy. This boy from Liberia is bigger and a lot faster than the other boys. He finishes the exercise and gets back in line. He waits to do it again.

The practice field is churned up from the army of cleats pounding out two-a-days, no time for the turf to recover and repair. *Crack crack, pop pop*, echoes into the morning haze. A water break is coming. High knees, pump your arms, get to the other side of the line of practice bags, the other side of the bodies.

Run Jehuu, run.

The churned ground, torn up by pounding feet.

The smell of sweat, of bodies being pushed.

The *pop* and *crack* across the field.

Run Jehuu. Run!

Jehuu, 1995

I sweat, deep and heavy into my uniform.

It's a flood in this heat. A single drop starts at the back of my neck and improbably moves up, against gravity. It settles under the lower rim of my helmet. I feel it as a foreign sensation, Sweat doesn't move that way. I frown against my facemask.

One drop of sweat ignores the natural flow of water seeking its lowest level. One drop that instead burrows back into the pores, seeps, sucks, drains. One drop and the flood of perspiration on this humid day on longer defines me in the here and now. One drop that triggers memories of the past.

. . . .

My sympathetic nervous system is suddenly flooded; fight or flight! There's that voice in my ear, old and hurried and urgent.

Run Jehuu. Run.

My eyes close on a memory. My brain folds over onto itself. The world is no longer in front of me, it's behind my eyes. My head swivels, side to side, looks anywhere but at the dead bodies at my feet. How did they get there?

Pop, pop in the distance. A voice in my ear.

Run Jehuu!

From somewhere someone yells, "Sniper. There! Get down!"

I peer across a city street, at the buildings where snipers settle, where they do their work, where they shoot your grandpa or grandma. I frown, confused. That makes no sense. I'm doing the bag drill. High knees, protect the ball. I shake sweat off my face, open my eyes to a different world. My helmet is a cave. It closes around my head. I feel it press my temples, push me down. From somewhere behind my eyes, there's a flash, a bright point of light. The ground jumps. Then that whisper.

Run Jehuu. Run.

Pop, crack, pop pop poppop. That's the workers at the school, right?

No. I know that sound. Those are weapons. Guns and bombs.

From somewhere in my past, my grandpa screams, *Ahhhhh. Hit!*

Run, Jehuu. It's time to run. Grandma Joanne in my ear, a whisper on the wind.

"Where, Grandma? Where should I run?" I am calm. I'm a good runner. I've run before.

To the other side Jehuu.

I see my sister and cousins flee across the narrow road, between buildings. The other side. Bodies lie in my path through the churned-up earth, holes made by exploded mortar. Some of the bodies are bloated from the mad heat. Insects infect the blue-black flesh. Some bodies are still alive, writhing. Stark, thick blood seeps into the dirt and gravel road, it pools in puddles and makes scarlet mud, like after a rain.

Lift your knees, pump your arms, keep your head up. If you trip on a body, get up before the they find you.

The bullet does not pick and choose.

Run Jehuu, run.

. . . .

"Jehuu? Son? Are you okay?"

Grandpa David's voice cuts through a buzz inside my football helmet.

"I think so. The soldiers? On the road?" I squint into a thick fog, but there's nothing there. I should see a street. I should see dull white plaster buildings through the smoke. I should see where the bullets hit people, see them on the dirt road, dead or dying. The guns *pop pop* and *crack*. I listen for the whistle of mortar. I know it's a battle. I know we're caught in it. I know because I was told to run. I ran to the other side. Knees high, arms pumping. Step and leap over the dead bodies, my backpack bouncing in time with my strong stride, my sneakers eating up space. My head is heavy, my neck aches.

There's a hand on my shoulder, I feel the weight, but not the touch. Grandpa leans close. He whispers. "There's no soldiers, Jehuu. There's no street."

That's not right. "No guns?"

7

"No guns. Just football." The voice is soothing. The hot breath on the side of my face is calm.

"Okay," I blink. There is no grandpa. No Liberia. No Odziki or Joseph or Mardea. There is only a football field in western, New York. Clymer. I sit in a grass field, not a city street. Coach Mac is by my side. He hunches in a catcher's squat, ballcap moved up off his brow. His maroon tee reads Pirate Football. Behind him, boys in uniform run the small hill behind the practice field. They strain to look my way. Coach frowns, concerned. "I'm your coach. Your football coach. You're here now. Safe. Up you go, Jehuu. You got your feet under you?"

"I think so." My legs are slow to cooperate. My eyes don't focus.

"Where did you go just now, son? Where was your head?" Coach grips my upper arm.

Liberia.

Liberia, 1992

A boy in Liberia, Africa, we'll call him Ghost, lowers his head between his knees, protecting his eyes and face from dust and debris falling around him.

The fallout of a mortar blast blankets his arms and bony shoulders. The debris takes a minute to settle. He flicks fragments of cement and gravel from between his *Four-Wheel-Drives,* the rubber sandals worn by the lethal *Small Boys Unit of Liberia.* He wears a t-shirt that will never be clean again. His elbows rest on bloody, torn jeans waiting for the next mortar to land.

It doesn't take long. The next concussion follows the sharp whistle of the mortar's lethal path, and the world in front of him explodes. He's showered again in soil and remains, construction debris, rebar, glass, parts of the earth, and pieces of human beings. *Bam,* a shell lands and rubble busts to smaller pieces. The air fills with fragments and more dust.

He's mostly gray now, the boy in Liberia, covered completely in dust, his black skin shows only where sweat washes away the filth. The blanket of detritus keeps the flies away and hides the tattoos and scars that marked him as a rebel. He's a wraith crouching beside a hole in the ground. He doesn't move. Clouds pass behind his eyes. Then a memory, another life, one where he has a family and a home, a toy, a bed, a front door. The memory squats in a corner of his crowded mind and fights to take hold, to plant a seed, to grow hope, but the ground is a burned-out, lunar, inhospitable place. Nothing good can live there. He ducks his head and whispers, *No Hope, only Ghost.*

Earlier that day, Ghost was one of the child soldiers that attacked the city from the south. He waded through the treacherous swamps that frame the capital city of Liberia. He fought government soldiers, firing his AK47, reloading, and firing again on the run. He staved off thirst, bullets, and the predators that took most of his squad. He survived.

Now, he hides in plain sight in the big city. He looks from his place in the shadows next to the ruined ocean-side resort where he sits in the dust, his back to the swampland, where a hundred -a thousand- boys were slaughtered, either by bullets or swallowed up by the creatures that feed in the everglade. No men, no officers were sacrificed that day, just boys. It took all his skills as a hunter and soldier to finally, impossibly, escape that nightmare. When he emerged, covered in blood and the grime of the swamp, he followed the overhead vapor trail and signature whine of the fifty caliber shells into the center of the city to this spot, unseen by government soldiers, the ECOMOG. Forty at a time, the shells fly through the sultry air, easy to follow. The boy knows where they'll land, so he goes to that place to watch.

He is, after all, a Ghost.

. . . .

When Charles Taylor's Liberian rebels, the National Patriotic Front of Liberia (*NPFL*), bombed Monrovia, the first shells took out The Ducor Hotel, a Liberian five-star seaside resort, built at the edge of the Pacific Ocean. (They were supposed to destroy a government airfield, but whatever.) The ground shook, and people scattered, screaming, covering their heads, dragging their young. The missiles produced devastating explosions, ripping concrete and rebar, shattering glass, throwing leftover furniture and the limbs of squatters (paying guests long gone since the siege of Monrovia) into the air, broken and lifeless. The next series of ordnance landed…in the exact same place, as if to prove a point that didn't need proven, pulverizing that which was already pulverized, making pieces into rubble, rubble into dust, dismembering what was already dismembered.

No one should have been surprised by the bombing. Ghost certainly wasn't. Public radio sent out a warning the day before the shelling started. The voice of Taylor's top general John T. Richardson said, "I suggest you move from there because tomorrow I'm gonna rain all hell on you guys." He'd later say about the bombing, "We were aiming pretty close. That's the best we could do. People were trying to kill us. We were trying to kill them back."

That was the warning. Where people should move, and who you guys were wasn't clear. But the radio blast came anyways, right in front of the cannon blast.

Past The Ducor seawall, a cement staircase winds from the hotel pool to the ocean. What was once an ornate passage from one body of water to another, for the rich and the foreign, was transformed into a gaping maw of busted architecture. The statues that once framed the walkway, mutilated. The people who inhabited the decimated resort when war began and the paying guests escaped, the same.

· · · ·

The boy, Ghost, remembers seeing the big guns when his squad bivouacked at the Firestone Plantation some sixty miles from where he crouches now. Fifty-millimeter cannons pointed northwest toward Monrovia. His commander said "Shells will be falling all over the city." The soldier aiming the big gun confided that the guidance system was frozen. The guns could only fire in one direction, one distance at a time.

So shells pour into the capital city, landing within meters of each other, and the boy sits still, while others scatter, trying to guess the time and place of each explosion.

After an hour of this puzzling practice and hundreds of shells sent into the resort ruins, locals gather outside the range of the blasts to whistle along with the entry of each projectile. It's a game to see who can pick the rockets out of the sky first. *There it is. Here it comes!* The smell and taste of metal fills the air. A large, feral dog (rare to see these days in the city where food is so scarce) runs into the ruin and grabs what looks like a human hand. The spectators howl with glee when the next bomb lands and the hound disappears in a red mist. The sultry Liberian air holds aloft the fine cement dust and red dog-mist, making a cloud. Dare-devils run up to the cloud, touch it and dash back to safety, making catastrophe into sport.

Eventually the mortars are re-directed. The carnage moves from The Ducor Hotel to Stockton Creek, then James Spriggs Airfield, pulverizing whatever is there.

· · · ·

This is the first stage of a military assault called Operation Octopus. It is the latest attempt by Charles Taylor and the NPFL to take over the capital city, the precarious seat of the Liberian government. It began that morning with a multi-armed offensive that attacked the city from all points of the compass. The confusion and tragedy of the assault is defined by this misguided shelling, and the massacre of the Small Boys Unit in the Monrovian swamps.

The Liberians watching this shit show, very accustomed to senseless chaos, smile at the firework display, as if it's staged for their personal entertainment, a Broadway show, a cabaret. When the missiles change trajectory yet again and land harmlessly in the ocean, they laugh and whoop at the spectacle of force and power that's swallowed by the sea.

They are tired, poor, starved, and wretched from the three years of war waged between government forces, rebel armies, hundreds of warlords, and any rogue with a weapon. Their city, the shining hub of western Africa, is a cesspool of disease and poverty. The beach that's smoldering in mortar holes is called Poop Beach because that's where Liberians defecate. Their city has no power, very little food or potable water, and definitely no septic system to remove waste. The city, their city, bursts at the seams.

But today, they are entertained.

1

Jehuu

"A little rain each day will fill the rivers to overflowing."
—*Liberian proverb*

MY DAD WAS Kru.

He survived an early wave of Liberian genocide, one of the regular cleansings that sparked so many of the civil wars in my home country. He was the head of security for Thomas Quiwonkpa, a general in the Liberian army. His association with the wrong people made his life in Liberia impossible. He fled, reluctantly, and we erased him from our lives, burned his pictures, threw his effects into the ocean, including a precious set of dog tags he left for me.

He was ambitious, General Quiwonkpa. When you're ambitious in Liberia's military, you better also have a good share of the guns and money. He didn't.

I was two when he fled the country, and to keep safe from continued retribution from his enemies, I gave up my given name, Jerome Blomo, and took on the name of my mother's family. I became Jehuu Caulcrick fulltime.

My mum was Bassa tribe. She moved to the United States shortly after my father left, looking for a better life for me and my sister. This was just before the second Liberian civil war arrived in my neighborhood. Her leaving was probably a blessing for her. She might not have survived the war. It was a burden for my sister and me. But Liberia is a country of big, ranging families, and we were left with my grandparents. It wasn't unusual. When she left we waved goodbye from my grand-parents front porch, and went back to playing with our friends. When you're seven years old you don't know what the world can do to goodbyes.

I only saw her one more time in the next three years.

When I was nine, on the refugee road, my grandpa was shot in the leg, a sniper bullet that was meant for the back of my head. Grandma pulled the bullet out.

When I was twenty-six, I played one down in the National Football League for the Buffalo Bills. My Blomo thighs now thunderous, rhinoceros-muscled weapons. I grabbed a football from a professional quarterback, plunged forward for one yard, a lifetime of running coalesced into that moment.

In between, a lot happened.

. . . .

I was born in Liberia in August, 1983. Dad was Jerome Blomo, and that was my name too. Mum and Dad weren't married, but they lived together off Old Road in Sinkor, a suburb of Monrovia. In Liberia, there are lots of different family combinations, parents married, parents not married, kids born to different fathers. My sister Mardea and I are *Same ma, Same pa.* Other brothers and sisters we know are *Same ma* or *Same pa,* but not both. My first name Jerome is Bassa-tribe. It means Holy Name. After my father tried to overthrow the Liberian despot Sam Doe, my last name became a death sentence.

My father's face lingers at the back of my memory. It turns to vapor as soon as I try to latch onto it, to name it. It dissolves as an echo. He left when I was two, him outcast from the Liberian regime at the time, me still in small pants. When he disappeared, it wasn't dad going out for a bottle of milk. His disappearance was the result of African circumstances that changed my name, changed my family.

I spent my infant years near Monrovia, a good life in the bustling city with plenty of everything, opulent by the standards of the structured Liberian caste system.

My sixth year I became Jehuu fulltime. My mum says I got that nickname before I was even born. In Bassa, it means fussy baby or naughty boy. The creolized dialect Bassa is a mix of African-Liberian and English. Americans can understand it, be able to communicate, but not easily. It's a sing-song language, full of superlatives, fun to hear and speak. We don't say "large", we say *big-big*. Instead of "I am leaving", we say, *I'm coming to go*. *Da-me* means "It is me". *Da-nat for* "That is not". We end sentences with *eh* and *oh*, language fillers that emphasize, question, or contradict; they can mean whatever the speaker wants, it's up to the listener to sort it out.

After my dad disappeared, we moved to the Firestone Plantation where my mum worked. I lived with my mum and my nanny, Thomah. There was a local girl who gave me school lessons. I loved to run, wrestle and fight, throw and catch, kick and jump. We were active, physical kids. Footraces, tag and tackle, real football (you call it soccer), *knock-foot* with my sister Mardea and so many cousins. We have big families in Liberia. Busy feet, busy hands. *You na sit still Jehuu. You go go go, eh.* I zip from one thing to another, never land on anything, go go all the time. Always somewhere else to be –football in the field, races in the street, *run, run.* I get in trouble, get scolded, little kid trouble; I knock stuff off the shelves when I blow through the house, slap my sister and cousins and run away, wrestle with friends. I'm a dark blur in white sneakers, green shorts high on the hips, no shirt (shirts are hot), hair cropped tight. I'm Jehuu the *water-bug*, low maintenance, smile full of teeth and mischief.

. . . .

My family was well-off. Before Firestone, Mum was in nursing school, my grand-parents were government workers and land owners. Dad had access to money and power before his exile. I

15

didn't know we were wealthy, I just knew I got whatever I needed; food when I was hungry, water when I was thirsty.

Life in that house was so different from being a refugee, it was hard to square the differences being that young. How to go from playing in a yard, to running for my life. From food whenever I was hungry, to rationing a cup of water for an entire day. From a soft bed to sleeping in a tree. We escaped Liberia right before the worse part of the second Liberian Civil War, at the age when boys were being recruited as child soldiers. Girls and women, just like my mum and sister, were raped and tortured at a dizzying rate.

When we arrived in the United States, I attended a small school in a small town. I was raised by a mother and sister who define perseverance and adaptation. We were embraced by community that recognized differences as an opportunity, rather than a defect. I was mentored by a village, neighbors, teachers, and coaches who demanded hard work and humility.

That was my fortune, a schematic for building a life, based on virtues like hard work, opportunity, good people, and luck.

Lots of luck.

. . . .

Escaping Liberia was luck beyond understanding, or possibly it was divine intervention, depending on your faith. My mum says Grandma Joanna is in direct communication with the Christian God, that she has tin-can-and-wire telephone relationship that stretches from Grandma's prayers to God's ear. The number of fortunate decisions, blessed turns, audacious timing, and happy coincidences that fell into place to get my family out of the teeth of a barbaric civil war was astounding. So many flukes, and providential twists of fate. It's hard to believe it was all luck. Our home wasn't destroyed when an entire neighborhood was razed by mortars, a bullet just missed me and instead lodged harmlessly in my backpack, a soldier was distracted so my family could sneak through the checkpoint of a warlord.

It all happened. Was that God working through Grandma's religious will? What about the others? What about Joseph, our family friend murdered by random bullets, shot through a door, then a chair leg and into him? What about the neighbor lady who was fine one minute and dead the next as my family treaded down-country, looking for shelter from the war?

The bullet doesn't pick and choose, according to a Liberian saying. Who decides when you occupy the same space as a bullet fired from a soldier aiming at something else or nothing at all?

. . . .

Many Liberian expatriates ended up in Staten Island, living in relative poverty among haunted child soldiers with no enemy to hunt, victims with scars that wouldn't heal. The refugees, still haunted by the war, move around the crowded island like zombies, looking for paths in life away from their only known home, away from their family, stuck in new worlds that looks like a no-man's land.

I could have landed there. I could have landed in any number of large cities, in school systems where they played soccer, my favorite sport. Southwestern New York, with its rural geography, has lots of schools. Jamestown High School, the largest in that area, just up the road, has hundreds of students in every class. Erie, Pennsylvania, a bigger city than the county I lived in, is close-by, with eleven-thousand students in all their schools.

Given the opportunity, I would have played soccer in the United States, not American football. But I went to Clymer, a school so small that it didn't offer soccer. There are ten or twelve schools with soccer teams within hailing distance of Clymer. Football might have never registered with me had my mom ended up living fifteen miles to the east or west. I loved my football, Liberian football. I understood it, had talent and experience. I would have found teammates in the world of travel ball and junior leagues. I would have climbed the soccer ladder. Who knows how that story ends up, how good I'd have been, how welcome, how capable. Instead, I played American football and ended up in record books, high school and college. I became a professional athlete. All those puzzle pieces clicked into place. Was it the culmination of God's plans? Haphazard series of coincidences, grand decisions, or luck? Or a universe bent on taking care of things in its own way?

The bullet doesn't pick and choose.
Does God?

2

Bonita

IN HER ACCENTED voice ("they" is "dey", "them" is "dem", and so on), Jehuu's mum Bonita, shares her journey from the United States to Liberia and back, summer of 1992. Equal parts humor and sadness, anger and resolve, confusion and surety.

After your escape, how did the kids react to life in the United States?

BC: When I finally brought my children out of Liberia to Findlay Lake, they were afraid at first, and then later not as much, my children. When it would rain and thunder. Lightning was worse, the flashes. I think it must look like guns or bombs, some explosion. Something they lived through while I was away in New York.

What about the time they were there and you were here?

BC: I was in agony. Daily dreaming of the world my kids lived in. Every single day, just the helplessness. No way to talk to them, were they dead?

And in Clymer, were they able to forget Liberia eventually?

BC: Yes, loud noises with light together were very bad for my children. Smells were maybe worse. They say the things you smell bring back the strongest memories. Dead animals along the road or something in the woods behind the house that went to rot. If Jehuu or Mardea smelled something like that, they'd go quiet. Maybe start to shake. What do you do when your children shake from some-thing they smell? What do you do?

How did you get them to understand that they were finally safe?
BC: I didn't know then, and I still don't, how to separate what you see and feel and smell then from now. You can tell them thou-sand times that the bad men with the guns don't exist here, rural New York, with its farms and forests. How do they tell muddy roads in war-torn countryside from dirt roads in Clymer? How different are the dead in your nightmares from the living in your waking? What's the real difference between hunger and thirst and sleeping on the ground, and the safety of real beds in houses. The places and the times melt together in their young minds, and it takes time to separate them. It took very long for me to ever find comfort. For me to step out of the guilt of mothers who abandoned her children in the worst place. No matter how many times you tell them, no matter how many times you show them. How could they know? They're so, so young.

They come to my bed late at night, and they shake. They hide their heads, burrow in. Jehuu's little legs jump and twitch. Like sleeping dogs chasing rabbit. Mardea older and a little stronger, holds back her tears.

It happens like this, to my children. They would go back, back to Liberia in their minds. Something reminds them of that life. Sounds, smells. Back to that world I didn't know (after the war started). Worlds I left them in, without their mother. No one should be without their mother, but Liberia is different. Families are big and very close. We do everything together. Everyone knows everyone.

3

Liberia

MOST LIBERIANS ARE indigenous ethnic African tribes.

The rest of the country is foreigners – Lebanese, Indians, and West African nationals. The tribes are very complicated to understand if you're not from there, all with their own dialects and customs. Kpelle, Bassa, Mano, Gio, Kru, Krahn. There's Americo-Liberians or Congo people, descendants of African Americans and West Indians. It's easy to mistake them.

It's also tempting for one tribe to try to take power from another.

There are sixteen of these tribes, and understanding their allegiances, their histories, their betrayals, their paths to loyalty, is to know Shakespearean tragedy. The ethnic relationships are ingrained into the collective memories of each faction. Conflicts, resolutions, and struggles for power have been waged in and among those sixteen distinct interests throughout the history of Africa. Treaties and promises, contracts and pacts, truces and violence, all declared and broken over and again. When the Americo-Liberians arrived from across the Atlantic with their notions of chauvinism, a class-system built into their governing, and corruption (lots of corruption), the country became fertile ground for consistent rebellion. It's the way of colonialization on the African continent and of most of the history of the world.

4

Bonita

Your parents lived just outside of the capital, of Monrovia? How was it growing up there?

BC: Mum's house outside the city was the daily place for people to go. It was the place we all learned how to work, how to keep busy, how to be part of Liberia. We planted all our own food, acres and acres of food. Everybody, all us Caulcrick's harvested food and shared with the neighborhood. We took turns wheeling it all around, dropping off mangos here, potatoes there. We planted casabas, edels. We planted eggplant and all the fruits and vegetables we ate. My mom would cook, and she'd make all us kids cart the food around all the neighborhoods. First, me and my many brothers and sisters, then all our kids.

Everyone had mango trees. We made donuts that we would go and sell in the market, in the open market. We made Kool-Aid in ice trays, those metal ones. We put them in ice jugs and we took them to market and sold them. All the kids did all of those things.

Except my Jehuu. They had to handle him with kid gloves when I left him off there to find place in the United States. Ohhh, he was spoiled. He was just coming into this life, the one of work and shared responsibilities. They thought he was the civilized one because we came from the city. Poor Jehuu, had to learn to share.

Your family was very religious.

BC: We were very religious, in that house, Christians, like most of the country. I believe almost eighty percent when I was there, probably more now. We knew Muslims, fewer Hindus, Sikhs, Buddhists. My father was in the St. John's Episcopal Church, and my mom was one of the ushers.

And your parents were professional? Government work?

BC: My dad was a health inspector. He worked for the government hospital, and then when he retired, he did theater recordings of weddings and funerals and graduations. My mom worked for the government when I was very little, as a teacher of home economics. When the government got rid of their schools for that, she opened her own, teaching natives, other tribes, people from the ghettos how to cook, bake, and sew. She'd make wedding dresses, and that's the wedding that my dad would go and film. She had the back of the school for the girls, and in the front, she used to bake bread. We owned a bakery.

5

Liberia

"Small shame better than big shame."
—*Liberian proverb*

LIBERIA AND ITS people present a perplexing contradiction.

There's natural beauty, resources, a variety of climates and habitats, an impressive array of indigenous fauna –lions, tigers, the pangolin, mongoose, hippo, crocs, African civet, two-hundred-some species of monkeys, and six-hundred-ninety-three different kinds of birds. Some you can pet, but many will kill you if you don't get them first.

The land can be magnificent, graduating from seaside environ, to mangrove-heavy forest, to inland desert and bush, to mountainous terrain, all within a hundred or so miles between the sea and the western border. Liberia has the largest natural harvests of Hevea brasiliensis (rubber tree) in the world.

The people are generally happy, thankful, gregarious, and hopeful. It comes across in their attitude of nonchalance and tolerance, their stands on things like language (verbose and elaborate), marital fidelity (laisse fare), commerce (barter-oriented), and the way they treat their fellow Liberians (generous and helpful).

But their acceptance of fundamental violence on each other can be disturbing. It's baked into tribal ethnic history, a primordial, generational bigotry toward different kinds, skin color, education, and inheritance. It's not just a Liberian phenomenon. Africans in general seem to accept, perpetuate, and endure a barbarous level of hostility, while maintaining a positive attitude. Charles Taylor's presidential campaign slogan, after he designed and carried out the bloody civil war, was some version of, *You killed my ma, you killed my pa, you get my vote.*

What is a world supposed to do with that querulous attitude?

Starting around 1980, Liberia spun into a killing-purging-rebelling-revenge-rinse-repeat cycle that was as bad as anything the continent had experienced previously. It was hell on Earth, no other reasonable way to describe it.

Jehuu Caulcrick's story is embedded in that violent progression. It is a lesson in what humans can choose do to each other, good and bad, mostly bad. The accounts of pain and suffering are eye-opening. The catalog of what Liberians have endured and survived is large –starvation, murder, rape, fear, and abuse were all part of their daily lives. It was their daily existence. But it's also a story of how the human form can adapt and move forward. When savages are gang-raping, cutting off your skin, amputating limbs, burning you alive, how do you possibly move from day one to day two? More to the point, why do you move from day one to day two? Curl up in a ball, and call it a day. Nobody would care, nobody would argue with you.

But that's not what most Liberians did.

6

Bonita

Where were you in 1980 when the Doe coup happened?

BC: In 1980, I was in Tubman Institute of Medical Arts. I was in nursing school in Monrovia. I'm working the late shift in the maternity ward. The women are happy this evening, but there is a pall over the ward.

The doors smash open, and the ward fills with people. It's Tolbert. In his white suit. There isn't a scratch on the man.

I was right in the emergency room when they brought Tolbert's body in. I slept in dormitory there, we were nurses in the ER. His body was in his white suit. His suit wasn't even dirty.

Monrovia in early 1980, before Doe, was a place of action, streets crowded with cars and motorcycles, called pen-pen. Roads lined with women selling food and water and whatever else they gather onto tables or blankets. There was everything you could imagine in other big cities, a football stadium, government buildings, shopping, fashion, clubs, banks, but hot and crowded.

What about Taylor? Do you remember him?

BC: I wasn't in-country when Taylor invaded. I don't know what I would have done, if the news would have been a warning. Most people did nothing, didn't see him coming. We'd been through wars before.

So Christmas of '89 when Taylor came across the border, you weren't there.

BC: No. No I wasn't.

There are some pictures from April of 1990. Would that have been when you were back?

BC: Yes. I came back for my sister's graduation. Travel wasn't impossible yet. I was working on the kid's papers, the visas to have them come back with me. They weren't ready. Nobody had any idea that the war would turn so fast, that things would get that bad.

7

Liberia

THE COAST OF Liberia, at the northern port in Monrovia, looks like a Disney property from the sea, from far away.

Straight white lines of surf cut the deep blue Atlantic cued to wash onto picturesque lagoons. The coast bleeds from beach to city to a green canopy of a dense vegetation. The coastline is marked with bright, ornately colored buildings that pack stretches of land.

Then you get closer, and it all goes away. The sea is a sewer, the beaches are junkyards. The city transforms into a third world's third world of poverty and decay. It's obvious something has happened to make this place a banquet for vermin and maggots. It's no longer the city of Jehuu's youth. His Liberia was a proud, pleasant world. Today it's 4.9 million people stuffed into ten cities. The rest of the country, decimated by scorched-earth warfare, is wind-swept plains or salt-resistant mangrove bush.

8

A Child Soldier

OUT OF THE Wuteve mountains comes a boy.

He is comfortable in the mountains, can wield guns, machetes, scythes. Can work all day. Can tend his own wounds, find water, eat off the land. His father, widowed, runs the reserve with the restrained competence of a Kru Liberian. The boy is *Hope*, called by his father, sometimes with obvious regret, strained through a clenched jaw. The Loma tribesmen who help on the reserve call him *Weeskind* (Afrikaans for orphan). The name is meant as tribute to the mother who died violently.

Hope, the Weeskind, grows up fast, sharpened against the wheel of hard work, inhospitable life. He knows the bush and the desert. He knows the wild beasts, cougars, gorillas, warthog and boa, can field-strip deer, break down, clean and rebuild weapons.

Today, Hope is at the watering hole. He throws sticks into a gnarly kola tree to shake out the cobra who lives there. He doesn't want venom dropping while he busies himself at the bush-line. The serpent drops and hisses. A slender mongoose appears from nowhere, gives chase. They scurry off through the brush, predator and prey. When Hope was a baby, his mother was taken at this same watering hole by two adult cougars. Since then, his father raised him in these mountains.

Hope climbs high into the vacated kola, surveys the watering hole. He has pockets-full of throwing rocks. He's there to watch the coming and going of the beasts. He'll count them and report to his father, noting any new species or newborn among the regulars. Best to come right before dusk, before bats arrive from their caves and dens –the woolys, yellows, hairys and fruit bats. They buzz your head to pick off insects that gather around your eyes and ears. Sometimes they come close and strike, leaving welts and small bleeding rips in the skin. Then you must go inside and clean the wounds before the blood-smell reaches other predators. Bats carry disease.

The rocks are a deterrent, Hope's arm is strong and accurate, not out of the question for him to hit a moving bat, but it's just better to avoid them altogether and come to the water before dusk.

The first to the hole is almost always the River Gorilla. He approaches horizontal on knuckles and feet with confidence. He brokers no argument. He sniffs as he arrives to drink, black eyes set deep in his arched head. Wary eyes, on a casual, nonchalant pivot, his great black mane hackled, declaring his alertness. He would rip your head off if he had to, but otherwise he's a fur-tuxedoed man-about town. He drinks, deep and satisfying. Then comes his family. Little ones, three, bundles of fur and energy, precocious and curious. The missus follows the brood.

This is Hope's bliss, watching and learning from the wild. The lessons of violence, submission, bravery, and futility will serve him well.

9

Liberia

PICTURE A MAP of Pennsylvania or Ohio.

Maybe North Carolina or Virginia in the east. Louisiana, Tennessee, or Kentucky in the south. These states have about the same land mass as Liberia. Thirty-six states are larger. Western states are almost all twice the size. Four Liberia's would fit into California.

Liberia doesn't change much on the coastal road, civilization carved out of a harsh world with anything that can hold form in hot, wet, salty conditions, a series of small ocean cities, a port here, a fishing village there.

Moving south are Buchanan, River Cess, Greenville, Barclayville, and a hundred smaller places in between. The ocean, the coast, has promise that inland, the bush, doesn't. If you care to learn the water, you have fish for food, transportation up and down the coast, port commerce, and trade. There is another whole world on the horizon to the west. Inland is where the heat goes to damp-blanket refreshing breezes, where predators lurk, where the bush grows thick.

Western Liberia starts a gradual incline from coast, to plains, to foothills, to the mountain ranges that define the border of Liberia into central Africa; it's basically downhill from the Wuteve to Monrovia, east going west. The plains are almost always wet, a few hundred inches of rain a year, 85-95 percent humidity, the perfect ingredients to make a swamp and raise wetland crops like rice, cassava, and sugarcane.

Moving east from the coast, from Monrovia, into Lofa County, woodlands dominate the landscape, the Bluyeama forest, and three reserves–the Wologizi Mountain, Wonegizi Range, and Foya Forest.

The Wuteve mountains border Sierra Leone, as northeast as you can get in Liberia. Lines of national demarcation are a vague thing in the bush, where deep forest and harsh climate at altitude determine how a man lives, not where.

Liberia has a larger population than only twenty-four states .It's older than twenty-three. Liberian independence came July 26, 1847. The Emancipation Proclamation was signed into United States federal law in 1863. Slaves from the United States were free in Liberia before most were legally free in their country of origin.

To get an idea of what Liberia is like, without having to land at Robertsfield Airport in Monrovia and negotiate a third world economy and infrastructure, you could do worse than visit Louisiana, which has almost the same land mass and almost the same population and density (104 people per square mile in Liberia and 108 in Louisiana). The climate is similar, if not exact, hot and wet with vegetation that thrives in that ecosystem. Both have a coastal presence on the Atlantic Ocean.

. . . .

Liberia and the United States are historically and inexorably joined. American businessmen, with the blessing and a few dollars from the government, sponsored an endeavor called the American Colonization Society, their goal to repatriate freed slaves onto the continent of Africa. The result is the country of Liberia.

Liberia is the only attempt by the United States at overt colonization. As with most nation-building, if you walk back the idea of Liberia the one the United States tried to impose, not the deep history of African tribal history you get a cloudy, disheartening picture.

In 1817, American Colonization Society ships, loaded with freed slaves and a few white advocates, set sail for Africa. The expedition was an opportunity to plant in the soil of another continent a so-ciety chosen by the ship's passengers. The goals of the expedition were threefold: to get the freed slaves out of the United States (their presence was becoming an international, unsightly blight as the rest of the western world outlawed slavery), to facilitate a nation-state on the other side of the world that would be naturally grateful and sympathetic to the United States, and to throw an anchor of de-mocracy and civility into a place where there was practically none. It was assumed that whatever society blossomed wouldn't support the same slavery these citizens just escaped across the Atlantic.

That opportunity was left at the shores of the east Atlantic when American Colonization ships sailed west for home, leaving their cargo to invent a new world. Between 1822 and 1861, more than fifteen-thousand freed and free-born Black people, along with 3,198 Afro-Caribbean's moved to Liberia.

A century or so later, the United States would add Liberia to the long list of countries abandoned in time of need. The historical ties between the two countries made this one hurt a little more, a parent stepping out for cigarettes and never coming back. When the civil wars inevitably bloomed and the bombs flew and the citizens were slaughtered, mom and dad stood aside and watched, to the convenience of some, the shame of others.

. . . .

The western coast of Africa presented itself to the American Colonization Society as an oasis, a cornucopia of resources. Fresh water, plants and animals, natural resources in lumber, diamonds, and a vibrant eco-system –an exotic home. But inside that vision was a typical African culture. What seemed like a convenient, intact, and picture-book setting for a new beginning had its inherent dif-ficulties. Indigenous tribes lived there for millennium, establishing a hierarchy in clannish schema, the strong and the weak. Basically, the same as the rest of the world, separated only by distance and unsophisticated travel capabilities but possessing wholly universal human qualities like jealousy, avarice, revenge, and creative violence.

When the American Colonization Society came, bringing their ideas of civilization informed by the southern plantation systems in the United States, they introduced the ethos that would manifest itself a hundred-fifty years later in the hot mess of civil war. The newcomers, called "Congo" more or less enslaved the local tribes, called "Country", and the wheel of human oppression made another rotation.

Satisfaction of the few, the strong, at the cost of the weak, breeds contempt. Contempt begets violence. It's been that way throughout history and was no different in a place like Liberia.

10

Bonita

How did Jehuu grow up?

BC: In 1988, Jehuu wasn't quite in school. I had him home tu-
tored. It was some girl who was helping right at home. He was five.
We were in Firestone. That's where I lived at the time. He went to
[a] day-care, kindergarten kind of thing. I was in customer service
at the golf course and at food services. Mardea was at her grandma's
house, in school there, a few miles up the road in Buchanan. She was
learning how to be around people. Jehuu was not.

He had a nanny, Thomah. His dad was gone three years or so
now, and here he is surrounded by women.

In the 1980s, rubber demand went down, and Firestone got rid
of thousands of workers, all Liberian, but kept their entertainment
and pleasures. They had golf, social clubs, sport fishing boats. They
had big houses, big parties. That's how I was hired, as food services
and hospitality. Luckily, I wasn't there in 1990 when the plantation was evacuated of Americans because Taylor and his National
Patriotic Front of Liberia took the plantation.

But I knew people who were there. I imagine they stayed at plantation because it was where they lived, and they probably thought
the Americans, the Firestone people, would protect them. Maybe it
was a place to stay alive if you know where to hide, where to get at
the Firestone supplies, food, water.

But when Taylor crossed the river into the plantation, the bloodshed started.

A little later Jehuu was in school, right? Like a kindergarten class? It sounds like he fit in, except for the infamous Skittles incident.

BC: When he was six and in school, he brought his favorite candy to school. Oh, that boy was spoiled. It was Skittles. The teacher, his teacher, took them from Jehuu. He knew exactly what to do. He came and told me. He tells people I had her fired. Oh my God that boy will never forgive that woman.

While he was in school, you went to the United States?

BC: So later that year, I met a man and left for the United States to see if there was a better life for my family. That was June. I arrived in the United States on the 25th. I was gone [a] long time, longer than I expected, but we were so much a big family, and my mom and dad had the best place to raise the kids. Lots of family, cousins and step brothers and sisters. Lots of good clean work, religion, everything. I came back in 1990 for my sister's graduation. Flew from New York into Monrovia airport. Saw all the familiar people, that same world I left. I didn't know that Charles Taylor was invading the country. Even if I knew, how was this time going to be different? People just live their lives. They watch men with power hand it back and forth. They watch them go by, they bother other people, not us in the neighborhoods. Warlords were just people we knew who had people around them. They weren't rebels. There was just the government.

But if I knew. If I knew that this time was different, I never would have left my children in that world.

11

Liberia

"Liberia's history after independence has been a tale of two cities and people. On one hand, an affluent minority with access to all the benefits of a free people, and on the other hand, a majority underclass, disenfranchised, and taxed without adequate representation in the government."
—*Ijoma Flemister (Republic of Liberia Legislator)*

RACISM IS A complicated structure in Africa.

Is a lack of enlightenment, specific to a cultural period of time, a moral failing worthy of scorn and resentment by those who come after and judge through the prism of hindsight? Or is it excusable, part of the fabric of society in a snapshot of time?

Can we look back and judge mankind from the comfort of a more tolerant, more informed world? Mankind is destined to get more enlightened, more informed. What will our grandchildren think of us?

The American freed slaves in Liberia had a chance, their sponsors did as well. As the United States was built on the ideal of democracy, so could those original settlers build a country based on humanity, democratic ideals. Foresight being exactly that, and the citizens of that time not being the same caliber of men as the founding fathers, the opportunity was lost to expediency and lazy thinking.

It stood to reason that as Europe abolished slavery in the early 1800s, and the United States after the Civil War, so would transplanted Liberians. But money and land and greed and rivalry and petulance and barbary and the lesser angels of human nature could not be overcome. Native Liberians (called Country) were not ancestrally equipped to give up on enslaving their fellow man. Leaders couldn't help but take more than their fair share of land and resources.

Those first families from the United States (called Americos), free of the yoke of slave-owners had every chance to recognize the scourge of slavery. They refused to embrace it in their new home. The first thing the Americos did was build an exact replica of the plantation system they'd left behind in the United States South.

The nation became fertile ground for class resentment and rebellion. The Americo-Liberians, incapable of learning lessons from their own slavery, backed by the United States and recognized by the world as sovereign, kept piling on the oppression. By 1979, four percent of the population owned sixty percent of the wealth.

The best example of this is a prime piece of seaside Liberian real estate originally owned by the Dey tribe. In the 1860s, it was renamed Bensonville after then-president Stephen Allen Benson, but the Deys kept ownership, the land benefiting their tribe and accessible to all Liberians.

When Tolbert became president, he confiscated and transformed that land into an African Camelot. Bensonville was renamed Bentol. It was transformed into a Versailles, Liberian-style, while the Dey looked on from outside the fences. Each Tolbert family member had their own opulent estate with high walls and security systems to keep them sheltered from the rest of Liberia. While bare-foot "Country" children begged on the side of the road, the Tolbert's built a private zoo and an artificial lake for motorboat racing and waterskiing.

The injustice couldn't be sustained. The animosity of the majority wouldn't allow it. Educated and oppressed is a dangerous combination in a populace; when mixed with the ability to raise tribal armies and buy cheap weapons, it's lethal. This is about the time when being President of Liberia became terminal employment. You could set your calendar by the assassinations. But the essential problem was that the men who turned over the government committed their coups with an eye toward owning their own Bentol, rather than for just reasons.

Tolbert was assassinated by Samuel Doe, Doe by a warlord named Prince Johnson, and then came Charles Taylor.

Yes, Liberia had its chances.

12

A Child Soldier

"Compelled to become instruments of war, to
kill and be killed, child soldiers are forced to give
violent expression to the hatred of adults."
—*Olara Otunnu (Union Nations Special
Representatives for Children and Armed Conflict)*

THE REBELS BUILT roadblocks to pick up stray kids.

They sent soldiers to refugee camps, schools, and orphanages to
"recruit"; any place where people congregate for food or water or
shelter. Even Red Cross shelters were places to find child soldiers.
When warlords ran out of men for their armies, they turned to children, unable to rationalize another solution, incapable of moral and
ethical awareness, cowards unwilling to back up their convictions.
Nearly all warring factions used child soldiers, as they were especially
energetic, ferocious, and expendable. Many were conscripted, some
joined voluntarily to avenge the massacre of their parents, siblings
or relatives, others joined the war because their parents were killed
and enlisting was the only option.

Over 50,000 would be conscripted into service for the war, boys
to carry weapons and supplies, girls to service men, both to use up
enemy ammunition. Recruitment was by any means necessary. If a
family objected, they killed the family, grabbed the child, or, even
better, have the boys kill the family to prove their loyalty. Child

soldiers made up ten percent of the combatants in Liberia's civil war, their victimhood a generational issue in the country. In their most formative years, it was demanded they become addicted to heroin and booze and sex. Then, to feed that addiction, they murdered, raped, and mutilated other human beings.

How do you sit in a school, live in a home, or contribute to a peaceful society after that life?

The pictures of these child soldiers of Liberia, found anywhere on the internet, are disorienting. Zoom in. That kid in a polo and gym shorts, a mischievous grin, all wiry and athletic, could be any kid in any neighborhood. Pull back, big picture, the grin is a leer, the thin frame is malnourished, that athletic pose props up an automatic weapon. The eyes, when not hidden behind oversized sunglasses, are red-rimmed and either watery and scattered, or dull and dead. Cheeks are puffed with swollen arrogance, necks and arms corded with muscle to hold both head and weapon aloft.

There are no fat child soldiers, there are no boyish grins.

Teenagers wear lunatic outfits, death masks, wigs, wedding dresses, told these are talismans, war-paint to protect them and to terrify their enemies, but they're worn as much to hide them from themselves, from who they should be –broods in a schoolyard, teams on a playground, players on a pitch. Here's a teenage boy, proud portrait of eating human flesh. An adolescent's skilled fingers packing a carbine with bullets. They're barely recognizable. Humanity has been carved out of them.

So many boys, with so many stories of how their lives were one way one day and different the next. The indigent and homeless rounded up first and most easily, kidnapped from broken homes and raided orphanages. Give rice and a bed to a boy who has never had a consistent roof over his head or tasted steak, and you can easily weaponize desperation.

13

Liberia

IT'S WORTH NOTING that slavery in Africa was, and has always been, much more prominent than in the United States.

It wasn't until cotton became king in the US South that the voyage across the Atlantic to the West Coast of Africa became a financially stable proposition.

Even then the work it would have taken to subdue a continent of peoples might have been too cumbersome to make the operation profitable if not for Africans willing to fill the cargo-holds of American ships with their countrymen. Historians estimate that some ten million Africans died being marched to the sea in chains.

Slavery has always had a home on the African Continent. The physical dominance of one tribe over another, resulting in genocidal killing, rape, murder, mutilation, and enslavement in Africa is notorious, part of the collective consciousness.

When slavery was abolished in the US and in Great Britain, so was it outlawed in Liberia. When goods and services and technology were developed and marketed, Liberia wasn't forgotten. Trade ships frequented Monrovia harbor, an oasis on the eastern shore of a hot, humid, and barbaric continent. English became the native language. Liberians modified the Queen's English into a more intuitive and efficient and playful and harmonic form.

But the sale of African slaves by Africans for profit ceased only when the rest of the world realized the wrongness of it and markets dried up. The deep-seated insistence that one type of person is somehow better than another, more valuable, stronger, and therefore, born with inalienable rights is ingrained in our species. But it battles constantly with the need to dominate and submit other to our wills.

The British outlawed slavery in the early nineteenth century, and they enforced the law in ways that other countries chose to ignore. So, British patrols seized slave ships, usually coming out of the mouth of the Congo river and returned them to Liberia or Sierra Leone no matter where the captured Africans came from. Around this time freed slaves from America arrived on board American colonization ships. All the new faces got lumped together. Country became a derogatory name for the natives of the Western Coast of Africa. Native Liberians were not happy to have freed people dumped onto their shores. They called them Congo. Congo and Country were the basic factions that would eventually make the opposing sides of Liberian Civil Wars.

14

Jehuu

MY MUM WORKED at the Firestone plantation.

This was in Harbel, about half-way between Monrovia and Buchanan, two other places I lived in Liberia. She managed hospitality and the golf course for Firestone executives and American businessmen. Harbel is home to the rubber-giant, employing lots of Liberians. My mum, beautiful and talented, from an honorable family had a good job. Most Liberians made forty dollars a month harvesting rubber from trees.

At Firestone, my mum met a man, and they decided to get married. Later in 1990, she dropped me off with my grandma and grandpa, her parents, the Caulcrick's. My dad was still in hiding. Mardea and all those cousins were already there, in Buchanan. Off she went to the United States to set up a new life.

Buchanan was hot-hot days filled with children-sounds and smells in a big dry-dust, wet-mud yard surrounded by neighborhoods of low houses of brick, mortar, steel roofs, and paint trying desperately to hold in the humidity of Liberia. Hot in dry months, hot and wet when the monsoons come October through May. But hot, all the time hot.

Grandpa was a food inspector, Grandma ran home-economics school. So many aunts and uncles and cousins and neighbors and students at my grandma's school, passing in and out like hotels, busy hotels. A house where I was only a guest, not the owner, not the little king. The women had other boys to look after, to spoil. The change was brutal. All of the sudden there were other people who had needs, not just me. I learned the sharing lessons Mardea and my cousins already knew.

Before Taylor arrived and put a tank in our yard.

15

Liberia

THE RUBBER TREE, Hevea brasiliensis, is all over Liberia.

It's a nuisance of a sapling, except that it yields latex in rivers. In 1926, Firestone corporation understood this and when the need for rubber exploded in the world, they leapt at Liberia, carved their own city out of the deepest Hevea orchard on the African continent, taking advantage of the historical relationship between the United States and Liberia.

Harbel is named for Harvey Firestone and his wife, Isabelle. It says something about the influence of the American corporation that they were permitted to name their own city in a foreign country.

Rubber is generational work for Liberians. After it's planted and grown for about three or four months, buds from a hybrid rubber tree are fused to it, and the tree is planted in long rows of fertile Liberian soil. It takes about seven years for that tree to produce mature latex. Harvesting the latex without killing the tree is a highly skilled labor. A tree can produce valuable latex for about twenty-five years.

The latex is collected in lumps and sent to central processing where it's pressed into large bricks easy to transport and use in future production. The latex is branded with a colored die to identify it as a Firestone product and keep poachers from selling it on the black market.

The plantation is its own world, crafted as an oasis of work and pleasure for Firestone executives on pristine Liberian soil and separate from the lives of the natives. For a reasonable fee and a few employment guarantees, Firestone was allowed to pick any Liberian land they wanted, so they took gorgeous coastal property between two rivers, natural borders that conveniently washed rubber and human waste to the sea. On a million acres, some four percent of the country, there were dozens of work camps and eight million trees in neat rows, the biggest rubber plant in the world, sold to Firestone at six cents an acre.

Liberians were told that this deal would be a financial boon to the government coffers and would trickle down to every Liberian in the form of jobs and social programs. Some eighty-thousand Liberians were employed at the plantation at the height of production, some thirty-five million dollars spent on making Firestone-in-Liberia a piece of United States soil. Petrol, food, housing, heavy equipment, a hospital and school, a modern communication system, everything you need to supply a fully functioning city.

Coincidentally, this was everything you need to supply a fully functioning army.

16

A Child Soldier

FIFTY THOUSAND IS a fair, agreed-upon number.

It's about how many children were recruited into rebel armies during the second Liberian Civil War. That number is probably low, since kids in Hell don't always raise their hands at attendance, but it has enough zeros to be acceptably accurate. A lot more than that were injured, orphaned, or abandoned during the wars, that number being such a moving target that no one has bothered to offer better than a guess. The National Military Families Association of Liberia (NAMFA) was created to provide for orphaned children. It registered thousands of street children, those with no families or homes. Over a hundred orphanages sprang up right after the wars in and around Monrovia, but with so many kids in need, resources were stretched beyond capacity, and those refuges offered little relief. Orphanages were also where warlords went first to recruit children for their armies, so kids learned to stay away from them.

The Liberian government gives no aid to orphanages. They are all supported by private donations. The orphans are viewed as possible troops in some future altercation between warlords or across borders to wars in Sierra Leone. Approximately twenty-one percent (4,306) of the combatants who were disarmed under the provisions of the Abuja Peace Accords were children under the age of seventeen, traumatized and addicted to drugs. International programs like UNICEF and other NGO's try to rehabilitate and retrain these child combatants into some semblance of normal life, but the government of Liberia has discouraged their efforts, concerned that they will be recruited into sub-regional conflicts and come back to terrorize Liberia. The specter of another home-grown rebel like Taylor returning to galvanize the populace into another hellacious rebellion informs their policy, even if irrationally so. Instead of protecting and nurturing their children, they have chosen to fear and abandon them.

.　.　.　.

Hope and his father walk the path from the warden station to the watering hole. From there, they will camp north, toward the foothills.

His father holsters his sidearm and carries a huge rifle. Hope wields his smaller weapon. Ranger, their Kru aide-de-camp, wields another small weapon and huge knife. The bush where they patrol is tight, dark, a wet tunnel. Every turn in the path is another adventure in claustrophobia and stress. The small rifle Hope holds is heavy, clutched tight to his chest, barrel pointed skyward. His father insists he keeps the safety on. This makes Hope nervous. If a cougar or lion rushes, he won't have time to react. His fingers ride the muzzle and feel the safety, ready to move it to life, his opposite index finger twitches on the trigger guard. He feels like his eyes will pop from his face if he peers any harder into the deep bush.

"Hope, stop your head moving," his father whispers from the trail ahead.

How does he see me?

"Use your eyes. Attacks will come from there," he points to the animal run. "There's no place for a beast to crash us through this bush, *eh*?" His father brushes his own rifle against the dense foliage. "When we see the path, then we are ready. Come to clearing, we can be rushed, then we are alert."

Hope nods, swivels his head side to side anyways. His father grunts.

To Hope, his father is the ultimate hunter, the top predator, more dangerous than anything in the bush. It helps Hope relax. *Nothing can hurt me,* he thinks. *I am safe.*

That memory will come back time and again in a sad wave of naivete.

The heat brings bees, flies, and mosquitos to investigate the three hunters so out of place. Covered in scat, mud, and urine they are able to mask human scent, but the swarms hover anyways. Bugs don't stay for tastes or pricks, but they tickle and scratch. Hard to maintain discipline. Hope wants to swipe and itch and brush pests from his eyes and ears, to do so would bring more grunts from his father.

From behind, he senses Ranger but hears nothing. How do they make no noise, these hunters? He wonders if Ranger is really a witch or a Negee. His own breathing sounds like engines to the ears.

"Toes. Pads of the feet, like panther and pangolin."

Hope looks back at Ranger. Says, "Lions roar, the gorilla bawls. They don't pad."

"Which are you *Weeskind,* lion or gorilla?" Ranger smiles, teeth white against his black face. "That's right, you are neither, you are a meerkat."

17

Jehuu

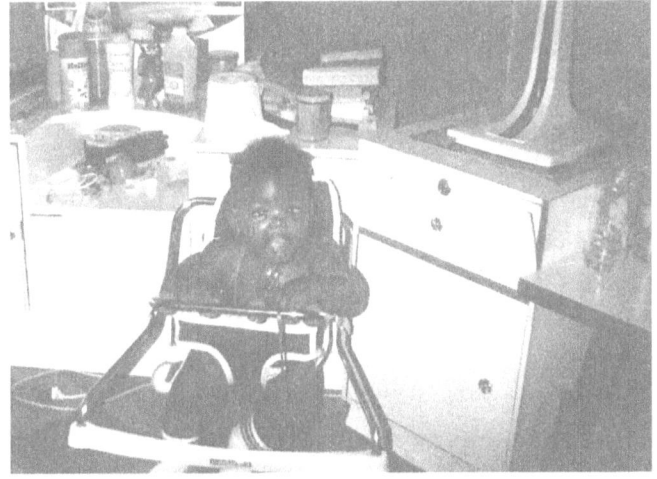

Jehuu baby picture

I WAS A healthy, happy, baby, thundering legs, big smile from the start.

No wonder my women spoil me. I get height from my mum, she's a tall Liberian lady. The rest of my size is Blomo, my father –thick athletic body, powerful legs and back. You aren't head of security for Liberian generals without big physical parts. I don't remember my dad in any way that would put a solid picture in my head, just that faint reckoning from stories, descriptions from family. We had to throw away all his pictures when he escaped Doe's assassins. When we were tiny, Papa and Mum took me and

Mardea places in Monrovia, the football stadium, to market, past government buildings and military barracks. It's hard to tell which memories are real, which come from the pictures and stories, but I believe those memories have context, if not detail, substance.

In mum's pictures, I wear bright polos and clean shorts, stiff shirts, brown shoes on church Sundays. Mardea wears dresses with frills, white stockings. Other pictures are different, very Liberian; scrub brush, dirt yards, thick mangrove forests, run-down buildings, white-washed churches. These come from the neighborhood in Buchanan, some from Firestone.

Then there are pictures of big cities. Those are third world. Crowded, pedestrians line streets, packed busses, old low-riding trucks, weighted down by people piled into cabs and beds, bikes and pen-pen carrying two-three-four riders, stacked on handlebars and laps. Cramped, painted with people, nowhere for your eye to pick out what the city might look like.

You see that and you say, *yes...Africa.*

Those pictures are before civil wars destroyed places like my neighborhoods and the cities where I walked on toddler's legs. During the war pictures of Liberia take on desperate, violent qualities, as if people are waiting for something bad to happen.

. . . .

When I was five, around 1988, it was just me, mum, and a nanny in the house in Monrovia. Yeah, I had a nanny, spoiled Jehuu. Her name was Tomah. I had mum to myself, only child with a nanny and a house, surrounded by women. I was the little king.

Everybody else was south in Buchanan, at Grandma-Grandpa Caulcrick's house. We couldn't be around my father's family, it was too risky. Enough violence came our way without having the Blomo name tied to me and Mardea. It was hard to tell who was safe. One of my uncles was detained by the government, beat up, and released. People saw the writing on the wall, the regime change, mostly Kru violence against other tribes, settling scores and pouring salt in old wounds.

While Monrovia got crowded and dangerous, Buchanan was a place for peaceful people, not as much hassle, more space, a garden, lots of family. It was communal. Mardea was there, learning to share, play with others.

18

Liberia

IN APRIL 1980, nineteen APL (Liberian National Party) soldiers seized on civilian unrest and took over the Liberian government in a bloody coup.

Samuel Doe was behind that takeover. He was supposed to be the liberator of Liberia. He was supposed to avenge the history of humiliation and abuse of indigenous tribes by Liberian Americos. His rebellion fed on distrust baked into the collective conscious of natives.

· · · ·

By 1821, the Mesurado tribes in Western Africa suspected the Americos from the American Colonization Society of nationalist intentions. They saw the westerners as intruders, as pirates.

When the Mesurado refused to negotiate, the Americos representatives, Captain Stockton and Eli Ayres, held a gun to the heads of the African leaders and made them sign over what is now Monrovia for six muskets, one box of beads, two hogshead of tobacco, one cask of gunpowder, and six bars of iron, in a Manhattan-like transfer. With that coastal foothold in place, the ships came from the United States. Liberia was declared an independent nation in 1847, much to the surprise of the indigenous inhabitants of the Cape.

Precedence for deception and outright robbery was set. That dynamic of wariness and bad faith never really left Liberia (the

Liberian Declaration of Independence reads, *We the people of the Republic of Liberia formerly citizens of the United States of America,* a sentiment that left little room for the ninety-five percent of the citizens who didn't originally hail from the United States).

Doe's coup of the Americos-centric Tolbert regime was supposed to be a victory for the indigenous tribal element that dominated the population of Liberia.

It wasn't.

. . . .

Doe's coup assassins, relatively uneducated and unsophisticated non-commissioned soldiers, had no real plan for what comes after a coup, what happens to a country with no government; who runs the whole operation, who leads?

As a Master Sargent, Doe was the most senior officer. When the killing was done, the eighteen other soldiers looked to him to lead. It never occurred to them that their new version of command and governing looked a lot like the old.

Doe, a Krahn from Grand Gedah County in Southeast Liberia, with a fourth-grade education, started his reign by killing people.

A lot of people.

Tolbert was assassinated in the initial raid on the President's Mansion. Other officials were taken to a nearby beach, tied to poles sunk into the sand, and shot by drunken uproarious soldiers, the massacre shown on TV broadcasts throughout the country and the world.

The next eventual coup was born that day as relatives from different Liberian tribes watched in humiliation and helplessness as their fathers, husbands, and uncles were executed to the cheers of a Krahn leader and men hand-picked to run the army.

Doe declared himself Chairman of the People's Redemption Council (PRC), and military ruler of Libera. The world, including a United States Embassy staff of over five-hundred, barely knew his name. He didn't show up on any military-coup depth charts. Promising to establish a commission to develop a democratic constitution, Doe instead found it impossible to relinquish power or to forgive and forget. He maintained a pro-U.S. stance (visited Ronald Reagan's White House in 1982) but surrounded himself with minority tribe Krahn acolytes. US assistance, money, and military flowed. Politics and human rights deteriorated.

In 1985, Doe won his only free and fair election with fifty-one percent of the popular vote.

He asked Amos Sawyer, a celebrated Liberian academic and leader of an opposing political party to be his vice president. Sawyer declined. Doe burned down his house and banned his political party from future elections.

When the new constitution was drafted, one of the items adopted came directly from the US constitution: the president of the country must be at least thirty-five years of age. The PRC political faction had gone to great propaganda lengths to promote Doe as the twenty-eight-year-old Master Sargent who liberated the Liberian people from the tyranny of Tolbert's regime. That made Doe, born in 1951, thirty-four at the time of the elections.

When the ink dried on Doe's brand spanking new birth certificate, he was now born in 1950.

19

A Child Soldier

"Child soldiers continue to be used throughout the
world. Militia commanders consider them ideal fighters
– cheap, nimble, and psychologically malleable."
—*Unknown*

THE LIBERIAN CIVIL Wars would not have lasted without child
soldiers, the Small Boys Units (*SBU*), the kids.

The *SBU* was a group of children forcibly recruited for the war.
In 1998, twenty-five percent of the soldiers fighting in the war were
under eighteen. Of those, fifty-percent were abducted and twenty-
eight percent were under the age of twelve.

The *SBU* sustained the energy, the rage, the fear, and the
cannon fodder for the war. They were the bullet-eaters. The men
who instigated and maintained the violent conflict could never
have sustained the murder of their countrymen without the kids.
Liberians are generally a jovial, rollicking, pleasant people. War
isn't sustainable according to their world view; they'd rather eat and
visit and dance and play while they build civilization collectively
and lives individually. Conflict doesn't necessarily fit. They haven't
the appetite. If they did, real soldiers would have carried out their
wars. It was the undeveloped minds and moral compasses of the
children that were hijacked, drugged to obey, and brainwashed to
murder, that sustained much of the actual conflict.

In one of the single largest and most atrocious recruitment raids, three hundred orphans were seized in a place called Chocolate City. More children were picked up as the rebels moved about the country seizing land and resources. Children under fifteen years of age made up about ten percent of the total combatants in Liberia's Civil War. Gathering and mobilizing them became an arms race for warlords. The tactics used to body-snatch child soldiers were nefarious and wicked. Some were flat-out kidnapped, like the three hundred from Chocolate City. Others were cajoled, looking for food and water after families were destroyed. Some joined voluntarily to avenge massacred relatives and friends. Some were forced to assassinate their own mothers and fathers. Enlisting became their only path to survival. The children were taught how to recruit others, how to kill, loot, and commit atrocities.

20

Liberia

JEROME BLOMO SR. was head of security for General Thomas Quiwonkpa.

Quiwonkpa was a Gio tribesman and officer in the Liberian Army. From 1980 to 1985, Quiwonkpa was involved in three coups of the Liberian government, once as an assistant and twice as a head coach. His record was 1-2. He thrived from the first, rewarded with a high government position. He survived the second, but was exiled to Sierra Leone. He was sacked after the third, in a very African way.

In 1980, Quiwonkpa helped Doe oust Tolbert in that violent and bloody take-over. Jehuu's father was by his side as head of security. Doe made Quiwonkpa his secretary of state, and Jerome Blomo went along for the ride. The relationship wouldn't last. Quiwonkpa was gaining popularity with the people and fellow soldiers. Doe was Krahn, a minority in Liberia. He didn't like or trust other tribes, especially Gio. Doe was also developing an unhealthy love of power, succumbing to the paranoia, obsession, and the suspicion that comes with governing a diverse African country.

By 1983, Doe recognized Quiwonkpa's popularity and saw it as a threat. He needed a way to get rid of him. Quiwonkpa recognized this and, to beat Doe to the punch, planned his first solo coup. The plot was uncovered early in the process and Quiwonkpa and his general staff, including Jehuu's father, were expelled from Liberia.

From Sierra Leone, Quiwonkpa returned to Liberia in 1985 with a dozen men to try another coup of Doe. Jerome Blomo did not return with him and good thing –the coup failed miserably. Now Quiwonkpa's coup record was one win, two losses. Grounds for dismissal.

Jehuu's father had attached his wagon to the wrong star. But there really wasn't a guaranteed luminary to lend your talents. Coups were abundant in Liberia, based on who trusted who, Shakespearean in their machinations. With Quiwonkpa's failure, Jerome Blomo was forced to leave the country, Liberia no longer his home. His family never saw him again. They disavowed him totally. They took all his pictures, his dog-tags from the military, all his papers, and threw them in the ocean.

. . . .

After the 1983 coup, General Quiwonkpa was captured, dismembered, and parts of him eaten by Krahn soldiers loyal to Doe. In response to the coup, Doe launched genocidal revenge against Gio and Mano tribes in Nimba county, Quiwonkpa's home. Some three-thousand unsuspecting Liberian citizens were slaughtered. Another brick was placed in the foundation of the next coup. In 1985 Taylor started his rebellion in Nimba County, understanding the significance.

Back in the Monrovia, Prince Johnson, a Gio warlord, recruited an emerging army, and formed an alliance with Doe. For this partnership, Doe gave him part of Monrovia to set up headquarters and continue to build his small army with the stipulation that Johnson's forces help Doe fend off future insurrection. Trusting a Liberian warlord with part of your city was not the best military decision Doe ever made.

It would wind up being one of his last.

21

A Child Soldier

HOPE IS TEN in 1989, older than Jehuu whose father disappeared into Sierra Leone.

It's not plausible to wipe out the population of wild cats, killers of mothers, in the Wuteve plains and jungles, but this doesn't keep Hope's father from taking one out every year on this horrific anniversary.

Hope is tucked between his father and Ranger. They walk slowly through a bramble path of broken plants, a pack-animal corridor between hunting grounds and a watering hole. More than one animal moves here but not at the same time. The men approach the clearing water bank from downwind, muzzles pointed forward.

"Loosen your safety," his father whispers. Hope's been waiting for this; his finger jerks the lever to the live position. His heart jumps in his chest, his ears buzz, he listens past insects, into the bush. He wipes a hand on sweat-soaked khakis, quick to replace his finger on the trigger. His shirt is saturated, heavy on his shoulders. He's careful not to get it stuck on anything sharp, tries not to disturb the plants along the path. Walk on my toes, like the panther and pangolin. His father and Ranger have tight britches and heavy canvas vests to tamp down their clothes. There is a sheen of moisture on everything, man and plant alike.

He thinks to be quiet, to stalk. His feet are soft pads he prays make no noise, leave no marks, not a single print on the face of the earth. Be a ghost. His heart beats hard. When they break through the high grass line, they will see something wild and untamed, watering holes in the bush are never completely empty, not in heat like this. Hope knows his own watering hole on the mountain, he doesn't know this one.

Hope brushes more sweat off his face to uncloud his vision. His father turns a corner on the path, lost to his line of vision, he can't hear Ranger behind him. He is, for a moment, alone. Insects buzz ears, eyes, nose. Nairobi flies, mealy bugs, blisters, he doesn't dare swat at them.

He stops and listens.

He knows better than to shout out in his brief isolation. The path behind him is empty. Ranger is gone, his father ahead somewhere. He hears a rustle in the grass where Ranger is supposed to be, around the bend he just passed. He breaks discipline and whispers, "Ranger. You there?" He starts, stops, looks ahead where his father just was. "Papa? Where are you?"

It's possible, but not probable that cougars hunt in ways like men. That they use subterfuge and distraction, reason and strategy. It's possible this was a clever plan laid out by a beast past its primal functioning of instinct and impulse and animal reaction.

Possible.

A cougar leaps from the bush. Hope dives to the ground and lands on his gun. As the beast flies by, it rakes Hope's back with extended claws. A voice screams in his ear, he realizes it's his own. The snarl from the cat is a roar. It's not the pain that rents the shout from his lungs, it's the sheer physicality and savagery of the attack that causes his involuntary scream.

The pain comes later.

22

Bonita

What was it like living in Liberia? Did you grow up affluent?

BC: Mum's house was very popular because we were one of the few people who had television. Every Friday and Saturday night my mum would make popcorn, and they would put out benches and the whole neighborhood would come over to watch *General Hospital*. And that was one episode, not one every day, we would watch one episode a week. We were allowed to watch *The Rifleman*, *Combat*, just those kind of movies. On Sunday, we were only allowed to watch the news at eight o'clock from America.

When I was little and growing up, we planted all our own food. Acres and acres of food. My mum would cook, and she'd make all the kids, everybody, cart food. Everybody would drop off food to the neighbors. Acres of land that we would till by hand and plant most of our own food. We had casabas, we planted eggplant, all the fruits and vegetables that we ate.

So I guess you could say we were farmers growing up. We certainly knew about the land. Wet season, dry season, our hands were dirty even though my mum and dad had government jobs and brought home money. When a child grows up like that, hard work comes natural. It's in their blood. Every place has it's lazy, it's thieves, it's ticks and fleas, but that wasn't an option at my mum and dad's house. You worked. It served my children well when they came to this country. They fit in with the other kids at the Clymer school. Hard working Liberians into hard working Americans.

What about Jehuu? Did he fit in with this lifestyle? You said he was pretty spoiled.

BC: Oh, yes. When I left Jehuu with my mum, when I went to the United States, he was spoiled rotten, so they all thought he was the civilized one. He was just coming into this, a place with other kids, with responsibilities, so they had to handle him with kid gloves. He had to learn to share and work. He was getting used to that life, and then the war came, and he had to leave, pack up whatever they could carry on their backs, and walk. There were no spoiled children walking the roads of Liberia, not then.

They grow up fast.

23

Liberia

"Liberia has become a casualty of the Persian
Gulf War. A distracted world has ignored its
suffering. It is one of the most critical and neglected
humanitarian emergencies in the world today."
—*Edward Kennedy*

CHARLES TAYLOR'S REBELLION was a devil's errand, masked as a grassroots rising.

It is considered one of the most tragic and homicidal series of human rights violations in the history of mankind with its escalation of murder, rape, and torture between one group of humans and another. When Taylor eventually filled his army with Krahn opposition and his personal Small Boys Unit of displaced and orphaned children, the back-and-forth battle with government forces began at a more lethal level, mostly for prized real estate in and around Monrovia. Warring armies –government, rebels, warlords– took turns committing atrocities on the population, all claiming to be champions of justice. The unrelenting catastrophe of barbarism was internally justified when the perpetrators invoked time honored phrases like necessary evils and this is war.

Many claimed to be Christians yet used juju and dark magic when it expedited atrocities. They said they were making a better Liberia for the children, yet drugged them up for battles they wouldn't fight themselves, saying they were better served in their armed services than in orphanages.

24

Jehuu

"JEHUU, THE CABLES. Here wrap them like this. Come now, we're late."

Grandpa directs Christmas day traffic at the house on Allison Street. Presents will wait. Now it's time to go to church and see the baby Jesus. The house on Allison Street has a bouquet of sweet smells that cuts through the usual odor of meat and herbs. My nose tingles, this is Grandma's work, better than candy, better than Skittles. It conjures gift wrapping and holiday decorations. It's hard to concentrate on church. Grandpa is patient, directing me and the other kids in the house to the jobs, Mardea, Joseph, Odziki and the rest. But I can see his patience melt, disappear, like frosting licked from a cupcake. Pure sweetness down to the real cake.

"When are we back from church. Papa?"

"The usual time."

"When is that?"

"Mind your work, Jehuu. And you others!" Grandpa hollers back into the house. "We will do our church service before we do our presents. This isn't your day, this is baby Jesus' day."

The morning is light and dry, the heat won't come until later, when it's time for presents. I hope for a football. I did recon of the house over and over again, but found nothing of gifts, no wrapping, not a roll of tape or scissors out of place.

Grandma tests us daily, hourly, it seems. "What is today, Jehuu? Why is it different than other days?" God lives at our house and watches over us. There is no voodoo, no tribal witchcraft, no *Heartmen.*

Heartmen are witch doctors who kidnap people, usually bad children, and cut out their hearts while they're still alive and use it to make medicine. They aren't supposed to be real, But I'm not so sure, the stories sound real to me.

We have the baby Jesus, Santa, presents, midnight mass. We have *Old Man Beggar.* His job is to make fun of people, then tell a story of redemption and Christmas miracles to redeem himself, lessons of humility. My family is among the over eighty percent of practicing Christians in Liberia. The advent season is as real to me as to you. "Merry Christmas" in the United States is *My Christmas is on you* in Liberia. We don't say two words when we can say five. Christmas meals, snacks, treats, holiday sports where we gather around the telly to watch our football, our national team, The Lone Stars. Their name is a tribute to our national flag. How can a Liberian not root for them?

Christmas 1989. Liberian Christians went to church, but it was not just another holiday. There was a tide building. You could feel it on the edges of our world, even when you're six, even when you have presents to open. It leaked from my family like dark smoke, whispers in back rooms, a father you're not allowed to speak of, the way people looked and acted when they spoke about President Doe, the sneers, the anger covering a veil of fear and paranoia.

Older Liberians will remember Christmas in 1989 differently than I do.

· · · ·

Not many people get more than one distinct life, one from a past, one from a future. Christmas is one of the few things that translated from Liberia to the United States. Sun only in one place. Sun, but also snow in the other. Church in both. Christmas commercials in the United States that hardly make sense. Ads on the

TV start around Halloween. It's more on the down-low in Liberia. In the States, I saw Santa Claus, presents, decorations, shopping and cookies, shopping and parties. In Liberia, it's more separated between homes and churches and neighbors, where four or five religions blend, all as fervently believed as the next. There's room for the baby Jesus, there's Muslims and Hindus, and there's an avenue for voodoo and shaman and witch-doctors.

Bumper slogans on buses throughout Liberia read, *Rejoice, God's Word Is the Best* and *Every Disappointment Is a Blessing.* Evangelical signs are a reminder of the important role that American Protestant missionaries have always played in Liberia. There is the *Eternal Love Winning Africa Missionary* radio station, the *Fullness of Time Evangelistic Ministry*, the *Living Water Baptist Church*, and *God's End Time Ministries, Inc.*

On another side of the coin, one used for expediency and, occasionally, terrorism, is the world of magic and voodoo. That set of beliefs have long been associated with Liberia's political culture, and its most malevolent practices —ritual human sacrifice and cannibalism, usually linked to people seeking power or to those who fear losing it.

Samuel Kofi Woods, the director of the Justice and Peace Commission, a human-rights organization run by the Catholic Church, blames Taylor for what he says is an upsurge of politically motivated ritual murders. Woods says that the consecration ceremony sent the message that Taylor believes in juju. In early June of the rebellion, there were several local news stories about Heartmen at large. Human hearts were reportedly being removed and eaten by candidates for various offices to enhance their chances of winning election.

And always the specter of the child soldier. *Suffer little children to come unto me, and forbid them not; for of such is the kingdom of heaven*, said Jesus. Saint Nicholas is the patron saint of children. Neither of those facts gave pause to the adults who used children to execute their civil war.

We all learned that Heartmen really do exist.

25

Liberia

JEHUU'S BABY PHOTOGRAPHS look like most kids at that age.

No way to tell they were taken in Africa –a newborn, eyes closed, swaddled against the world. An infant on his mother's hip, in a bathing tub, in his high chair, running restless in the yard. The child, Jehuu with those thundering thighs, healthy, strong, well fed.

There are few clues in the Polaroids that show they were taken in Africa and not Florida or Texas. A yard void of grass could be the panhandle instead of a Liberian suburb. The clapboard siding could be rural Arkansas or Georgia. Jehuu's Liberian surroundings have the feel of a home in the United States. There are photos of Jehuu playing on a clean hardwood floor, eating in his favorite high chair, a fully stocked kitchen in the background. Your prejudices evaporate; they could be your baby pictures.

Pictures from April of 1990 when Jehuu and Mardea were seven and nine years old. They show peaceful domesticity, two kids showing off nice clothes. Jehuu's growth plates stretching up into the world, legs already thick and muscular. Mardea slim from top-to-bottom, a half-head taller than her younger brother. There's no stress, no fear on their faces.

Other pictures show the family on their way to church, Mardea proud of her lace dress, Jehuu barely in check. It's obvious he'd like to take his Sunday clothes into a wrestling match or game of rough-house. Grandpa, David Caulcrick, wears a dark suit, red-striped tie, his VHS recorder on his shoulder. On Sundays, he tapes church services with his personal video and sound equipment. All the kids from the Allison Street house are responsible for transporting the gear to and from church, everyone has a job. Jehuu carries a microphone stand and rolled cables.

April 1990, Sunday church is still a thing for the Caulcrick family. Bonita is in the United States building a home for her children. Jerome Blomo is exiled to Sierra Leone.

The rumors are out there, in the wind. A rebellion is coming, fighting in the North. There have been rumors before. There's no way to understand the growth of the movement, the power of Taylor. No way to see into the future. No way to know that the people in these pictures will soon be on the road, where clean clothes and church are a memory, smiles rare, Polaroid pictures impossible.

April 1990. Charles Taylor is four months into his rebellion, energizing the country against the Doe regime. Charles Taylor, marching south from the Nimba county where his swelling rebellion just finished a series of indiscriminate massacres of Krahn tribes.

26

A Child Soldier

WHEN HE LOOKED back at it, the ambush was a classic operation, easily foreseeable.

He didn't have the sight then, no experience with man as animal, only animal as animal. Papa was foolish, a mountain-bush man with no clue of war. No idea how to stay alive outside of keeping clear of the watering hole during feeding time and staying off the animal runs. Respect the gorilla, cougar and panther, avoid python nests, and the cobra thicket. You don't rush into blind spots in the bush, and you don't slow down for blocked passage out on the road. You always leave a way out, backward, forward, sideways. You keep your weapon on your hip or back, fully loaded, safety off. You empty rounds and rounds of ammo at any noise you don't recognize, and you step on the gas. You move fast to the other side.

And you don't trust men.

Lessons Hope would learn. Lesson his father would not.

. . . .

Christmas 1989, a *Maharratan* sandstorm comes from the eastern desert. The northern side of the mountain will soon be an air-sea of sand. The tempest will originate in the Mojave and sweep west across the continent. In a Maharratan, you have to cover your mouth to breathe, or eat sand, one or the other.

Hope rides in an old Jeep with his father, away from the mountain range. Wuteve, part of the Wologizi massif that borders Guinea and Sierra Leone, is the highest point in Liberia at 1,440 meters. Both the boy and his father are Kru tribe, a secret they know to keep.

Satellites on top of Wuteve in the Ivory Coast have been sending weather signals for days. The national preserve where the boy's father is head ranger battened down, equipment and windows covered with tarp and wood. The rangers have supplied the outer barracks with food for days of refuge in case travel becomes impossible. The mountain will most likely stall the sandstorm system, dumping sand and debris over square miles of elevation. The mountains usually protect inner and coastal Liberia, down-mountain where Liberia changes to foothill, then to bush, mangrove forests, and eventually the sea.

Hope and his father use this excuse to take a Christmas trip into the capital to deliver unnecessary reports from the mountain preserve to government agencies that won't understand them, but demand the paper be used. They'll gather supplies, buy a few Christmas gifts for the assistant rangers and staff.

. . . .

Hope sits in the passenger seat of the Jeep, gazes at his father, the bright sun washing his dark skin in light. His father frowns, says, "Wha you looking at boy?" Hope rubs the white puckers on his arms, those cougar scars from the hunt. His father smiles, reaches over and touches a scar on his face, "You the great hunter. Almost lost you that day."

"Nah, you and ranger were there." Hope shrugs and looks out the windshield of the open Jeep.

"Cougars don't care we there or not. Smart cats. Those scars, they still hurt, *eh*?"

"Nah, they just bumpy. It hurt when you burned them shut. More than the claws." Hope thought back to the mini-triage on the cougar hunt. The cougar had mauled him pretty good, his back and face were shredded. His papa and ranger had to solder them shut. He wandered in and out of consciousness with the pain, the smell of his own flesh burning. When he woke up, he was back in the barracks on Wuteve Mountain.

Wrapped in a cougar pelt.

. . . .

A few clicks short of five-thousand feet of elevation, Mount Wuteve, in the far north sector of Liberia overlooks the neighboring countries of Sierra Leone and Guinea; the peak is much more a part of Guinea since its parent range sweeps from Guinea Highlands east towards the West Africa Mountains.

The drive down the mountain is slow and deliberate, picking the way through brush and boulders. The road is empty from Wuteve toward Gbarnga. Then Lofa county to Bong in Northern Liberia, going south toward the capital city of Monrovia where the government waits for its annual wild-game reports from Papa's sector of the national preserve. Phone lines and communication are down, possibly because of the Harmattan. Rumors say rebels cut all communications with the South to isolate the Liberian government from the North. Rumors of attacks, one tribe killing another tribe.

The people in Nimba county had heard it all before, a coup is afoot, an uprising. It was none of their business, unless Doe's forces came charging into their neighborhoods, then smart people take to the bush and let the violence blow over.

Hope and his father are government servants and bush people going about bush business, removed from politics.

But this time was different and very few saw it at the start. The knocked-out communications was one sign. The quiet in the small villages they passed driving down from the mountains was another. There where were other signs, warnings a Ghost soldier might notice. Nothing for Hope, the twelve-year-old son of a park ranger, to worry himself over. Papa should have known, Papa should have sensed the danger. But Papa was a man of the bush, not of the world. He knew animals, not men. He should have protected Hope so they could run their simple errand and get back to Wuteve, back in the barracks close by the watering hole. Back by the other Wuteve men who looked after the jungle, close by the Sierra Leone border.

27

Liberia

"War won't end here as long as these people are armed."
—*Unknown Liberian Quote*

THE OUT OF control, spiraling nature of Liberia's Civil War was gruesome.

The day Taylor crossed the border with his hundred well-armed insurrectionists, a human tragedy was set in motion, a clock started that ticked toward the mortality of a nation susceptible to cruelty in that its peoples are generally genial, and trusting.

At first Taylor's rebels were welcomed as a guerilla force weeding through Doe soldiers, a noble and efficient knife carving up the corrupt regime, the Poncho Villa/Fidel Castro of modern Western Africa, a romanticized bush warrior hero.

Doe, responding in the way of violent dictators unable to understand those he governs, and wielding an army filled with minority Krahn soldiers, sent his military to Nimba County to quell the rebellion. His troops were not welcome, the Gio and Manos living there remembered all too well the 1983 genocidal revenge Doe perpetrated after Quiwonkpa's coup attempt (coincidentally the year Jehuu was born and Hope chased cougars in the bush). When three-thousand of your neighbors are executed for reasons you don't fully understand, you hesitate to help your government stamp out rebellions.

When the Liberian army was unable to find Taylor's rebels in the deep bush, their frustration and bullets were spent on other tribes and non-combatants, the 1983 massacre repeated. Krahn soldiers were sent into the bush to kill the enemy, and finding none, they went after old enemies, real or imagined, innocents sitting in the cross-hairs. To please Doe and his regime, they killed a few hundred (mainly Gio and Mano) they claimed were rebels. When the local clergy complained and asked for the removal of Doe, they killed the clergy.

The purge had begun. Name them, and Doe had them killed. There was no safe place if you were caught off guard, or if you wanted to try to protect a home or belongings or loved ones. Sanctuary was nonexistent.

Taylor now had more fuel for a civil war, capturing the hearts and minds of the majority of Liberians and further isolating Doe to the confines around Monrovia. Taylor's campaign quickly jacked up the body count, nine-thousand killed, tortured, or stolen into his army. Internationally protected Red Cross retreats were especially soft targets. Refugee camps became slaughterhouses, the vulnerable horded into convenient pens. In the Harbel refugee camp alone, six hundred were executed, five-hundred wounded, two-hundred abducted.

By the end of the first surge of violence, fifty-thousand were dead, eight-hundred-thousand displaced. One million ended up homeless, one-third of the population. There was no place to go for medical attention, no food if you were starving, nobody to see.

By the end of 1990, every single person in Liberia was dependent on international food aid.

.   .   .   .

The country swooned under the random violence by Doe's government, aimed at non-Krahn tribes, but hitting all walks of Liberian life. The outrage and helplessness of the population found their salve, their aloe, in the idea of the *NPFL* and Charles Taylor, who told the people what they wanted -needed- to hear, did all the right things.

His first assault was on a Doe-held military post in a place called Butuo in Nimba county, on the Sierra Leone border. Taylor attacked Christmas eve 1989, and when Doe's forces fled instead of fighting, there flashed a pen-light ray of hope for Liberians not aligned with Doe's government. Doe's soldiers ran, Taylor's forces prevailed. Is justice possible? Is Taylor the savior? Is this a chance at a life out from under the thumb of a paranoid despot? Taylor's campaign was supposed to be a Liberian grassroots rebellion against the Doe government and its mounting atrocities. But Taylor's story has enough mysterious elements of geo-political convenience and coincidence to make a reasonable case that his rise to power was part of a multi-nation, coordinated effort to clean up Liberia. Was Taylor's rebellion a case of nation building?

The political and military maneuverings were all news to the Caulcrick's in Buchanan and Bonita in the United States.

28

Jehuu

IN SPRING 1990, my mum came back to visit us in Buchanan.

She came for auntie's school graduation. She traveled all the way from the Erie, Pennsylvania International airport to Robertsfield in Monrovia, Liberia, then on to Buchanan where we all lived. She was gone almost a full year and still the Visas for Mardea and me were not ready. She couldn't take us back when her visit was over. She left without us…again. We were in no hurry to leave for another world. Liberia was still child-friendly, the government intact, Grandpa working as a food inspector, Grandma's home-school prosperous, the neighborhood full of friends, in and out of our daily lives. Liberian football, church, plenty of good food and drink.

But Liberia was changing fast, just beyond the grasp of the people. We were used to conflict and upheaval ever since Doe assassinated all those people in his coup, and later. Charles Taylor was building an army of rebels, gathering momentum as he made his way south from Nimba County into Gbarna in central Liberia. Taylor set up a base of operations there, able to branch out into all parts of Liberia.

Picture the state of Pennsylvania. It's approximately the same size as Liberia, tipped on its side, a quarter turn counterclockwise to see the shape of the country. Taylor enters Liberia around where Philadelphia is, and sets up in Harrisburg. From here raids into Pittsburgh, and Erie, access to Altoona, and State College is convenient.

Meanwhile warlords, in control of their own parts of Liberia and representing in some combination all sixteen tribes, are reading tea-leaves, smelling the air of rebellion, and consolidating power of their own, forming allegiances, stockpiling arms, preparing for the day when Doe and the sitting government is inevitably attacked. Doe, for his part, threw as much gasoline on the fire as he could, with his Krahn-heavy military. Reacting to Taylor, and instead of hunting down the rebellion forces, he used the Liberian military to terrorize civilian tribes that were not his blood. This made Taylor's recruitment easier. His ranks swelled. As Taylor gobbled up land and resources, his war-chest grew, and his army did not want for weapons and supplies.

My mum left Liberia with this potion of rebellion brewing, never able to imagine that she would not be able to return for another year and under the most dangerous conditions imaginable. Maybe for the best though. If she stayed or came back before the Civil War broke, she might be dead now.

Threading that needle.

29

A Child Soldier

LEAVING WUTEVE FEELS like an adventure.

They drive down a canopied dirt road, lined by thick mangrove bush, leaving Vahun city, where residents, instead of waving to the Jeep as it passes, peek from behind thatch-beaded doorways. The next city is Gelahun. There is barely room for two vehicles and the bend in the road makes his papa slow down. The report of a single rifle shot, a second before the front left tire of the Jeep blows out, is registered by neither Hope nor his father. It sounds like a branch breaking in the jungle, nothing else.

Papa says, "Tire going flat." A grumble. "Hope, sit. I'll look."

Hope gazes into the bush, close by the road. He sees the trees move, a rustle that is too big for the deer or the fox. A gorilla maybe? "Papa?"

"Fix it and be going." Papa gets out of the Jeep and the bush comes alive with black faces, cartoon clothing, hats, wigs, a full-length white dress on a stickman, metal, gun, and machete. Papa looks up, then back at Hope who rises from his seat to see better. Papa holds his hands out palms down, a hushing gesture. Hope leans so he can see, but stays in the Jeep. Sweaty boys with white and yellow teeth shine against the jungle backdrop.

Papa shows the boys his hands. He whispers, "Sit Hope, don't move."

The boys surround Papa, a man in full-dress military uniform splits the crowd. Points a big gun, bigger than Papa's hunting rifle, "*Eh*? Who are you traveling this road? What's your tribe?"

Papa shrugs. "We from the reserve, up the mountain." Papa's khaki clothes cling tight to his big muscles. He hovers over The Man. Hope notices how big his Papa's hands are, paddles of flesh.

The Man makes a face. "What are your weapons?"

"No weapons," says Papa. His hands are up, but his face is easy, a hunter's eyes that move to the boys, back to Military Man.

"In da Jeep, with the boy. Wha weapons?" The soldier pokes Papa in the chest, then lowers the rifle, crooked under his arm, one handed. His beard is dark against his face. His eyes are rimmed red, muscles cord in his neck and arms.

Papa's hands lower slightly. "No weapon Sah. He's a boy. We're rangers, government. We're driving to…"

The Man raises his weapon slightly. It goes *POP*. Papa falls onto the dusty road and screams, *AIEEE*, he grabs his leg. Hope jerks at the sound, frozen in the Jeep.

Now the Jeep is surrounded by boys, they paw at Hope's backpack and the tarp covering the government papers, the sleeping kit, the hunting rifle. The boys smell of shit and sweat and something sweet. There's a sheen of moisture on them, their lips cracked into hideous red smiles. One jumps in the front seat, plays on the steering wheel, "Beep beep," he says. An older boy, orange shirt, long camo pants and a black skull cap, teeth yellow, face pocked with sores, reaches in the back, and pulls out Papa's hunting rifle.

"Weapon here, Sah," the older boy holds it up in the air for the man to see.

Papa lies on the road, rolls in the dust. The Man pins him to the ground with the point of his weapon in his broad chest. "No weapon, enh?"

Hope shakes himself, "No!"

And *pop pop pop* goes the gun. Papa screams.

Hope knows shotguns from the range on the mountain, he does not know these guns, too big for the boys, slung over their backs, they touch the ground. He can't fathom what has happened, doesn't recognize the report of this weapon, so unlike the hunting rifles, the genesis of the violence. He wonders, How do they hunt with those guns?

The Man leans over Papa, and prods him with the gun. "So, we have a weapon. And we have a boy." He rips at Papa's shirt with the barrel of the gun. Blood seeps into the dusty road. "What tribe are you? What tribe da boy?" He snaps a signal at a boy who stands by with a red container. The boy empties a clear liquid over his father, soaked head to foot. The soldier flicks a lighter, "Last chance for you."

His father groans. He reaches toward the truck, one imploring hand. Hope, he mouths. My Hope.

Hope tries to look away, but his head won't cooperate. He closes his eyes, he is slapped from behind. He glazes over in panic and stress. He's slapped again, hard enough to make his eyes water and focus. He goes slack, his body giving up. He tries to melt into the truck seat. Hands yank at him.

The fire takes almost no time to build. Lots of gasoline and just Papa for fuel.

30

Liberia

CHARLES TAYLOR'S MOTHER was Gola, one of Liberia's most indigenous tribes. His father was Americo-Liberian, one of the least.

That mix gave him credibility on both sides of most tribal conflicts. He was educated in the United States at Bentley College in Massachusetts, been-to as Liberians called people with the resources to find education in Europe and the United States, giving him another fundamental source of legitimacy. He was intelligent, charming, manipulative.

He started his rise after Doe's coup of Tolbert in 1983. He was given the position of Director General of the General Services Agency (why use one-word titles when you can use five?). He oversaw purchasing for the government, where he embezzled more than a million dollars. The Liberian way. He was booted from Doe's government ostensibly for theft, but, like Quiwonkpa, more for his popularity with the people, a potential threat to Doe; one too many Liberians of consequence sided with him one too many times in internal governmental power struggles for Doe's liking. The hypocrisy of the charges on Taylor of government theft by Doe was not lost on Liberians. Doe was a notorious master at throwing a fit because someone else dared infringe on his own stolen bounty of national resources. Doe maintained, like most despots and dictators, that he was the sole interpreter of who could and could not steal from his citizens.

Taylor fled to the United States, back to Massachusetts where he was promptly arrested by US Marshals and sent to prison to await extradition back to Liberia and Doe. His death sentence.

Instead, he escaped prison, allegedly and legendarily by cutting through iron bars with nothing sharper than soap, dropping twenty-five feet from his cell, landing unhurt, and fleeing to South America…from Massachusetts. Then South America to Africa where he trained and outfitted a band of heroic rebels to take his country back from the oppressive Doe regime.

A superhero origin story.

The truth is probably closer to a conspiracy where United States intelligence agencies engineered his improbable escape so they could weaponize him against Doe who was becoming a thorn in the side of the United States with every human rights violation inflicted on his perceived enemies. Perpetuating its sketchy record of propping up the wrong side in foreign governments, the United States paid some sixty million dollars to the Doe regime, allegedly to keep communism out of Liberia. Spies in the Reagan administration went so far as to help Doe survive early coup attempts in the early 80s. But the 1982 attempt by Thomas Quiwonkpa, that came oh-so-close to eliminating the increasingly paranoid and oppressive Doe, was a bellwether event that set Doe aflame. The human rights atrocities he committed sending soldiers to Nimba County to slaughter rival tribes, further embarrassed the United States, and primed Liberian soil for Taylor and the National Patriotic Front of Liberia. Doe had to go.

It was Nimba County where Taylor crossed the border and started his own righteous rampage, symbolism not lost on the rest of Liberia.

With implicit support from neighboring African nations and a large section of Liberia's opposition, Taylor's NPFL rebels rapidly gained the support of Liberians because of the repressive nature of Samuel Doe and his government. Several unpredictable and untimely events, like the Gulf War and the consequent United States disengagement from Liberia, coincided to turn that invasion into a protracted Civil War. Intervention help came only from West African Economic Community of West African States Monitoring Group (ECOMOG).

31

Jehuu

WHEN NO ONE'S looking, not Grandpa, not Grandma, not even Mardea or the cousins, I go!

The forest out the back of the house on Allison Street is thick, root-heavy, trippy and sultry. Trees, low hanging and spread wide, easy for a boy to run under, harder for a grown man to get through. The shade keeps you chill if you stay low, a canopy keeping out the sun.

Rainforest covers more of Africa than any other habitat, some twenty-nine percent of the continent. For Liberia, it's almost forty-five percent, rubber trees, cocoa, and timber for export, much of it grown and forested on farms in neat rows. Mango groves cover some eight-thousand acres. Where rubber, timber, coffee, and coca are the main plant exports, mangroves are mostly left to grow wild.

The jungle behind the Buchanan house is dense, those gnarled trees heavily rooted, crisscrossed, covering the forest floor with bush and vegetation, thick and rough. No animal stirs my forest. No rustle of the wild boar, no wisp of snake, no mongoose, no monkeys in the trees.

This time it's after church. Sundays are chaos at the house, work to be done, meals to prepare, people everywhere. I change fast out of stiff church clothes, into my fast shoes, bright yellow shirt, high-pocket orange shorts. I start by the edge of the guava field, people gathering crops for after-church lunch, paying no attention to me. When no one is looking, sneaking, I dash into the mangrove forest, under the branches. I leap and hop and scatter from tree to tree without ever catching in the brambles, nothing touches me, I barely touch ground between trees my feet are so fast. Obstacle course, amusement park. Tubman Field, Little Jehuu is the best goal scorer The Lone Stars have ever seen.

I'm not supposed to be in this forest alone, been warned many times by mum and grandpa, and even Mardea. "Don't go by yourself in there, Jehuu. You get lost and Heartman will come take you. Maybe sell you, maybe eat you!"

The mangrove forest is too much fun to resist. For Grandma and Grandpa I say, "No I won't go."

For Mardea or Joseph, I say, "I go if I want."

The trade-off for being a spoiled only child is that your whereabouts are constantly monitored. You get what you want, sure, but you never get very far out of sight either. Those same people (women, in my case) that make you feel so special, dote on you, smother you with affection, but also stifle any rebellious wanderlust you might have. When your imagination shoves you into the open or into a mangrove forest, there is a tether of concern to reel you back; *Jehuu, don't wander too far. Don't touch that little one. Stay close.*

When you're one of many, like my new life after mum left, the leash lengthens, the line isn't held as tight. More eyes doesn't necessarily mean being seen more. Too many other little ones need attention, not just Jehuu.

So, here's my chance to go!

32

A Child Soldier

"They're not babies. They're not ten years old. The
AK47 weighs maybe ten or fifteen pounds. If this
young fellow feels like he doesn't fight, he will be dead
anyway, he comes forward to do what he has to do."
—*Jucontee Thomas Woewiyu*
(Charles Taylor's Second in Command)

THE DAY THAT his father was killed, Hope slept.

There were no dreams, those would come later. This sleep was the body and mind of a young boy shutting down, switched off, with the real possibility that it would never be turned on again. Can a brain, can a body, can a heart just decide to stop, to remain without power, to be blacked out?

Not for Hope. He wakes in the back of the open jeep, his head a mush of brains and blood. He tries to sit up. Dirty plastic sandals push him back. Pinned on his back, he looks into the treetops passing by. A soldier smacks him in the mouth with the butt of a rifle, a tooth loosens and lodges in the back of his throat. He coughs it out, blood soaks his chin. Another boy cuffs him in the ear, and the world goes silent. He closes his eyes again and sleeps.

This time he dreams.

33

Jehuu

IN THE FOREST by myself. No animals, all scared away by the war.

The constant and familiar *pop pop pop* of weapon fire -always in the neighborhood now- chases me into the mangroves. It's good to be away from real life. Two phantom football defenders get left in the dust on my way to the goal and the Champion's trophy. One long leap to a root the size of a man's torso, two more stutter steps through a snarled patch of roots weaving on top of the brambles and grass thickets. The heat baking the forest floor forms a haze of humidity. My shirt sticks to my back, familiar sweat, but I'm winning my fantasy game. I'm flying like Tarzan, like Reynaldo, my favorite player, weaving to score another goal for Liberia National team in this mangrove forest.

The *pop pop pop* of war grows faint. I run hard, revel in the freedom of flight. Trees defend my goal, gnarled roots make a pitiful defense, try to trip me. They're jo match, I'm Jehuu, savior of Liberian football! Gnarled branches grasp like arms to slow me down. They have no chance. Tree after tree, through the brush, goal after goal, until my energy finally gives out.

I stop, hands on hips, bent double, big smile. I look up at the sky through thick tree limbs and a leafy canopy. Blue and hot, cloudless. Hot, so hot tucked in this forest. Thirst catches me. Hunger not far off.

Uh oh. Where am I?

. . . .

They look many hours for me, lost in that mangrove forest. They call my name, they curse and promise and say there's candy at home if I come back. It makes me smile to have them all search for little Jehuu. I know I have to go back, when I get too hungry or thirsty, and I know I'll get finger-shaking from aunts and uncles.

But for now, things are easy here in the forest. There's no way for me to know that later, when we walk, when we're on the road and the *pop pop pop* of guns is so close it sounds like right next to you, that my grandma will want me to run to the mangrove, she will tell me to go hide. This time it's just me. No guns popping, no mortars landing, no soldiers squeezing triggers. I didn't know that this was training. I was preparing to run, and jump, and dodge. It was training to keep me alive on the road. Leaving the road, running in the bush, dodging and moving, keeping ahead of the bullet, the soldier. Then finding a way back to my people.

I was training for running with a football someday, too. I could never have known that.

34

A Child Soldier

HOPE WAS CAPTURED by Taylor's rebels like so many other children of Liberia.

When the soldiers finally got around to stripping him down, they saw the scars on his back, those soldered gashes and the bleached white-worm puckers that closed the large wounds made by the cougar claws.

They didn't know what to make of wounds like this. They looked into Hope's eyes and saw grey pupils swimming in a dark red bloodshot background of hate. Not fear, as they were so used to seeing. Not supplication, not surrender.

Under normal conditions, they would have shot him in the heart, but the commander happened to be Gio directly from the bush, a place where the old spirits had a firm foothold. The black magic so obviously seeping from this boy was too attractive to snuff out with a bullet. If officers could tame it, harness that hatred, that ju-ju, they might have a good boy soldier.

So, Hope was packed into a transport with other boys who were grabbed along this rebel caravan from Nimba County to Gbarna, where they could be trained into Charles Taylor's army, the involuntary recruitment to build the ranks of the Small Boys Unit of the NPFL.

Off to *Zero Week*.

· · · ·

Hope is given a bright yellow too-big shirt that read *Shit Happens* word-ballooned from a round smiley face, orange capris that hang off his waist, the tag still on (twelve dollars from *JC Penny*), obviously meant for a young girl, orange rubber sandals. He looks like every other child soldier grabbed by Taylor's NPFL, like a third grader might dress for school.

He doesn't get a weapon. Not right away. But he is given the name *Ghost*, for his white scars and those dead eyes.

Ghost is different than the other boys, the ones taken from inside towns and villages. When his commander yells, "Ghost! Here!" he doesn't always answer. Then he is smacked or punched, hard in the head. He doesn't mind; it makes him feel alive. He knows if he lets blood drip from his mouth, they might stop. Or they might not. He rubs his scars, the ones from the hunt with Papa and Ranger, he gets new welts from training with the rebels. They held together to make his skin seem unreal, like armor. Now there is a look they give him, a sideways glance, never straight on.

It's fear.

The soldiers say, "If you leave us, run away, desert, you burst into flames. That's the juju you have today, eh." Ghost nods and smiles. They give him the look. He already won his protective juju on the mountainside of Wuteve. It was burned into him by his father.

Day after day they train –how to crawl, how to form up, how to call the officers Suh, and to salute. How to make camp, dig a latrine, build a fire, set guards and watch for enemies. How to cook, how to clean weapons (no ammo yet). How to take the needle, to drink the jungle juice. Day after day, the new recruits line up. Officers point their AKs at them. When the safeties are off, the eyes go wide, and the boys shrink into themselves. Some cry and blow snot, hold up hands to stop the bullets. That's what Hope did, the first few times. Guns go off and bullets whistle through the leaves above heads, throw dirt in front, blow the bark off trees. Some hit the boys, the little ones who can't carry their weight, boys who can't make it, who cry all night for their mommies. Some boys pee themselves, their water flows down their legs and soaks into the soil. Some shit their pants. Those boys have to stand all night outside, among the beasts and bugs, until the piss and shit dries.

Ghost stood there the first night, the smell of his own urine calling the mosquitos and chiggers. He spent the night scratching and fending them off, refusing to sit. That was the last night he cried, the last night he believed his life was worth anything. The idea that his life was over was like lifting a cloud from his eyes, like when the Harmattan finally blows from the Wuteve and the dust settles and the sun comes out. He could see, *he can see!*

The next time he's lined up for the shooting, he smiles. The time after, he growls at the soldiers and their guns. His cougar scars protect him. Or he dies. The difference was nothing to him.

When lineups are over, the boys who are shot are pushed over a hill into a stinking pile, their names forgotten. You are allowed to go get clothes and shoes off them if you want, but their talismans have to stay in the pit. They don't work, the dead tainted them by not being believers. When it's over, every day, Ghost turns and goes back to the crowded tents to sleep with the other boys.

35

Jehuu

"If the townspeople are happy, look to the cook."
—*Liberian Saying*

WHAT ARE YOU up to little- pekin?

Grandma hums a Gio folk song, sing-song from her throat, the music fills the room like vapor. You can see it if you look hard. She stops to look at her Jehuu.

I squint at her. "Hungry. Peanut soup." Then, "Please," because I remember my new manners.

"Tell me how to make it." She looks into my eyes with a sly smile on her pretty face. She wipes her hands on her favorite flowered apron, brushes black and grey hair from her face with the back of her hand.

"Grandma, I'm hungry." I swing my legs under the wooden chair. My stomach growls.

"Come on boy. What's peanut soup?"

"I don't want to say all the time how to make it. I just want soup. Peanut soup."

She cocks her head to the side.

I sigh. "Ham-hock?"

"And?"

"Chicken peas, I know that."

"Um hmm."

The kitchen at grandma's house smells of spiced curry, fish, she-meat, some squirrel. My stomach growls again. The kitchen is comfortable, the chairs, the big old, worn table is covered in food all the time, and places where your water glass goes. Those smells are part of me, that place where I took in nourishment, meals and wisdom.

"So here it is, Jehuu. Peanut soup." Grandma smiles and picks up a piece of food, shows it to me.

"That's ham-hock." I say.

"Yes." She drops it into a boiling pot of water that smells like garlic and heat. Next ingredient.

"Beef?" I frown.

"Yes, beef." Drop, splash, hissing water. "Next?"

"Fish."

"That's fish," she repeats, and drops it in the pot. "Next."

"Nuts?"

"Not nuts little Jehuu. These are chick peas."

"Chicken peas."

On it goes, bell peppers, habanero -Grandma tries to get me to nibble these, but I know better- okra, and finally the peanut butter. I get a spoonful and sit watching her stir and fuss over the pot.

Grandma's house is a food factory; go hungry here, and it's your own fault. There is enough money in the family to buy what we need, and she runs a cooking, sewing, house-chores school right there on Allison Street. The house is separated for the students and the family, but it all blends into people coming and going. The front rooms have a couch and tables and chairs. Back part of the house is a kitchen-classroom.

Now Grandma sets down the spoon, hands on hips. She smiles with her eyes. Her thick Caulcrick lips and broad, smooth forehead is framed by jet-black hair with sprinkles of white salt on the sides. Her apron is a pattern of flowers scattered over a green field, her long sleeves impossible in the heat of the kitchen.

"Everyone is inside, right Jerome? Mardea, Joseph, them?"

"Yes grandma. When's mum coming back?"

"No one out front da house. That street is no good."

"Yes grandma." Not listening, eating. "But when?"

"I don't know. She finding a place for you in America. But no football outside now with soldiers here, *eh*?" Her shoulders sag, she moves back to the sink. You don't have to be more than six years old to know that's not good.

The dynamics of my world at Grandma's house are peaceful, a child's adventure, wake every day with the purpose of negotiating a world I understand. That changed when the soldiers parked a tank in the front yard. One day they are not there, and the next, they are. Guns and soldiers in the streets.

36

A Child Soldier

ANOTHER WEEK, MARCHING, starving.

The small boys are thirsty all the time. When new ones come, they walk the gauntlet, beaten by the older boys with whips and sticks. They are worked the hardest; they are taken, killed during the night. Some are taken by the animals around the camp, some just sit down and quit. They feed on what's left over from mess, wild berries or some old cassava. They die doing ropes over burning barrels of oil, when their arms give out. Those screams are the loudest. There are girls, too. They are mostly in the tents of the officers, but some become fighters.

The new ones don't get guns, just heavy wood to carry. More marching in formation, practice disappearing into the bush. Come back to formation. They all learn the ambush. Ghost realizes how clumsy he and his dad were to fall into one. They learn guard duty, how to patrol, how to clear a neighborhood. They get their warrior names, favors of the Gods, new clothes, and talismans, giving them new abilities –identity magic.

The boys line up every day before dinner bell. AKs aimed at chests. Safeties are popped off. *FIRE.*

Another splat! Another boy down. *Boy's not a believer. He thinks he can escape. He thinks he doesn't have to obey.* They throw him in the bush. Next day same.

Ghost doesn't understand how some boys are splattered into the bush and not him. He isn't a believer; it's fine if he dies. I don't understand. How is God not killing me? I don't believe. Why am I not in the death pile and the other boys can have my shoes, my clothes?

La God one know, a Liberian saying, *Only God knows.*

37

Jehuu

FOOTBALL IN GRANDMA'S yard.

Today, the fighting moves a few blocks away. Aunts, uncles, neighbors rush to and from the gardens gathering food. They laugh and joke, a welcome normal day after the war pushed us inside the house, cramped and anxious. The *pop pop pop* is a soft chorus on the horizon, so quiet you don't flinch. It's the music of revolution, today played in another place.

For me, it's football in the yard -the last game I remember there. Me, Joseph, Decontee, Terry, Jerry and Ozidiki. No girls. This is boys only, three v. three. The yard has a whisper of grass outline, a trampled playing field, sometimes dust, sometimes mud. Terry and Jerry are brothers from down the road. I think of them as the same person sometimes, close in age, except Jerry is faster, so he plays with me. Joseph is on my side, too. I call him my brother, but he's a cousin. Decontee is a giraffe, tall and gangly. He's second best (Jehuu is best, *eh*?). Ozidiki is bad at football, but we need him for sides.

Shorts and shoes, no shirts. It's hot. We have small goals set up twenty meters apart. Santa bought them at Christmas, and a new *Adidas World Cup* football. It's new and white, ready to be beaten to a dirty brown. Heat cooks everything, the crops, the football field, the people rushing around our game, to and from the crops. Sometimes they stop and watch and cheer. The football field is framed by a fence on one side, neighbors on the other, and the back stretches to the huge Caulcrick gardens. After that, the mangrove forest. Don't kick the ball over the fence or in the bush. Kicker has to get it.

Kick it Jehuu! You play like Weah.

Joseph, you look ready for the arena!

This is when I play my best. I'm a show-off, *eh*?

The score is close, and I sweat into my socks. My shorts are soaked. The same with everyone. Heavy breathing, some shouting Here, here, pass it here. Ozidiki tell jokes, he doesn't shut up, but he's *sooo* slow. I never want him on my team. He only cares about people laughing, not who wins.

I stick close to Decontee, mark him. When the ball comes, I shove him hard. He flies sideways, and the ball is mine. He whines, "Jehuu you cheat!" I ignore him and score. We argue, I count the score over and over until he gets mad. Same game, different day.

Then the gunfire, just up the street.

"Wha…?" Joseph stops and looks toward the house.

"No, Joseph! Don't stop." The score is tied. "Pass! Pass!"

Deconte steals the ball from Joseph and races to my goal. I give chase.

More weapon sounds, closer. A truck rushes past the front of the house. Deconte stops, the ball forgotten. Everyone stands still, looking, listening.

I score into the empty net. No cheers. No one cares.

Pop pop. Pop pop pop poppopopop. Gunfire is so close. It's right here.

Grandma at the back door. "INSIDE!"

"Awww." I start to complain. People from the field rush past me, right across the field, and run for the house. I stand, waiting for my cheers.

"NOW! Dammit." Grandma stands in her apron, holding the door open. She looks right at me. Her hair is flying, crazy.

She cursed. Grandma does not curse.

I run.

. . . .

War came, and with it a world I struggled to understand. The obvious violence, the dominance, the muscle and weapons those soldiers commanded was intoxicating. Us boys swore we'd be part of that, the arrogance of youth. If you're good at football, you're good at war, *eh*? Run, jump, shoot people. Ride in a white truck. The weapons, the uniforms, the swagger of them, it was exhilarating, boiled our blood. Kids all over the world played at war, at dominance, at killing. For us, it was right outside the window. Words like murder and rape and blood and massacre weren't mentioned.

The world gawked at pictures of child soldiers in Liberia, those crouched, athletic, snarling devil-children, firing a huge AK47 at unseen targets. The pictures showed ammunition shell casings litter the ground at a boy's feet, some caught suspended in air by the shutter, photos of those remarkable savages, so young and still so fierce. Those pictures you saw, can see today, in magazines from the time, on the internet, the kids with no names, those pictures frighten and repulse grownups. Those pictures have the power to excite and enthrall children. *Why not?* We asked. *Why not me?*

Adults say, *How can such a thing be? How can little boys live like this?* Reasonable, civilized thoughts.

I said, *That's me.* Those are my friends, my neighbors, the boy from down the street. I saw him at Firestone, in the city, at a football match. Maybe I went to school with him or his brother. Wasn't he at my house on TV night? Soldier boys!

Me and my cousins pretend to shoot those big loud guns *bang bang*. We say, *We going to fight, get guns, and be soldiers, oh? Help the rebels.*

Grandma says, "You not goin' be soldier Jehuu. All you boys just be still. You end up dead, *eh*?"

That's the way we thought, we thought being a soldier would be the fun, exciting.

Until Joseph.

38

A Child Soldier

"The elephant never gets tired of carrying its tusks."
—*Liberian Saying*

GHOST PLATOON.

War is exciting, so is killing people. The heat of battle. It's the day to day that's hell.

Look for food, look for water. Try to stay alive. Wait, then wait some more. Ghost knows this. He knows when you're not warring and killing may be the most dangerous times. He knows to put his head on a swivel, eyeballs on everything, like when you hunt the cougar. Especially the older boys, the ones close to the top. They shoot and kill when they're bored, no other reason. No one cares, another body at the bottom of the pit. Just to see the blood, just to hear their guns pop. Shooting is fun, and there are plenty of bullets. Finding food and water, sleeping, that's the hard work.

There's just so many in this platoon, so many guns, so many fingers to pull at triggers. Kids so young and ignorant they can't reload. Kids so stupid they wander in the wrong places. So many get killed; then they're just dead. Only the living are left. What's so good about that, about being left? Some days Ghost couldn't sort that out in his head. Kill someone else and stay alive? How is that good?

It's as natural in Liberia to be killed as not to be killed during his war. To be alive and to be dead are different only in where you stand. Every boy in this war, by natural course, has shot people. Every girl has been penetrated by a man in a uniform in the presence of a knife or gun and other men.

In the tent, Ghost sits, fingers a necklace made of bones. He took it off one of the boys who wouldn't come out of the sleeping tent. The pekin lay there, and he cried and cried. Soon a Suh came and pulled him out, and they shoved him down the hill, onto the dead bodies. Ghost doesn't know what happened to him, but his necklace is safe.

The boy called Shooter told him they were enemy bones, from a Gio tribe, carved out of a man while he was alive and so blessed. Ghost was sure they were animal, maybe chimp. He wasn't exactly sure what "blessed" meant either, since both the animal and the pekin in the death ditch lost them. He said so to Shooter, in his quiet voice.

"Ghost, you stupid. Nuttin' hurts you when you wear them. No bullet hits you. No machete cuts. Everything bounces off, *oh*. Armor, magic armor."

Ghost frowns, looks around the tent at the others who share the sleeping space, Trigger, Bug, and Chaos. "Dat true?" he asks. He knows they'll agree, all on jungle juice, and they don't like to argue with Shooter.

They all nod, up and down, like the crane stalking water-bugs in the marsh, glazed eyes fixed on the bleached bones threaded on a black leather lanyard, hands absently seeking their own talismans.

Everything in this crowded tent stays dirty, the canvas, the pot for boiling water, the plates for eating (no forks, no spoons, and definitely no knives). The tent is hot and damp, but it's out of the sun. Clothes hang off the gaunt boys. The ones getting better at formation, at carrying the fake weapons, at standing at ten-shun, are stronger, leaner. The boys who can't keep up are kicked and beaten. They are the last for the mess tent, the last to get new clothes or shoes. The flies buzz constantly around these boys, their arms too weak to swat them. Bugs know where the meal is easy. Bugs are brutal.

The boys are kept in their place with jungle-juice, a mixture of cane juice and gunpowder. They get as much marijuana as they can stand, and amphetamines called "bubbles". Before a battle they would be starved, then hammered with drugs, aimed, and fired at the enemy. A starving boy high out of his mind is a formidable weapon, easily replaced, disposable.

Child soldiers all get new names, their old names cast away like their previous lives. Their new names turn them into ferocious warriors, a new person. New name, new life, new purpose. Favor of the Gods. It took him time for Hope to get used to being called Ghost. At first he refused to answer to it. Hope is a kid from the Wuteve, with a father and Ranger and the watering hole for a home. A kid with a past. Ghost is a soldier who moves only into the future. Ghost is a warrior. He's rewarded with the spoils of war, food, water, women.

He was named Ghost in *Zero Week* because of his scars. The ones he got on the cougar hunt a lifetime ago, back when he worked and played in the jungles and foothills of Wuteve. Those scars made him Ghost, but that wasn't all. Not just the scars. There was something else.

Zero Week, the training of new recruits, wasn't hard for him. He was not impressed with the work and the ritual. Soldiers kept waiting for him to be amazed, by the drills, the weapons, the discipline, but he found it easy and routine. He was built for this type of life, the camping, training, shooting, if not the military purpose behind Zero Week. He was a boy of the hunt, of survival, of the bush. If you cover yourself in mud and animal urine, the mosquitoes don't bite. You find the biggest leaves in the bush for a blanket at night, no matter how hot, and they soak up the mist that seeps into the body and causes mold and fungus. If you wrap your hunting boots in heavy cloth, you're quiet when you walk. He knew things the other boys didn't, and that made all this easier for him.

There was something in his eyes, a dark hopeless desperation that bordered on dangerous. The soldiers talked about killing him outright, right in front of him, no secret. That Ghost. Get rid of him now, before he causes trouble, *eh?*

Eventually, he refused to flinch or cower when the guns went *pop*, or when the machete whistled past his head. These were just men, definitely not better than his father or Ranger.

Something wrong wit dat boy. Meant to scare him into submission, to wipe the forbidding smile from his face, bright white Cheshire teeth framed in his dark face, bordered by new pucker scars on his chin and forehead from repeated beatings.

Nah, he's a weapon, our Ghost, oh! They talked about pointing him at Doe's forces and letting him loose. By the time his scars and his dark eyes and his calm suffering, his devastating ability to survive, were seen and pressed on the other boys in the training cadre, it was too late. He became a talisman for the troops and for the officer commanding him. It was decided he'd become the point on any and every mission, the spear. If he died doing that, even better.

It's easier to watch a Ghost when it's in front of you.

39

Jehuu

WAR IS ON our street now, almost every day.

We stay tucked in houses. Outside is hot, inside hotter. We sweat and try not to move, fish sucking at the sky, like the world is exhausted, out of breath. Power is out, no fans, nothing moves air. The world pushes on you like hot hands.

When war comes home, you're supposed to hide, away from windows, in closets, behind doors. My place is in the kitchen cupboards, with the pots and pans. Then you wait for all clear so you can come back out.

The bullet does not pick and choose.

Sometimes war doesn't pass. Sometimes it comes right in, not even knocking on doors. Soldiers drag us outside, ask us our tribe, who's our warlord, who protects us. Boys have to strip down, stand still in the yard, breathing and sweating. Soldiers go up and down the line, you feel them in your nose and your hair -ghouls, Heartmen, warlords, rogues, Negee. They smell like dead dogs, like rotted mangos. Shadows of their big guns play on the dirt yard in front and behind you. They look for tribal marks, tattoos or scars to tell them if you a Krahn or Mandingo. They yell in a boy's ear, Which tribe you? You Krahn boy? I'm quiet, nothing marks my skin, I'm too young. But they look, and they yell anyways. When soldiers look for Krahn marks it means they're Taylor's boys in crazy clothes, bright pants, wigs, horror masks.

. . . .

I have a small statue from my grandpa, a talisman. It's a little *pekin* like me, fits in my hand, white and grey and smooth. Grandpa says it's made of elephant ivory. He says to keep it safe, then I'll be safe too. I worry the ivory, rub it with my hands, smooth out parts. It slows my breath, it sends me calm, my statue.

Today, I'm in my grandma's kitchen, I wait to be spoiled. Grandma is with neighbor ladies, cooking. They talk low, whispers, no laughing ignoring Jehuu in the room waiting for treats. They wipe sweat from heads, towel off legs and arms in the heat. They sit at the big table in the middle of the room. Others hover over pots and pans on the large stove. Grandma has the biggest kitchen. She teaches people to cook. Her house smells like food and people all the time.

A soft rap at the door. Everyone stops, standing still, a frozen picture. All eyes go to Grandma. Soldiers come for food and water? They usually come to the front door and bang their way in. The silence is like a sentence, then a paragraph. Tap-tap on the door again, a whisper on the other side, "Mama Joanna. It's Finda. From da street."

The women thaw, hurry to the door, past the stove where cassava and bitterroot boil.

"Finda? Why you outside? Oh Girl come, sit, oh. Give her room, get water."

"I come to the kitchen door. Soldiers, boys on the street front." Finda's voice is dead, a low whoosh inside a wind. She's hunched and ragged inside her clothes. Her eyes dark inside her head, they flit to the doors and windows. They stop on little Jehuu, a ghoul looking through a dark cowl.

"Hush. Get you some tea first."

Finda from the street sits at the table. She moves slow, sleepy. Her clothes are ripped. She holds them over herself with one hand, the other in her lap. A blue dress, no shoes. The ladies buzz around,

108

a hive of bees. Grandma wets a towel at the sink. She holds it to Finda's face, she is light-skin, a Congo-lady. Her face is scratched. Her lip bleeds.

The guns *pop pop pop* outside.

"Finda dey get you, huh?"

"Yes, mama Joanna."

"Where's your man? Where's Quincy?"

"He gone. He gone."

"Na ya mind girl. Drink some water, clean up. We'll get you clothes."

40

Bonita

Bonita

When did you first hear about the war?

BC: One day everything is fine. One day I can call, I can write, and know they will get my letters. One day I can picture myself flying back to Liberia, to Monrovia, out of the snow and cold of New York. Out of this world of paved roads and grocery stores and dentists and doctors and a dollar bill. One day there is all that. One day I can go get my children and bring them out of Liberia.

The next day it's all gone.

This is November, 1990. The war over there has been growing, raging since middle summer. There is no phone on the other end. No flights can be bought to Robertsfield airport.

So around the holidays in the US?

BC: It was so hard. You know at Thanksgiving, there's so much food. And at Christmas, there's so much food. I was sitting here, just me and my husband, with a twenty-pound turkey and wondering if they had any food today.

41

Jehuu

"WHERE WILL YOU go Finda?"

"To Sierra Leone." Finda's eyes never ever leave the floor. I shuffle my own feet at the door. I want to hear, don't want to hear.

"You got family?"

"No. But I go eh." Finda is young, like my mum, but not pretty. Her eyes are dark holes, puffy cheeks. Her hair, a doormat.

"How are people passing there, Finda?"

"La God one know! I will walk, maybe ride."

"Stay here?"

"No. I'll go. Not staying in Liberia, not near Monrovia."

"That walk, it's long. Weeks."

Finda is silent for another paragraph. She says to the floor, "A grave out back?"

Grandma frowns. Her dress is sweat-soaked to her knees, the floral pattern is creased starting at her waist. She sips at her cup. "People are going back to the city, to Monrovia."

Finda finally looks up from the floor. "You know people can't stay here, *eh*?" The ladies are quiet. "They'll come get you. They'll come get the boy." She looks where I stand. I reach for my statue.

42

A Child Soldier

"If you try to cleanse others -like soap
you will waste away in the process."
—Liberian Saying

GHOST IS AT rebel camp, this is his life now.

He toys with the bone necklace, rolling it in his rough hands. Instead of reverence for these talismans, he found them funny. He looked at the boys in the tent. "You sure this is good juju?"

"It is." Shooter puffs his chest. "Blessed by God and the Colonel himself."

"God and the Colonel?" Ghost suppresses a grin. "Dat so?"

Shooter frowns, confused. The older boys ignore Ghost and the necklace, lounging on cots, fidgeting with weapons. The younger boys lick chapped lips, and gaze at the bones in Ghost's hand, curious, covetous stares.

"Na mind." Ghost says, and a grin tugs the corners of his mouth. He breathes through his nose and holds the necklace out to Shooter, reaches for his sidearm, a Glock he took off a dead ECOMOG soldier. He keeps the Glock because it's a NATO sidearm, and ammo is easy to find. "I believe you, Shooter. Here, hold it", he hands the necklace to the boy. "I'll shoot."

Shooter's eyes go wide. He licks patchy lips, scratches at his shirt, two sizes too big, and rubs his shaved head. He's called Shooter

113

because he started Zero Week as the best with the AK47, stronger and able to hold it longer on target. The officers took to him, made him platoon leader. He lorded the position, punched and tripped the younger boys, stole their food.

But since then he rides the needle hard, never off it for long. Now he scratches all day, snores at night, and picks at his skin.

And he talks too much, pretends to know things.

Shooter looks from the necklace to the gun, back to the necklace. He swallows from a jug of juice, scratches at his open wounds, scattering the flies lodged there. "Wha you mean?"

"Hold the juju and I shoot you. No harm." Ghost shakes the necklace at him.

"You hold it Ghost, I shoot you."

Ghost frowns, scratches absently at the snarl of scars on his face. "No Suh, Shooter. I don't think it's good juju, like you do. I'm not believing what Colonel or God say. Both of them want me dead, so this one won't work for me." He shakes the necklace made of bones so they rattle. The small boys gasp, eyes wide and hands move to clutch their own necklaces and rings made of bones.

Shooter looks around the tent, red eyes peering into the corners, seeking confirmation, hoping for help. The older boys, Chaos, Trigger, Little Mosquito are amused. They shake their heads, grinning. Shooter looks to the little ones. His eyes brighten. "Bug, come here", he says. "Put dis necklace on." He motions at the talisman.

Ghost cocks his head to the side. "Shooter? You're not trusting God? Or the Colonel?"

Shooter blushes, but he waves Bug to the center of the tent.

Bug starts to cry.

Ghost walks up to the little boy. "Shhh…make you a hero." Ghost winks. Shooter waits, arms crossed.

43

Jehuu

WAR COMES TO Allison Street.

When we woke one morning to find an NPFL tank on the front lawn there was no longer any way to deny that war had come, in my neighborhood, right at my grandma's house. The tank was huge, soaking in all light with dark metal and sharp lines. What did I know of tanks and war? When soldiers patrol up our street, they stop at the house. They point guns and sit on the tank. They drink from dark jars, cans of beer. They spit and laugh and make animal noise. Grandma says they're dangerous. The guns look important, shiny, fun. I grin and elbow cousins Decontee and Ozidiki. Look, I whisper, I want one. Grandma stands nearby and hisses. Hush!

Another time, the boys come inside the house and steal food and water. They leave, to go fight. Grandma and Grandpa fret and worry, they say one time we're not so lucky.

"Soon one soldier goes crazy," she says. "One gets mad, or takes you boys for the war. Maybe one pulls a trigger, or swings a machete and someone is hurt. Or maybe it's a Krahn patrol that comes looking for Gio. Then we're not lucky or blessed," she says. "Then we're in real trouble. Liberian trouble."

The soldiers scare Grandma and Grandpa.

They don't scare me. I have no marks, so they don't know me. They don't know I'm a Blomo.

· · · ·

115

A band of soldiers sweeps up Allison Street, guns popping, horns blaring. "Here come more soldiers, them." Grandma says. We go to the window on the side of the house and crowd her. I want to see the big guns, the boys in trucks, others walking and shooting and whooping at the sky. I wear my white basketball shoes, orange shorts, loose blue tee shirt with Adidas on the front and Got Futbol? on the back. I can see the soldiers on the road. Boys climb on the tank in the front yard, lazy smiles, slouching confidence, glazed looks of something I can't name, cool and comfortable.

I want to be part of that. I want that easiness. I want to hold a gun, climb a tank, and be in a war. When the weapons go off a charge goes in me. When they fire off guns the older people move back and shrink, shoulders hunch, hands to their chest, cover their heads. I move forward, my eyes grow big, my mouth dries up, I reach out, my hands spasm, imaginary trigger fingers pull.

"Get back, get away, eh. Get your face from that window." Grandma shoos us. We crowd anyway.

This time soldiers are Taylor NPFL, not government, not the Nigerian Peacekeepers called in to protect Monrovia. If they're Taylor's, it means Krahn and Mandingoes are being hunted. Maybe Kru too, me and Mardea's tribe on daddy's side. That's why we're Caulcrick now and not Blomo. Before, when Doe's army was mass killing Bassa and Gio and Manu, being a Blomo was okay. Oh, you need a scorecard to know who's killing who. We're Bassa on mum's side, so if this patrol is NPFL, we might survive if they come hunting inside the house. Or maybe they just shoot anyways, your tribe doesn't matter, make up some reason to kill you, take all the boys away. This is our existence now. Unpredictable.

"Who you going to shoot Jehuu?" My Grandma says. "You shoot Bassa because you're Kru? Shoot your grandpa, your cousins? Or you shoot Kru because you part Bassa? Shoot your sister? Your Pa?"

The thought confuses and chills me. "Won't shoot either."

"Then they shoot you. Hush now. This war is not for you."

We stay by the window and watch. The house is hot, sweaty, heavy. We haven't been outside in days, not allowed, not safe. The same home that Grandma and Grandpa made for people to come and feel safe now smells of too many peoples and ruined food. Grandma-Grandpa's house isn't the place of kids and fun anymore. It's a prison.

The soldiers slide by. Grandma sighs. We slip back into the interior of the hot, *hot* house and wait for something to happen.

. . . .

Joseph was my cousin, but we called him my brother. That's the way it is in my grandma's house, in Liberia. Everybody the same family.

Joseph.

He's here, then he's not. We play football in the yard, we run through the house, we watch T.V., eat meals, and have sleepovers. We laugh. We make fun of Odziki.

Joseph.

He's here with me every day. And then he's not here anymore. That's what death is. A person exists, then they don't. They are in your life, then they're a memory only, a picture frozen in your mind, a ghost.

And if you go on living, if you walk a country filled with war, death becomes something else. For those people, death is a bloated body covered in insects, one you step over, so you get to live. It's a grave you dig in your back yard, where the dead are dropped and covered with dirt. Death is in everybody you pass, every set of rolled-over-white lifeless eyes you look into.

. . . .

"Jehuu, let's go. Hot back here."

"Not supposed to."

Joseph shakes his head, rolls his eyes. "Come on Jehuu, too many people, *eh*?" His hands are alive, fidgeting, snapping fingers.

"Soldiers are out front. You hear them? Grandma says stay out back."

"You do ever-ting Grandma Joanna say?" Joseph knows where to push. "Beside, we not going outside, just to the front inside, where the food is."

I'm seven years old. I'm Jehuu-naughty-fussy-boy, hardly capable of resisting a dare. Grandma is nowhere to be seen, Joseph is right in front of me, wagging a finger, smiling ear-wide. So, instead of staying in the back of the house on Allison Street, we weave through hallways past adults leaning against walls, talking softly, drinking coffee and juices, the sounds and smells of this home.

The large house sits low on Allison Street off the main thoroughfare of Tubman Road in Buchanan. It spreads out in the neighborhood, a distinct home because of its size, geniality, ease of access. My grandparent's house was the hub of the Divine Town Community, where people simply knew to visit when there was gossip or trouble, inviting and safe. The activity in the house was unmistakable, a neighborly trademark in peaceful times, a beacon for security in the middle of trouble. Part of it was the school, part of it was Grandma and Grandpa Caulcrick who brooked no nonsense in their Christian world. My mum says my grandma has a direct line to God, that he listens to her prayers different than other people. Maybe that's also why people came to her house. Maybe they wanted access to that halo, that spiritual umbrella.

The problem with open invitations is that they're open.

The back of the house was for living, bedrooms, kitchen, common rooms. The rooms smelled of people. The front was a culinary school; it smelled of food –palm butter cooked into crawfish, beef, pigs' feet, and suck-suck. Palava sauce made from jute leaves melted into stew. Bitterleaf greens, shellfish, rice, fufu and fermented cassava dumplings.

Me and Joseph headed for the smells, dragging other kids with us–Akeelah, Kenneth, Albert and Odziki. Kids looking to escape the adults milling in the back of the house. The gunfire was outside on the street, but that was outside, and we were inside.

. . . .

On a global scale, the AK47 is considered the finest urban assault weapon in the world for its sheet-metal cast designed for mass production, on a singular scale for its reliability, and on a killing scale for the terminal ballistics. You can make a lot of them fast, get them in the hands of people, use them to kill. Liberian guerillas preferred heavier ammunition rounds, those produced more efficient penetration, suited to circumstances for a soldier to shoot through heavy foliage, walls or the metal body of a standard vehicle. The kids wielding them didn't know the difference; they just knew how to work the trigger, reload, and work the trigger again. The weapon makes a distinctive *pop* when fired, recognizable when you hear it day after day. Rounds make audible snaps in the air, a warning of where a bullet might finish, not picking or choosing.

. . . .

The bullet that picked Joseph in the front room of Grandma and Grandpa's big house on Allison Street most surely came from that coldly efficient weapon. It was in all likelihood a 7.62×39mm M43 projectile, the heavy ballistic most likely to hold its line and least likely to fragment or tumble. That's probably the round that tore through a pane of glass, a wall, and a table leg to end up in Joseph, what killed him while I sat alongside, giggling and laughing. We had fooled the adults and snuck to the front of the house, Joseph sitting in the wrong place at the wrong time, one seat over from me. Bad luck colliding with a world where bullets fly.

Joseph was there, and then he was not.

. . . .

Go ahead, dig a hole six feet deep, eight feet long by three feet wide. Technically that's two-thousand cubic yards of brush, soil, rocks, roots. Set that earth aside. Feel the dirt cave under your feet, understand how high you have to toss dirt to get it out of an eight-foot hole. Break up hundreds of mangrove roots, gravel shards, and stone.

You probably know by now you're digging a grave. On the T.V., digging graves looks easy –quick shots of the shovel breaking ground, followed by a person shoulder deep in the earth flinging dirt into the air. Nothing in between, takes too long. You don't see the straining arms and back, the sweat and the grief and the breaks for water. It takes a long time to dig a hole like that.

Now, put your brother in the hole, wrapped in a sheet from a bed you've slept in. Set him down carefully, respectfully. He's not light, not at all, your brother, but he is stiff, implacable, like a board, because he's been wrapped and kept inside for a week now. You can't go outside and dig a grave when the bullets are picking and choosing.

Then pick up that same shovel and refill the hole you just dug. Mind you that all the excavated dirt won't fit, because the body takes up space.

That's what we all did –brothers, cousins, uncles, aunties– when we could finally get outside and bury our own. We cleaned his blood from the floor, we wrapped him up, and then we dug his grave. I learned how long it takes to make that hole, how much sweat, how arms ache, how backs bend. I know how hard it is to throw dirt six feet up. I watched, knowing we shouldn't have gone to the front, knowing it was a mistake.

44

A Child Soldier

GHOST PLATOON HELPED softened up the Monrovia suburbs, clearing them of enemies.

On important missions like this, these soldiers, these rebels, these children liked the word patrol. It spoke to them of military engagement, noble, important, grown-up stuff, exercising the thrill of power at the end of a weapon. They were still baked on heroin and jungle juice, but patrols were different. There was a level of care, some caution, some restraint, some discipline. It contained, barely, a defensive posture void of the usual cacophony of charged ammunition and war yelps. The officers, the master sergeants, the commanders, the corporals, kept a tight leash on this group of child soldiers. Trigger fingers twitch, safeties are forgotten, hallucinations from drugs and fatigue shake impulse control. Sometimes guns just go off. Rebel commanders count on that random violence and unpredictability in most forages into the suburbs, youthful urges of destruction, ferocity and aggression needs to be nurtured and tolerated lest it turn on you in its own rebellion (discipline, terror, toleration and drugs in equal doses to keep these human-weapons in order). *Weapon discipline.*

Monrovia was only a few kilometers to the north. Government troops were holed up in the capital with peace-keeping forces, mostly from Nigeria. So far the peace-keepers hadn't branched into the suburbs to try to reclaim neighborhoods from warlords and NPFL, but that was just a matter of time. This suburb was close to Monrovia, a few, short kilometers from the ECOMAG forces maintaining order in the capital city. If that army decided to send out a force, rebel patrols in the suburbs could get dangerous.

45

Jehuu

"When the elephants fight, the grass suffers."
—*Prince Johnson, Liberian Warlord*

JOSEPH IS OUT back, under dirt.

The rest, the living, are inside, not allowed to play, not allowed to look out windows or go to the front of Grandma's house. Hot in the house, stuffy, too many peoples, always bumping me, but I stay around the grown-ups. Safer. I won't be running in the bush today.

Guns go *pop pop*, all the time. I wonder where all the bullets go, where they land, if any more will come into the house. One found Joseph. Can one find me?

"Mardea, where all them bullets go?"

"Hush Jehuu. Don't want to think about that." She moves away from me, both of us wear easy, light clothes. Sweaty anyway. She's my older sister, but she doesn't have answers.

"But they go someplace."

"Yes, some place." Mardea looks at the floor, not at my face. Her hair sticks up, sweat holds it. She's pretty, my sister. Like our mum.

"I hope I'm not in the way of a bullet. I hope I'm not shot."

"So much blood." She shakes her head, her hair doesn't move.

We hear soldiers, them. Trucks, cars coming up the street. The *pop pop* is loud today. Mardea hurries to the kitchen, looks for Grandma.

A truck stops outside the house. A knock on the door, loud. Nobody moves, we are statues. Another knock, louder. Pounding. "Out! Out! Everybody out this house. NPFL is here!"

"Go away," Grandma is mad. Grandpa is not home.

"Open up lady. Are there boys in this house?"

"Nah, this my house! Go 'way." To us she hisses, "Stay quiet." Her eyes are angry, they say worry, crinkled around the corners of her broad face. Her hands wring in her apron. She stomps in place. Small gray hairs flash in the light as her head moves, eyes dart around the house, to the kitchen, to the front door.

"We not going 'way old crow." The voice at the front door is harsh, gravel under a wheel. "We stay. We see your peoples, who's in there? Open up, eh!" Out the windows on the front lawn I see soldiers. More faces look in windows around cupped black hands, blurred by dirty glass.

They fire guns. *Where them bullets go?*

"Okay. Stop that! We'll come. Hold you!" Grandma yells, mad again. To us kids gathered at her aprons she whispers, "All you kids, come on here eh. All you boys line up, we going out. Just do what they say, don't talk. You hear me? Don't talk! Girls stay with me. If them boys do anything, I will yell, but you keep to yourself. Don't say anything. Don't look at them." She looks into our eyes, holds each for a second then moves to the next child. She shouts at the door, "Hold there. Coming out! Don't you break my door!" I line up with the boys, grandma pulls me aside.

"Jerome, you remember where to hide? In the cabinet under the sink?" She looks old, heavy eyes, her jeans under the apron are baggy on the sides, shirt damp under her arms. She wipes at her lips with the back of her hand. "Remember how quiet you can be? When we can't find you?" I nod. "Now listen Jerome. Listen like a good boy. If them soldiers come into this house, you go hide. You understand?"

I shake my head, "No no! I stay with you and Mardea. I hold your foot."

124

"No son. Your papa is Kru. These boys don't like Kru."

This makes no sense. "I'm Bassa, like you, like mum."

"You Kru too, and you Blomo. You have Blomo face, Blomo hair, Blomo legs."

I look at my hands, at my legs. Blomo face? What's a Blomo face?

"Now go stand in the kitchen. If you see me wave, you go hide, okay? Mardea and me will be fine. You hide if the boys come toward the kitchen. Make sure soldier boys don't find you. Be Jehuu and hide. Nobody finds you."

I don't know what to do. I can protect Mardea, Grandma, but not if I hide. Grandma says, "Like a game, *eh*? Hide and seek, or like when you go to the forest. Nobody finds you there, *eh*?" She tries on grin, strained over her gaunt face. The door pounds again and we both jump.

"A game?"

"Yes a game. But a serious game."

"A serious game?"

"A game you need to win" She licks her lips, glances at the front door. "You go be Jehuu. From now on, you can be Jehuu, not Jerome."

A game to win. Yes. "Okay." This time I grin my Jehuu grin. Hiding from boys.

A game.

. . . .

The guns outside rage. One man stands in Grandma's doorway, the rest behind, looking into the house. He wears khaki pants, dark green t-shirt, and a vest that looks like the forest. A big, big gun on his shoulder, another, smaller on his hip. He raises the big one when the door opens. He pops it into the air and smiles. Smoke whispers from the muzzle and hangs there, in front of my grandma, nowhere to pass in the heat, then it floats away, reluctantly, on a puff of breeze. Grandma flinches but her sandals stay planted, balled fists rise slowly and punch into her sides, bunching her sweaty summer dress under the apron, the one she always wears in the house. She makes a face, the one where you watch out if you know what's good for you, *oh*.

The soldier sees her eyes and his go wide, his head moves back, but his feet stay put too. He's a big man, rough black beard on his face. He looks over Grandma's shoulder into the house. His yellow teeth flash inside is deep dark face. "Den send out dem girls, oh?"

Boy soldiers laugh. *Yes, send dem girls! Gives us dem girls.* Guns *pop-pop* in the air. That breeze again, ruffles at their ridiculous clothes, bright colored t-shirts, grass skirts, funny hats, wedding dresses. That breeze from nowhere (is a storm coming?).

"No girls," Grandma growls. "The boys will come out, but you don't take them. You just look."

The Command Sergeant makes a face, "Your people Krahn? Or Kru?"

"No, man. We Gio, some Bassa."

"Then no worries, Old Crow."

Grandma slips out the door. "Go away boys. This is God's house. No place for you." Grandma is a fearless woman, what Liberians call a *Big Jue*. I squeeze my eyes, hug my tummy, bunch my hands, hold my legs, curl my toes. My lucky statue makes marks inside my fist. *Go away*, I say inside my head. *Go to another house. You scaring my people, grandma, Mardea, my cousins.*

They come anyways. Wishing doesn't work.

The soldiers rush the house. Straight inside, no talking, no more knocking on doors, no warning. They shoot their guns, loud inside the house, ceilings and walls explode, a heavy spray of plaster settles to dust in rooms. *Wha you tribe?* They shout. *Who your ma, who your pa?* Soldiers cough through yellow teeth, sweat-sparkly skin, eyes red and watery, like the Negee in books. I'm supposed to be in the cupboard hiding, but I stand frozen in the kitchen doorway.

My feet won't move, my hands shake, I am so scared and mad at the same time.

"Go 'way!" Grandma shouts and shoos. "No soldiers here, just old peoples and babies. Go 'way!" She holds a broom like a shield, swats at the space between her and the rebels, not quite touching any of them. They shrink from her anger, her authority, but they keep moving into the house, slowly. *Who is this crazy Big Jue?*

"Where are your men? They will come outside now, so we can see," the man officer with the black beard shouts. He wears fatigues, sleeves rolled over veined arms, a flat red hat riding low over one eye. The smoke from his cigarette rises slowly. He reaches and grabs a cousin, yanks at his shirt. "Off with them clothes," he yells, "we'll see your marks!" Inside our house, some soldier boys growl and howl. Some just breath heavy and sit on chairs, grandma's chairs. Some point fingers at my people, eyes dead like a black fly. One squeeze is all it takes, one trigger and people get shot. Like Joseph.

Then more noise from outside, different soldiers, whooping and yelling, trucks and cars roar up Allison Street. The soldiers jump off chairs, look at each other, look at the officer. He waves his hand at the front door.

"Patrol out!" They run outside guns leveled, eyes crazy. Once outside guns explode, muffled by walls and windows.

"We'll be back", shouts the man.

A firefight is right in the front yard of Allison Street, boys and soldiers living war. Bullets thwack into the house. We all run to the back. Soon the *pop pop pop* of weapons fades, moves off down the street, soldiers chasing other soldiers.

But the damage is done. The spell of safety on Allison Street is broken. War is here.

Time to go.

. . . .

The elephants trampled the grass in my neighborhood in October, 1990. We were about to suffer. First they put a tank in my yard, then they brought guns, then they broke through the front door. Grandma couldn't hold them off anymore with her Big Jue routine. She was, after all, just one woman.

Soon the suburban warfare really started, a daily reminder of big guns and the soldiers who carried them. Every day. All day. Who knew there were so many guns in the world. Who could make so many bullets that spent cartridges piled ankle deep in a street, metallic wind-chimes singing under your shoes, so thick sometimes you had to wait until they cooled to wade through them after a close battle. Me and Grandma, Grandpa and Mardea, cousins and friends stayed as long as we could in the house, and then we left.

When the war first came to us, down the street but not into our home, I think it can't get worse, stuffed into the house, no places to go, no football, no mangrove forest. Nobody to visit, mum gone, almost no air to breathe.

Then Joseph is murdered.

Then they come inside and shoot up the house.

I was wrong to think inside the house was bad, because it got worse.

. . . .

"Jehuu, where are you boy?"

Grandpa calls into the back of the house. I hear him but don't answer.

"Jehuu! We have to go!"

I can't find my shoe. I can't find my shoe and all the house is ready to go. I looked and looked. What will I do with only one shoe? They're going to leave me here, leave me with them soldiers and the guns and the knives. Leave me in this house that is so bad now. Leave me with rotten meat and cassava soup. Leave me with no candy. I search and search but there's no shoe. Just one for my foot.

My people are outside with the backpacks and cases, baskets on heads, towels wrapped with clothes, only what they can carry. We don't have a car or a truck or a wagon. Just what's on your back.

And I have only one shoe. Maybe I can walk barefoot, maybe nobody will see. Except Mardea will see, and she'll tell Grandma, and then I'm left on this street, in this house with the tank in the front yard and the grave in the back.

Grandpa finds me, stands with hands on hips. He makes-angry face, right at me. "What are you doing Jehuu? We have to go."

I try not to cry. Mum is gone to America. Daddy is gone to somewhere. Now we are supposed to walk, to leave the house.

Grandpa comes to me, leans down and puts his hand on my back. "Are you scared boy?"

"I, huh, can't, huh, find…"

"This?" He has my white shoe. He smiles, it creases his hard face, touches his eyes, and goes into me.

Okay. Now we can go.

. . . .

Allison Street is no longer safe, the comforting glow of the house ruined. Doors and windows and walls can't block out the war, the soldiers, the bullets.

Taylor's rebels are gaining on the capital, and Buchanan is in the way, a suburb to be cleansed on a march to war with the government. We survived patrols so far, but the next one might be different, hunting Bassa and Gio. It's impossible to say which army holds which neighborhood at any given time. So we pack up and we walk. Grandma and Grandpa know people in the South, relatives and friends where we can stay maybe away from the bullets and bombs and roving rebels. Maybe out of the way of the elephants fighting so we don't get trampled.

The Liberian Coast is four-hundred sixty miles (740km), give or take. War steers the innocent, the non-combatant, the refugee. You move to stay alive, away from the irritant, gunfire, explosions, fire, and death. You are funneled toward the light, away from the dark. You look for hole in the carnage.

But decisions have to be made nonetheless, countless decisions. Move inland, or hug the coast. Bypass cities, or seek refuge there. Turn right and run into a spray of bullets. Turn left into a stray mortar. It's not like in the United States, not like the choices you have here. You choose to drink and drive. You choose to smoke and get lung cancer. It's your choice to find trouble; you can almost always shy away from danger. Our choices were base, elemental, where to turn, where to walk. Who to trust. Which tribe to claim. All choices are of a degree.

The rumors coming from the north –Ivory Coast, Guinea, and Sierra Leone– are about genocide, killing Kru and Krahn along the borders. In Monrovia, the government is holed up, a politician named Amos Sawyer inserted as the interim president after Doe was assassinated. Doe was killed publicly and gruesomely, like he did with Tolbert's regime. Goes around, comes around. ECOMOG soldiers were supposed to guarantee an element of safety.

Not so.

Monrovia was a mess. People lined streets filled with human shit and garbage. The sick and dying went there, looking for a hospital, finding none. There was no relief for them. Instead of finding a healthy remedy, people went to Monrovia to die; there was nowhere to move, nowhere to thrive, nowhere to live.

That just wasn't for us, not for Caulcricks. We walked south instead, away from the capital. My grandparents made a good choice. We joined the hordes, long lines of quiet travel, away from Monrovia, away from the government.

I was seven years old and a war refugee. I walked from place to place, away from the war, Red Cross camps, NCO shelters, homes where they let us in, maybe a night in the bush, sleep in a tree to stay off worn paths. It was confusing, all the walking, all the people on the road. Going where, all these people?

And all the dead bodies along the roads.

You still had to know warlords or soldiers to get around inside the country, they were there before the war, and they worked to consolidate their own power as the rebellion grew. We had friends on most sides of the war, because my grandparents were so generous and were community people. But you never knew when you'd run into the crazy boys or someone on a killing high. You had to know the backroads and paths through the bush. The direction we went was an easy choice; we walked away from the sounds of battle, of gunfire, shelling, the trucks loaded with wild-eyed boys. My grandparents being in the government all those years knew plenty of people all over the coast, inland too.

In the years I was a refugee, I took maybe a million small steps up and down Liberia, across borders, to neighboring nations, and back in the country. I don't remember a lot from the walking days. It seems like I was always tired, always thirsty. Someone on the road would give you a cup of water and you'd share it. One cup. How do you go from never tired, run all day, to tired all the time? Go from a house filled with food, drinks any time you needed, to constant thirst and an empty stomach?

I'm sure while I walked there was beauty, sacrifice, humans doing remarkable things, and the Liberian coast and countryside showing itself as a natural wonder, but I don't remember it, not enough to tell. I question sometimes what my eyes saw and my brain refused to register. It's mostly all blocked out, hidden away. A protective veil of darkness that won't let me, to this day, relive all but the most eye-opening experiences, sharp snapshots of passion, hostility, or generosity. What do you remember from when you were seven? A birthday party? A Disney vacation? A trip to the candy store? Your first bike?

We walked down the Liberian coast from Buchanan, my grandparents, sister, cousins. Mardea remembers, Soldiers watched your every move, you were rarely on the road alone. It can be a lot of stress walking around guns and soldiers all the time, and you don't know what they will say or do. A neighbor of ours passed out on the road. We went to pick her up but the soldiers were like, "Keep moving! Keep moving!" When we came back that way later she was on the side of the road all blown up.

Looking at a map, hearing stories from my family, I figure I walked seven-hundred miles (over 1,000km) in a little less than two years. I walked down the coast, back up the coast, into Ghana, out of Ivory Coast. I changed. When you're that young you don't consider that you're becoming a different person. A numbness replaced my energy and mischievousness. There was no more Jerome the football star, zipping in and out of the house in Buchanan, playing in the yard, helping in the fields, watching TV on Friday nights, going to school. I became Jehuu the Walking-Boy. My life blended into the dust, the mud, the thirst, the hunger, and the oppressive, tedious fatigue. For over two years, until I was almost ten, I mostly tried to stay alive, walking miles and miles every day. Some days I walked hungry, some thirsty.

Most days, both.

46

Liberia

SOUTH FROM MONROVIA, by car or bus, cycle, or on foot.

Traveling that direction takes you to United Nations Drive, an interstate road. North takes you to a place called Clara Town and then into the heart of Western Africa. If you go south, you choose between Benson Street and Sekou Toure Avenue as UN Drive terminates into Central Monrovia. Follow either of those main arteries or take the myriad cross streets that they intersect, and you find a bustling, crowded, third world. It feels like every person in Liberia is trying to get into Monrovia.

Outside of the center of town, you can pick up Tubman Drive. Now you move through the suburbs of the capital of Liberia, and you end up in Buchanan. There's a wave of people walking this road away from the city, choosing a different way to escape the elephants as they trample the grass.

This is the wave Jehuu's family rides.

In Monrovia's city limits, a Shakespearean tragedy is being played out. There is deception leading to murder, dismemberment, executions, and a most public case of regicide. Doe's reign of terror comes to an end in a most horrific and upsetting way when Prince Johnson, a warlord, kills him on camera for the world to see.

The Caulcrick's initial exodus takes the family south, on the coastal road, away from Monrovia where government and ECOMOG forces are holed up against rebels and local warlords fighting for their share of Liberia. They travel past Harbel and the

Firestone plantation where Jehuu's mom once worked, and where Taylor is setting his sights on an ambush of the American rubber company and its vast resources. The coast is war-busy with ports for weapon deliveries being exchanged for Liberian natural resources.

Taylor's rebel headquarters are in Gbarna, north and east of Monrovia in Central Liberia. This is where President Jimmy Carter visited Taylor in 1990 and was scammed by the charismatic leader into believing the NPFL had an interest in uniting the nation, rather than mass homicide and raping the country dry. From Gbarna, Taylor gathers support from Liberians at the four compass-points. So, the southern route of escape, hugging the coastline, holds promise that the north and east do not.

Liberia is a brutal country, except for the coastline. Jehuu's grandparents knew this when they started walking, the path of least resistance from war, safety seeking its own level. The Caulcrick's share the road with many of the 875,000 fleeing their homes from in and around Monrovia. Some 325,000 run to Guinea to the northeast, 300,000 to Cote d'Ivoire to the southeast, another 125,000 to Sierra Leone, the nearest border from Monrovia.

Jehuu and his family eventually wander across borders into other countries, looking for quiet, running, dodging, escaping death and mutilation and abduction.

In early 1991 there are rumors on the roads of a cease-fire. Lots of refugees start back to their homes, carrying fewer supplies than when they left. The cease-fire sells hope to people starved for relief. It is, like so many other peace-plans in Liberia, summarily ignored. In fact, by March of 1991, Taylor instigates the opposite of a cease-fire. He takes the civil war over the borders into Sierra Leone, set on further destabilizing West Africa for his benefit. His pretense is the extinguishing of a possible resurgent, counter-rebellions, but everyone knows he wants more resources, money, and diamonds.

Taylor's Small Boys Unit becomes a cadre of sadistic teenage killers, sporting names like General Fuck Me Quick, Babykiller, and Dead Body Bones. They are completely out of control across the countryside, arbitrarily executing civilians and decorating check-points with human heads and entrails. These murderous adolescents rape, pillage, and slaughter at will. Many engage in cannibalism, eating the hearts and genitals of their slain enemies, invoking dark magic to enhance their power.

The deck is reshuffled when Sierra Leone is no longer safe. Next stop, for both Liberian and Sierra Leone refugees is Guinea. Packing more refugees into West Africa increases the burden of already poor countries exponentially.

. . . .

Doe's inevitable assassination came in 1990. It was especially public, cameras running. It's on the internet today.

"I want to say something if you will just listen to me." Doe pleads, kneeling shirtless in blood-soaked pants.

"Wha you say? Wha can you say to the people of Liberia?" Prince Johnson, lounges smugly in military camos behind a large desk, a machete rests nearby, a can of Budweiser beer sweats in a paper bag. A woman in a blue dress fans him adoringly, moving hot air and flies.

"Let me, just let me…" Doe says.

Johnson leans forward, waves a dismissive hand. "Cut off his ear." You can barely hear the words, barely understand them. They don't make sense on a live video, something you see in the movies.

"Ahhhh. No!" Doe screams.

"A test for black magic." Johnson settles back into his chair.

Soldiers pin Doe to the floor, hold him down with heavy boots. It's an expressive and disrespectful act for a Liberian to be stepped on. They preen for the camera before pulling out a knife and cutting off Doe's left ear.

"Who's protected by magic?" Johnson sneers.

First one then the other ear is removed. Doe cries out. There is a brief silence, then applause from the soldiers filling the small office where Johnson looms so large. They mingle and celebrate. Civilians stand nearby, one appears to take notes, a pen poised over a pad of paper. Others crane for a view of the butchery. The crowd sweats visibly.

Prince Johnson leans toward Doe, "We are asking you in a polite manner now, what did you do with the Liberian people's money?"

Doe bleeds onto the floor. He spits out blood that has seeped into his mouth, making his teeth red. "I have only $500 in bank. One account." The audience laughs. Doe must know his assassination is playing out in front of his eyes. Surely he can see, surely he remembers the first days of his own revolution. A microphone is thrust in his face. He is forced to repeat the words, "I Samuel Kenyon Doe declare that the government is overthrown. I am therefore asking the armed forces to surrender to Field Marshal Prince Johnson."

The video ends.

Later that day Doe is finally murdered, along with seventy of his soldiers. He is stripped naked and paraded through the streets of Monrovia. His bloated naked body is photographed for posterity.

47

Jehuu

THE STREETS AND roads of Liberia are paths pocked with the results of war, ruins from exploded mortar.

The dead have been dragged off to the side, left there to decompose; town to town, camp to camp. There's just no way to get yourself in a position of consistent safety. We're almost always monitored by soldiers on the road. They keep us moving. When we happen to go unwatched for a few miles, we send older boys ahead and behind to scout, runners. Sometimes the fastest is a girl, and we send her. The job is to see people coming, maybe soldiers in cars or trucks, maybe soldiers on foot, maybe other refugees. Maybe, who knows? If they can tell which tribe or if it's government on the road, that is best. That way we know what to do. Runners hurry to us when they see trouble ahead or coming from behind on the roads. We dissolve into the brush, hide in trees and sometimes in a ditch with the dead. It's hard to stay quiet when you're seven, eight, nine years old. If soldiers are government, we move to other side of road and slouch, head down, feet in the dirt. Maybe rub mud on our clothes, make no noise, no eye contact. The very young and the very old disappear, become invisible. Open areas have much more danger, when there's nowhere to hide, no trees, no bush, on roads framed with wide marsh on either side or near the coast where the Atlantic Ocean is a natural barrier.

The distant claps of firing pins pushing lead is constant, the sounds ubiquitous and repetitive, the background music of my world. I shuffle my feet, marking my trail in the stones. I wait to be scolded, a sheepish smile curls the corners of my mouth. I can't help it.

And, of course, it comes. "Pick up your feet boy, I take your shoes you not gonna use them." I plunge my knees and march, arms swing by my side, my backpack swivels, the grin stretches my lips.

"Oh you sometin' boy, you something all right." Grandma looks away, but I see her smile.

Guns clap closer now. Actual fire-fights are rare outside the city where Daguda men use buildings for cover; they hide from snipers and roving militants. The bullets we hear are outside Buchanan where we just left the house on Allison Street, probably child soldiers wasting bullets in the sky or target practice on a house or street sign.

Maybe they're shooting another man, though.

Walking is easy for me, but I still want to run. The grown-ups won't let me.

The first night on the road we stop at a relief station. They take names, mine is Jehuu Caulcrick; Jerome Blomo is gone. Then you pass the main gate, move on, and find a tent. You take off your backpack, feel the sweat. Take out your extra clothes and bunch them up and go to sleep.

We are all tired, this first day.

48

Liberia

ALL CIVIL WARS are hard to survive.

In Liberia, death and randomness are a Venn diagram where the circles almost indiscernibly overlap; any person in the wrong place at the wrong time has a one-in-three chance of being killed. Take the wrong turn, enter the wrong village, the wrong house on the wrong street, choose the wrong path in the bush, and the chance of dying increases or decreases exponentially, and there isn't much you can do about it.

Two-hundred-fifty thousand Liberians counted dead in ten years of constant, consistent, pervasive civil war that tore up the country. Seventy-five percent of the women raped.

Breathe the wrong air and you could share space with a bullet, a machete, a human pyre.

A soldier recognizes you from the wrong neighborhood, dead.

Wear a tattoo or a piercing that strikes a rebel wrong, you're murdered.

Carry a jar of peanut butter that a child soldier wants, and your arm is hacked off.

Males of a certain age, stolen in the night and given a weapon. If you refuse the offer, your throat is slit as your best option, skinned alive, limbs hacked off as a consolation prize.

A woman of any age and you're raped, only a one-in-four chance of missing out on that torture.

There were so few good guys, on either side, nowhere to seek relief, protectors and rebels alike killed and raped at will. Peacekeepers, in acts of convenience, killed plenty of people without due diligence or any recognized system of justice. They contributed to the chaos, to the civilian death toll. Tragically, they contributed to the number of people who mistrusted the government, and emboldened Taylor's army. This brutal state was perpetrated over an area roughly the size of Pennsylvania, inhabited by two million people. The places to hide, to escape, were few and far between. The numbers strain the imagination, but those statistics don't touch the berg of ice hiding below the water. The mortal ripples continued for decades. They are still being felt. The wars brought the depletion of resources. Taylor stole from the country –diamonds, gold, lumber, and rubber. A generation of youth left without a chance of contributing anything unspoiled to their home country.

49

Jehuu

TODAY WE WALK again, the refugee camp is unsafe.

I hold people's hands, but it's so hot. Skin touching skin makes heat. Heat makes itself, people say. Don't need help from people.

Dust from the dry road fills my mouth, my nose, my ears, my skin. I am part of the dust, or the mud when the rains come, for days at a time when I'm no longer Jehuu, when I'm the *Walking Boy*.

We look for food or water, you drink whenever you can. The only thing there is too much of is dirt, dust or mud, dry or wet, and bullets, plenty of bullets.

The heat has nowhere to go. It wraps your shoulders like a blanket then leaks a slow, dripping, broken faucet, soaking your hair, down your shirt into your pants, down your legs filling your shoes. Anything used to stem the sweat, a sleeve, a towel, a flick of the wrist, is a wasted resource. So you let it come. What else can you do? The heat, the baking sun, the air filled with moisture brings the stink of human suffering. It brings with it the carrion smell of the dead, underlaid with the salt of the sea when the wind is from the east. The dirt road we walk frames the coast of Liberia. It's called the Freedom Highway. It takes you places if you're strong and extremely lucky, but it doesn't release you from the heat. Or the smell.

White trucks pass, and we jump from the road. We keep heads bowed, eyes downcast, step by step. Jehuu wants to be big, tall, fast, strong. *Walking Boy* needs to be small, unseen, a ghost.

Convoys are packed with boys and guns, spilling out the sides, hanging on for life, going to and from the war. Boys will shoot right at you when they pass. They lower guns, laugh, and fire. Your eyes go automatically to these boys; they are funny and strange and scary and power-filled, but you learn to watch the weapons, where they are pointed. You jump if you have to, slide away, crawl into a ditch.

We cross a threshold from the destroyed road to streets of a blown-out city, I don't know which one. Buildings just spring from the land. Nobody here, no animals, no cars, no windows, doors are kicked down, roofs caved in. The *pop pop pop* from the guns, distant when we were on the road, is louder here, it echoes off the buildings that line the narrow street. I can't tell where they come from, but we know that bullets are close by.

The bullet does not pick and choose.

. . . .

"Keep up and hush them! On the road. No strays. Get your hands on Jehuu," Grandma's harsh whisper hisses in the heat. We've been lost and found more times than I can count. I always know where the road is, but in the mangroves, in the bush, the way gets confused. Usually you can follow the guns, *pop pop pop,* those will be near the roads and where people walk. Grandma Joanna has no way to keep us under control all the time. Ten or fifteen cousins and friends, walking the roads. Imagine how hard it is in a mall or a park, keeping your Jehuu or your Mardea wrapped tight. Now imagine them loose in Liberia.

Grandma says, It's very difficult to describe. Living there, you could die at any time. You went to bed with your clothes on because you might have to pick up and go. We would just leave everything behind. It was leave everything behind or die. The children were small and we were trying to hide them. There would be shooting and the kids wanted to get up and see. They were kids. They didn't know how dangerous it was. Keep quiet. Keep down. There were dead bodies all over the street.

. . . .

The walk is a desolate experience when all you want to do is run. I am forbidden to run, except on command. My legs, those Blomo thunder thighs, ache to give wing. But running is no longer freedom, sweet pumping of legs and arms, wind-in-your-face, gliding across the Earth. Running for fun is showing off, calling attention. It's catches the eye. Running makes you a target, either to be picked off with a weapon or to be singled out as capable and strong, and valuable. Every time I run, Grandpa or Grandma yells. Jehuu, be still.

How can I be still?

So, I don't run. I walk. The slow foot-sliding tramping of the Liberian refugee. Grandma says it's okay if I kick a rock along the dirty roads, as long as I don't get behind. It keeps my head down, tracking a piece of rock on and off my foot. I'm forbidden to give chase, either with a rush toward the imaginary goal or off the beaten track to retrieve a sideways strike.

Kick, walk. Kick, walk, into the dusty road.

50

A Child Soldier

IN THE TENT, Bug cries softly. Shooter folds his arms and grins.

With his back to the older boys, Ghost slips the nine-millimeter shell out of the Glock chamber. He's good with guns. He covers the sound with a cough. Bug stops crying long enough to frown.

"Take the bones, Bug. Hold them tight." Ghost hands over the cherished necklace.

Bug shakes all over, a wet-dog convulsion that runs through his whole body. His eyes roll, and he whimpers again. Ghost leans in close, "Bug, believe," he whispers as he places the necklace around the boy's scrawny neck, "in me."

Quickly, he pushes Bug to arms-length, "Give me six feet", holding the boy's dirty shirt in a tight fist. He places the Glock on his temple and squeezes the trigger.

Click.

Bug falls back into the canvas of the tent. Urine trickles down his leg. His eyes squeeze shut. He opens one, then the other. Feels at his chest, touches the necklace made of bones.

"Give it here," Ghost holds his hand out for the talisman. Bug slips it off his neck and holds it out, still lying against the side of the tent, unable to move.

Ghost takes it, "Go get clean, Bug." He flips the necklace in the air. Shooter takes his eyes from the boy lying against the tent side just long enough to snatch it from the air.

"Your turn, Shooter. Do you believe? Like Bug believes?" Ghost racks a live round into the chamber of the Glock, the *cha-chick* is loud inside the canvas tent.

Ghost has taken charge of these boys.

Training is over. Time to fight. In the bush near Gbarna, the boy soldiers break Zero Week camp. Where seventeen boys started, nine remain, ready for combat. They'll be first in and last out of fire-fights.

Ghost patrol.

51

Jehuu

Mardea

FOR TWO YEARS, we walk.

Two years. I don't know days from weeks from years when I walk. Up and down the coast of Liberia, walking, riding when we can, hiding, living. Chaos, torture, rape, murder, hunger, disease, accidental and intentional consequences. The devil occupies so much space, you have to be the luckiest of the lucky not to be in the same place at the same time as evil. In civilized places, mortality and daily human existence overlap much less than Liberia during the civil wars. For the average American to cross the path of a bullet, a mortar shell, the blade, a fire set to burn human flesh, dysentery, starvation, the bloodlust whims of a twelve-year-old with a weapon of destruction, is all very unlikely, almost impossible. You'd have to be very unfortunate to be burned alive, garroted, hung, starved, or eaten.

In Liberia, it happens every day.

. . . .

Today we walk in rain. Soaked from head to toe the second I wake. The rain is the worst for moving about, except it's a little cooler than the sun-scorched days. It slushes your shoes, makes your clothes heavy. But mostly it dampens noises, makes it harder to read the road, the soldiers, who's coming and who's going.

Liberia has humidity that melts people, it feels like you can drink the air. Grandpa says when we get to River Cess town we can stop. "I hear there's a camp. Or maybe friends will take us in. I have relatives. Maybe even a night in a house."

But today, this walk is hard. It drains us all. We pass Taylor-people two times. They pay us no mind.

For now.

. . . .

The canopy of mangrove trees are still a few meters away, and my feet aren't moving fast enough to cover the distance. Gunfire is so constant that it's a part of the landscape, part of my consciousness, like traffic in a city, crickets on a farm. You don't hear it unless it pierces your consciousness immediately –a car coming close to you on a sidewalk, the distress of animals in the country. The magazine of an AK bursting close enough to smell the powder is something that makes you sit up and take notice.

And then run for cover.

A minute ago, one of the older boys ran back down the road to warn us. His name is Christian, and he says soldiers are coming our way, on slow patrol.

Run Jehuu, run!

I haven't been allowed to run for days, and now when I do, my feet feel slow. Most of our party of refugees head for the open fields, trying to outrun the advancing army. They dive into bushes, hide in ditches.

I sprint for my mangroves.

Pop pop pop, the reports are loud. The patrol rounds a bend in the road. I don't look back, hit the forest, dodge and duck, leap over bramble, my football game is now a run for my life. A quick glance back and I see soldiers through the thickening trees. Hunched over their weapons, they walk toes-first, feeling their way. One lowers the gun and fires, no aim, no purpose, just fire.

None follow me into the bush. I climb a tree, high enough to see the road ahead, behind. The city of River Cess on the horizon. I see smoke, buildings. Guns explode, more soldiers pass, maybe twenty, maybe thirty, can't count them, can't tell which army. They aren't government, on account of the young boys, and ECOMOG doesn't come this far south. Maybe rebels. Maybe Heartmen, warlords looking for sacrifices. I think about Mardea. Is she safe? It's good to be in a tree. If I make no noise, they won't look up. It's hard to be quiet and invisible on the ground. Harder for Grandpa, Grandma, Mardea, Christian.

The soldiers pass, but nobody moves back onto the road. We stay in our hidey-holes. I wait to hear from my people, maybe Grandma, *Come back now Jehuu, Come back to the road.* I wait and wait.

More soldiers come from the other direction, from behind. A fight, a battle, boys and men dive for the bushes, some stand in the road and just shoot and shoot. The *pop pop pop* is steady, a thousand crickets. How can there be so many bullets?

I remember how I always wanted to be big, like my cousins, like soldiers, and the Liberian football team. Tall and thick and strong.

Not now. All I want is to disappear. *How small can you be, Jehuu? How to make no shadow? How to be a ghost?*

. . . .

When the fire-fight is over we come out. We listen, we smell, we look up and down, take small steps back to the road. No way to tell who won and who lost, bodies scattered all over the road. Blood seeps into the Earth, boys and men cry out, shot, wounded. Most are dead. They are face-down and face-up. Some look like they're sleeping, sprawled with arms and legs stretched. If you look into their open, empty eyes, you know it's not sleep. It's dead.

Grandpa gets my hand, covers my face, and we go look for the others. We're happy to see Grandma and Mardea. Step over bodies, ignoring howls from the wounded, start back down the road toward the city.

Outside River Cess, there's smoke, smell of potash, dead fish, more dead men. We walk into the city, guns now faint in the distance. Grandpa can't keep his hand over my eyes forever, I peer around corners, into broken buildings. More dead here. The road shines, burnt orange, light reflects with a wet-sheen.

"The roads are gold," a cousin says.

My eyes brighten, the street is shiny, glints from the sun. *Gold?* "Is that gold?"

Grandma frowns. "Not gold, boys."

We move into the street, between buildings. Shuffle my feet, kick at the hollow metal.

"Bullets," says Mardea.

"Shells," Grandpa. "Bullets that were shot"

"So many," Grandma sighs.

The metal sings with every step. *Swoosh, tinkle, clang. Bullets, shells, oh eh,* I sing as I go. A big kick stirs up enough to see the road. *Swoosh, clang, tinkle* as the shells settle, seek their lowest level, like water filling a dry creek bed, like the blood that soaks the dusty road.

"Shells as far as you can see. So many."

"A big battle, *eh*?"

The town is empty except for scattered bodies, all those shells. We wade through.

To the other side.

.　.　.　.

We walk with as many other refugees as we can find. Big groups, long lines help you hide. Hard to pick you out of a crowd. More targets. Many times we are made to stop, either roadblocks or passing armies. Checked for our tribe or for valuables. Checkpoints are the worse, always something scary, never just walking right through. We are lucky, our small group from Allison Street. Soldiers don't want an old lady, an old man, a baby boy like me, or small, small girls like Mardea.

Grandma and Grandpa are scared for me and Mardea. Boys get taken up, girls get raped. Less along the road or when you can hide. The stories are bad, rumors that have truth. Heartmen looking out for the very young, especially girls, to sacrifice. Black magic, voodoo, war, an end to civilized Liberia.

So, we walk with as many as we can find, with larger groups. Form a line, walk on to the next place. War funnels all refugees to the same places, as far away from fighting as we can get. That means south now. Battles wage through Buchanan into Monrovia, past Harbel, north into the bush, as far as Gbarna, then Nimba and Wuteve, into the mountains.

I wonder about grandma's house, the fields of food, my football pitch. *Did someone find my World Cup ball? My goals? Did they take all the food and water?*

It's impossible to get clean on the road, not your body, not your clothes, not your teeth. If there's water, you drink it, you don't run it over your body, you don't flush it down a toilet. This isn't a life you can picture; it is a life that must be lived to understand.

Take your child to a dentist, to a dermatologist. Get them shots for measles, mumps, rubella. Buy clothes from a store or get hand-me-downs. Wash hands, brush teeth before bed, toothpaste, run the water in the sink, two minutes, long enough to sing your ABC's.

All things you teach children.

A list of school supplies from a teacher: pencils, paper, binders, glue, crayons, a lunchbox. Kids in the school play pee wee soccer, little league. They dance; they learn the piano. Grandparents babysit on weekends.

During the long walk children wait all day for a drink of water. No place to learn to read and write. No dentist, no doctor. If it isn't on your back, if you can't carry it, you don't own it. If you cut yourself, you don't get a band-aid. There's no place to go that isn't different than the place where you stand.

. . . .

In this dream, I drink. Right out of the ocean. I know I'm not supposed to, Grandma said so, but it's good, there's no salt, just cold. I stick my face right in and no more thirst.

Except that's not true. Still thirsty. I stay thirsty no matter how much I drink. Mardea is here. She stands beside me; she won't drink. *You have some*, she says, points at the ocean, but then go 'way.

Staying, I say, *and drinking. All day. All the water in the whole sea. All the way to America. To mum.*

There's a big fish in the ocean, tail under water, head in the air. *No more ocean water, Jerome*, says the fish, except his mouth doesn't move. He calls me by my old name, the boy I'm not. *Enough*, the fish says, *Now go before they eat you.*

Who? Who goin' eat me, fish?

Dem men. Dem boys.

Why? I don't understand this fish.

They eat everything. Everyone.

151

Clouds darken over the ocean. Fish shows me big razor-teeth. *Eat you.*

My shoulders tighten, I bend at the knees. I can run if I want. Nobody will catch me. I don't want to be in the ocean. I don't care how thirsty I am. I turn to run but my legs are too heavy, my feet don't move in the water.

Through those sharp teeth Mr. Fish says, *Go 'way. Run 'way before they eat you...*

. . . .

I wake in my tent, family spread out on cots all around. The air is cool inside the canvas, but heat comes off sleeping bodies. People make sleepy people sounds, snore, soft cries, weeping into the gravel floor and then the earth.

A dream. The Fish Man.

Eat you...

I sit up. Her back to me, Mardea sits in the entrance of the big tent. I recognize her outline. The shape of her head, her hunched shoulders. She talks softly.

"Now go" she says. "Go 'way."

Am I asleep? Dreaming?

"Mardy? Who's there?"

"Shhh. You wake people."

"But who is it?" I whisper. It's a quiet, crowded tent. The air will be heavy soon, hot and soggy. Backpack will be damp this morning. Makes me want to bust out and breathe before the tent is too hot and sticky. But my eyes are heavy from sleep, my legs carry the weight from my dream. I pinch and rub them to make sure they work.

"Settle down Jehuu, don't wake people." I remember Fish calling me Jerome. He knows I was Jerome. It's a startling thought.

I scoot along the tent to Mardy, my legs work free from the water-dream fugue. People sprayed all over the tent, arms and legs here and there, open mouths, eyes closed in slumber. Reminds me of bodies on the roadside. Chests rise and fall. There's life in these people, sweat and odor, but not rotten. Everyone here is alive, just asleep.

Mardea sits cross-legged, the dawn light frames her back. Soft breezes ruffle her clothes. A ball of fur with a nose sniffs, favors her outstretched hand.

"What is that?" Eyes go wide. I haven't seen animals in forever.

"Shhh. He's hungry."

"Me too. Where's food?"

"Just crumbs from my bread."

"Wha's he doing here?"

She ignores me. I watch in awe as the fur-ball licks crumbs from my sister's hand. She crumbles up more and holds it out.

. . . .

We settle in this camp for days now. Resting mostly. A whole village, town, except no roads or cars, or real buildings. I learn my way around and am allowed to escape every now and then to explore this new world. Oil lamps light the camp, fires at night. People sell water and food at some of the tents. There is a real place for breakfast and dinner, even though it's cooking in a tent and taking the food out.

You hear the school building before you get there, whirrs of a generator. Me and Mardea sit and try to learn, but it's hot and loud. Grandma, older cousins spend time with us, reading, learning numbers and colors, animals and plants. We don't stay long enough to get comfortable in schools. We've lost something that makes us students.

War news comes. I don't understand, but adults talk, names like Taylor and Sawyer, government and ECOMOG. I can see places like Buchanan, Firestone, Monrovia in my head. Places adults say are now war-zones.

This camp has TV, in the big tin building that frames one end. They turn it on once a day when the generator pushes electricity. It gets so crowded that little people can't see or hear.

At night, teenagers play music, older cousins dance, pass cigarettes, and be loud. I'm allowed to watch, but not all night. This city isn't real, but life moves, people do things. There's a tenuous sense of safety, a strange normalcy, feelings of life that's not constantly fearful and alert, slightly, not completely, restful. The people flock to places like this, embrace it. That's the way of Liberia.

. . . .

Through the tent opening, a narrow band of the refugee camp stretches. Dirt lanes framed by tents. Trucks and a small stage end the lane, a large sign stretches between rickety wood posts. There's a red cross painted on it. The cross is supposed to mean safety and home-free. Sometimes, the red cross is a target. In the distance, the usual *pop pop pop* of guns. No trees, no bushes, no plants of any kind, just a dust city of tents. Not like Buchanan, not like my grandma's. I have to pee, not allowed to go outside myself. Soon, I'll have to ask grampa to take me. For now, I let him sleep. I look at Mardea's pet.

"Think they'll eat him?" She looks at the animal.

"He should run 'way," I say.

"I know," she says.

Animals don't last long any more. We haven't seen anything except dogs for miles and miles. Too many hungry boys, too many guns. Smart dogs stay out of sight until trucks pass, then they come to look for scraps of the dead. Dumb dogs get ate. Boys eat anything they can shoot and cook. Even rats, racoons. There's no sugar cane or mangos or corn in the fields. It's all taken for the soldiers or burned. Waves of brown lands by the roads, tortured grounds, looking like pictures of the desert or the moon.

"Is it a rat?" I frown at Mardea's pet. It stretches out, long tail twitches. It rattles and purrs, like a cat. Rats in Liberia are big, some like small dogs. I didn't ever eat one, but I bet you could. They don't look like cartoon rats, some have snub noses and lots of soft fur. This is maybe a rat; it looks soft, like it would want to be a pet.

"Mongoose, I think. They eat snakes." I reach out to touch it, Mardea says no. "And they bite fingers."

. . . .

Water is scarce, food hard to find. Cups of water here, bowls of rice there, shared as many ways as people. All Liberia is like that. Money doesn't matter on the road, jobs, titles, parents. There's no currency. Depending on where you walk, who you see on the roads, your family name can get you food and shelter or the sharp end of a machete. All except a very few are fed, safe from violence. Those are the people with guns. The rest of us walk, a million refugees, one-third of the population.

Automatic weapon fire is so constant you don't even notice it. You can only flinch and cower so many times. Through the days and nights, somebody always shoots, like by a busy road, noise is constant. You ignore it. You see dead people, all day every day. So many people killed, more than you'd believe really.

52

Liberia

THE MAN ON the side of the road, shot through, eyes open to a blistering sun, is dead.

He's been kicked toward the ditch, but not enough to go in. He lies on the edge and looks, his lips parted in surprise. Whatever blood might have come from his wounds has long since seeped into the dusty roadside. The unfeeling earth soaks, sucks, and melts his flesh and bone and sinew, muscle and organs as soon as his cells and tissues stopped receiving oxygen. His brain was the first thing to die, halting electrical firing within three to seven minutes. His bone and skin cells might survive for several days still, but he's not coming back. Zombies, animated Negee don't really exist. His blood has drained from capillaries, pooling in lower-lying portions of his body, creating a pale appearance in some places and a darker appearance in others.

About three hours after his death, muscles stiffen, and rigor mortis sets in. Within a day, depending on body fat and external temperatures, all internal heat is released in a process called *algor* mortis. Bacteria will begin breaking down all his cells. His body will take on a gruesome appearance and smell. Decomposing tissue emits a green substance. His lungs will leak fluid through the mouth and nose.

Insects and animals will take notice of all this. His body will provide sustenance and a great place for insects to lay eggs. In the intense sun, his body will mummify quickly, within about three months. After that it will take a long time for him to decay finally, definitively. If he's buried, or moved to a shaded area, he'll become a skeleton in three to four months. In general, bodies decompose faster in hotter, more humid climes than in colder, drier places. This is a hot, humid place.

In most civilizations, his dead body would be attended and never get the chance to become a skeleton in broad daylight. The dead are buried or cremated, or otherwise disposed with ceremony and veneration, the value of a human life recognized, and the ending of life treated as a source of reverence.

In Liberia, the human form is just another obstacle, a mass to be stepped over, without the compunction even to push it aside. Detritus, trash, roadkill.

Plenty of skeletons in Liberia.

53

Jehuu

Walk again?

"Yeh, Jehuu. We walk." Grandma gives the look that says, *I know I know*. Also it says *Get your butt off the ground, put one foot in front of the other.*

I don't like the walk; I'd rather kick soccer balls. But it's not bad, only a walk. I don't know how much we walk, but it's a lot. Days are the same as the next, nothing to tell one from another unless something happens –a jug of water from a stranger, meat, or a piece of candy to eat. A gun battle marks a day as different. Maybe someone gets cut or shot, violent collisions between soldiers and refugees, bloody sights.

It's always hot. We try to be quiet, but it's hard. Busy hands is what Grandma says, "Jehuu, you got busy hands! Keep to y'self." How do I keep hands to myself? Using hands, that's what they're for.

I kick rocks down the road. How far can I kick one? How many times can I kick a rock or a stick or pieces of trash? I count my steps up to a hundred, two hundred. Can I kick a rock three hundred times? Let's see.

Today on the road is me, Mardea, Grandma, Grandpa, Odziki, and Lonny. Others too –Larry, Donny, Scout, one called Hemmer and a girl called Sunny. Scout is the biggest, he leads down the road. *Pop pop pop* go the guns, ahead and behind, both sides of the road.

"There's nutin' backwards," says Scout. "Might just as well go up roads than where we came from." He's older than me, Mardea, and cousins. I don't know how he isn't a soldier. He's the right size and age.

We walk, hot and dusty, wet with sweat, and the dirt sticks to everything. Mardea looks like a skeleton, her clothes stuck to her. She kicks at dust, pretty dresses and Sunday shoes all gone.

Scout comes back from scouting. "Soldiers ahead. I go around, through the bush. You all stay on the road." He smiles, even with soldiers nearby.

We round a bend; the smell is bad. Something is dead here. My nose scrunched. Grandma looks, "Jehuu, don't make your face up. You ugly." She tries to smile. There's people laying in the road. Flies swarm bodies. I hold my nose, no matter it makes me ugly. No matter what Grandma says.

"Who them people Grandma?" I try not to look, but people cover the whole road.

Go forward. Don't look back.

"Just bodies. All dead", says Sunny. "I can't count, so many." Sunny is not like Mardea, younger, short and round in places.

"Too many", says Grandma. "Too many eh." So many bodies we step over them, can't go around. The flies buzz when you rustle a body, you have to shoo them away, or they land in eyes, fill your ears with buzzing. Then they go back to the dead.

"These bodies been here a long time."

"Not so long. Sun and rain."

"But it smells so."

"Sun and rain. Sun and rain, and flies."

"Blow flies, the green ones get here first. Then maggots, beetles, vultures."

"Hush you all", says Grandma. "These are dead people. Show respect." She closes her eyes, says a prayer, "And the dead bodies will lie in the street of the great city which mystically is called Sodom and Egypt, where also their Lord was crucified."

I saw a lot of dead bodies in my life. More than you.

.   .   .   .

The road is mud today, not dust. We leave another refugee camp at sunrise, slip from the tent, past wire and parked trucks and dirty Red Cross flags hanging limp in the morning ooze.

We are part of seven-hundred-thousand Liberians considered refugees, the result of Taylor's civil war. We seep into the countryside, dodge battles, seek comfort in neighboring countries, the common denominator is movement, displacement from homes. My family trusts instincts and contacts better than ECOMOG or the Liberian government. Rumors of what "peacekeepers" do to native Liberians not much better than how warlords act. My family knows people. We built good will through the years by being generous and giving. We don't know or trust the other side, that's why we pick our own way around Liberia.

.   .   .   .

Rain.

It fills the potholes with brown, brackish scum, the color of a penny. Dark water unwilling to reflect light. Look in it and see nothing, a broth of filth, a door to nowhere. I look at water as a base element, mixed rain and death. I drop rocks into puddles, get back evil ripples, stench of rotten meat. It's a mockery of the water I loved to play in when I was at Firestone and Grandma's –pots, barrels of rain catchers, mirror-water, see my face look back, broad lips, high forehead of my father, a Blomo face, smile fixed. Water you can drink from in gourd-bowls mum fills for lunch, with slices of berry and coconut. Snacks of craw, salted rice on broad papa leaves, and on the side, gummy bears from the grocery down the road.

Not here. The dead pile close, bloated corpses melt in the rain and heat, leak into the water, make it poison. Be careful, don't touch it, no matter how thirsty. It's hard to walk by rain-filled puddles of mud. La God one know I am thirsty.

"Why can't we drink, Grandma?"

"It's bad, Jehuu."

"It looks wet." Why if it's wet it's no good?

"See them people there. The dead ones, *eh*? They in the water. Their souls"

"Oh."

"You don't want to drink dead ones, do you?"

"No."

And on we walk.

That bad water, gets your blood, your mouth, holes in your shoe, cracks in your skin. Dead spirits in your blood.

So, you walk in the rain, head down, watch where you step.

Africa is not dry heat.

. . . .

November bleeds into December, then January. Rain and heat become just heat. That layer of child-cuteness, that desire to run and race, bright eyes, all dissolve from me into the Liberian countryside, dusty roads, random violence, incessant gunfire. Walk is a slog, one footfall followed by the next. Step after step is all there is, no imagination, no joy, no fear. Dead bodies along the side of the road decay in my path, not people anymore, obstacles to my next step, like rocks or potholes; lifeless wads of flesh, homes for insects. Dogs pick at corpses, maybe a brave gibbons sneaks from the bush to inspect, a snake sets up home in a rotting body. We step over them and move on. Adult torsos are too big for a toddler to step over, so they weave between legs or over necks or heads. Look careful so something alive doesn't jump out at you.

It doesn't take long to go numb. Spirit and curiosity, tapped-out energy extinguish pretty fast when you are so thirsty all the time.

161

The heat pushes, drives you into the road, takes your breath, and doesn't give it back until a cup of warm, dirty water passes your lips.

And then all you really want is more dirty water from a plastic cup.

. . . .

I wake with a start, bolt upright. The tent is hot, of course, and close. Bugs flit in and out of ears. I brush them away, crawl from under netting.

The guns are close. The sounds of battle. When guns are far away, you can relax, but when they are close, it's time to move somewhere else. I scout a place to run, in case guns get too loud, too close. My family, all packed into a small tent. I rise, close the tent flap to keep bugs out, listen hard, look at the camp. It's mostly silent except for boys moving in and out of other tents. Rub my eyes and yawn, make faces at them. If they come here, I will protect us. Kill them, even if I'm just a small boy. Yawn, stretch, breath deep. Go lay back down. So tired.

I had a dream. Something about candy and Mum. I want to go back to sleep and see her again.

. . . .

Travel is all walking. Cars or trucks are stopped confiscated for the war, different tribes or military. Roads are so beat up that driving is slow, then it's dangerous. When trucks move fast there's no time for soldiers to eyeball you. When trucks are slow, they look long. They look in your eyes, see what's there. They point guns. When they're slow, you look at the road, at your feet.

We move south, close to the coast. Beaches aren't safe anymore, there's nowhere to hide, and they're a favorite place of soldiers, warlords and Heartmen. They go to the ocean to catch cod and tuna and to execute rivals, for blood sport. Rockets from nameless ships off the coast blow holes in the sand, nobody knows why. We see all of Liberia on our walk, coastal roads, inland trails, and paths, except for mountains north in Lofa and Nimba, we don't go there. (I will pass those places later when we try to escape.) We walk past buildings and houses in Buchanan, soaked marshes of River Cress, rain forests in Greenville and Barklayville. Past plains once filled with sugar cane, heavy thatch, cacao, bracketing the roads and paths, further and further from home, from the world we know, from my mum. Into and around the African bush with bamboo, oil palms, and mahogany that's not yet torn down. Rebels and the government will loot everything they can sell. The rainforest and valuable timber will be stripped bare, harvested for profit to buy guns and ammunition and drugs. But the bush is a hard place with worm-snakes, cobras, mambas, adders, and rock pythons.

One time, when nobody can see, my family sneaks off the main road to the beach. I watch the ocean, the waves. "Why does the ocean come here, then run away?" I ask.

"That's the tide, Jehuu."

"A tide?"

"Tide is when the water comes here to the beach, sees Jehuu, then runs back. Afraid of the big, strong boy." Grandma smiles down at me.

When you're seven or eight, that's special. The ocean afraid of you. I flex my arms, jump in the sand. I yell at the waves, *Come! Now go!*

Then we're back on the road.

You take your next step. Then your next.

. . . .

Here is a road block. Here is a tank, a real army tank, taking up half the road, stopping traffic, foot and truck and pen pen, and rickshaw. Single file we pass the point controlled by a few boys with big, big guns, holding jungle juice in clear plastic cartons. At a roadside table sits a man, an officer, with piles of paper, rosters, lists, pictures of peoples. Holding the papers in the hot breeze is a large, rusted machete.

No way around, we have to go through and show papers, hope there's no pictures of Blomos or records of us as Kru.

"No other way south, except to go back," our scout whispers. "Have to go through, but these boys, dey tired, lazy. Taylor's rebels, dumb kids. But we can't be Blomo here, *eh*? We can be Caulcrick, Coopers. Bassa and Gio."

"You hear, Jehuu? Mardea? Sunny, Hemmer and the rest?" Grandma taps us each on the head. "You stay quiet. They ask your name, you say Caulcrick. They ask where your mum, your daddy, you say they gone."

Scout says, "If shooting starts, there's nowhere to run. Deep ditches on both sides, with men there. If you hear the guns, if you see bad, you have to run through or back, straight away. You can't go sideways"

Our line of refugees is long, it runs back up the road, weaves around a bend, disappears. Boys, girls, young, some old. No young men, they're all gone or turned into soldiers. Some women, some with babies in their arms, cuddled in pouches.

The tank and roadblock loom. Taylor boys sit atop the tank. They wear funny clothes, they smoke, all have a knife, a gun, a cigarette. Their eyes droop, they look yellow. Some sleep with flies, bugs landing on their skin.

This is the coastal road halfway between cities, Barclayville and Harper, as far west in Liberia as you can get without meeting the ocean, and south before you cross into Cote D'Ivoire. The ocean ports here are too far from the fighting for supplies, the roads are too bad to fix. Food and water supplies as scarce as the desert.

We walk like lazy people. It's easy in the heat, the sun takes away your lifeblood. The guns, the boys, the tanks, are electricity itself. We drag our feet, slap dully at bugs trying to infest eyes and ears.

We hood eyes from the world, try to disappear, leave no footprints, breath no air, we cease to exist. We die a little.

But we move, we keep walking.

. . . .

On the side of the road, a man talks with Grandpa. His pants are ripped down the side, shows a leg that looks like a skeleton, all bone. He smiles wide, teeth that are spread out –white, black, white, black, all the way to the back of his mouth. "Here is something for you, friend." He presses a jug of filmy water into Grandpa's hand.

"*Eh*, God will bless you," says Grandpa, bowing a little at the waist. "God will bless you much."

We drink the jug almost half-way down. Grandpa ties the jug off his belt, saves half. My throat is wet at last.

This is not a good place, not a safe checkpoint. It's tense, metallic, the Sulphur smell of fired weapons. Boys look and smell of killing, clothes streak crimson, blood, crusty and flaky, drying flesh stuck to crazy clothes, crazed hats, white dresses, chests crossed with bullets. Dark boys, shiny, bumpy skin, red, red eyes, yellow, yellow teeth. No light skinned Congo-boys, no Krahn, no Mandingo. All Gio, or Bassa. They wear masks of every menacing Liberian wraith known –Heartmen, rogues, shades, phantoms, ghosts. Young boys shout, laugh, run around with guns, machetes. Shoot in the air, at the feet of us refugees. People jump and them boys laugh.

Boys ask for papers. Grandpa whispers, "Keep your head down. Look at the road, not at them. Don't talk. Keep moving."

My backpack is heavy, sweaty, my shirt damp. I brush flies from my face; they find my ears, my nose, flick in and out of eyes. More flies here than other places on the road. They hover in a black cloud, a buzz-wave that settles in the deep ditches framing the road. Piled bodies there, probably lots, you don't need to see them to know.

Cousin Ozidiki walks with me. "See that gun, Jehuu", he says. "See how big?"

Hiss, Grandma says from behind me. "Stop talking you two. Now!"

"I didn't talk! It was Ozee."

"HUSH, Jehuu." She's mad, I pout, kick the road, raise dust. Mardea has her hand over her mouth, giggling. Shutup Mardy.

A boy on the truck snaps his head, looks at Ozidki, squints, tongue darts out and licks air, a snake tastes a mouse. The boy jumps down, gun slung over his back. His eyes are black, slits against sunlight. He wipes his nose on a dirty brown shirt, snot and blood soak the sleeve. His tongue clears red lips, takes in blood. He shuffles to us, plastic sandals on dirty feet. He smells like boy-sweat and smoke, dull eyes, dull voice. That tongue moves and darts, feeds blood into his mouth, coating teeth and gums in a bright red hole. "I take dat." His voice is lead, cloudy, talking through gauze. His gun looks heavy, weighs his skinny arms down, the barrel comes up, points at Ozidiki.

"Un nuh. No." Ozidiki backs away.

"Nah, I that, eh. Gimme here." He points his gun at Ozidiki's side. For the first time I notice he's carrying a big plastic tub of peanut butter. The boys eyes are dead, unblinking.

"This is mine." Ozidiki cradles the peanut butter.

I look from the boy, to my cousin and back.

Grandpa stops. "Give the peanut butter, Ozidiki. Get you more." He sighs.

"But da butter, dats to me." Ozidiki looks at Grampa.

The boy raises his gun, so big up close. His arms are thin, bruised. His blue-jeans are frayed at the knees.

"Ozidiki? Give it to him." Grandpa's eyes don't look like his voice sounds. They go wide, back to the gun, pleading with my cousin.

"Nah, Grandpa David. Don't make me. I hold your foot. I traded clean socks for this. I carry it all this way, oh." Tears well in his eyes, he hunches over his prized possession.

The soldier boy lifts the gun higher, points at Ozidiki. I freeze, think, *This boy will shoot Ozidiki, Pop, pop. Then me and then Grandpa, then Mardea and Grandma. Everyone. And here I stand, can't even move to help.*

A vision of Joseph comes into my head, the blood, his dead eyes. I try to brush it away, my hand to my forehead. The boy darts a look my way. Odziki will be Joseph now. Will we bury him? Or will he go in the ditch? Bugs fly in and out of my earholes, my nose. I want to slap them away, but my hands are frozen. I don't want that boy to see me, to look into me. Everything is petrified, no wind, the air is a blanket, roadside trees periscope close, box us in. The dead in the ditch peer over the rocky ridge, crowd us.

Give us your cousin, Jehuu, they breath into the air. *Then you come. You can rest here, with us. No more walking.*

I look for a place to run.

Run Jehuu, run.

A shout from the truck, "Lady comin' with a belly!"

The gun pointed at Odziki and Grandpa drops. The boy flicks his tongue, eyes come alive. He turns, forgets us. "A baby? Woman *eh*! Na Ya!" He charges back at the truck, arms flail as if he was jump-started with a battery, infused with energy.

We hear a commotion, laughing, and shouting from the soldier boys.

54

Bonita

"Let your love be like a misty rain, coming softly,
but flooding the river."
—*Liberian Saying*

After about two years in the United States, you were finally able to return for your children?

BC: I flew into the Ivory Coast, and I had to go by road into Liberia. That was not comfortable travel. Nothing is paved. Big holes that shake and jump the cars or trucks you have to ride in. You find rides, hitchhike, pay off drivers. You get stuck when it's mud, you can't see when the roads go to dust. Vehicles coming to Sierra Leone to dump off refugees. I'm looking into each one to see if my family is there. The panic of crossing them here is big in my heart. I'd come in and they go out?

How did you get to your parent's house?

BC: I managed to get there and go to the house. My mum's house. Nobody was there. The house was still standing in a place where every other house was ground into the Earth. It was a miracle. I knew my mum was responsible. She talks to God. She made sure I have a place to come back to.

Some people I know squatting in the neighborhood, nowhere to go. You can't go into the city, people there dying every minute of every day. A million in a place meant for half that. I used to live there, had a house in the city when I was in nursing school and Jehuu was a baby. Monrovia was crowded then. I try to imagine this whole neighborhood and all of them in between squeezing into that place. The hospital will be over run, the apartments full. The streets filled. Where do they eat? Where do they toilet? Where do the sick go now?

I asked if they saw them, my children, but they were all displaced. I asked why these people stayed here. They said where else? So, I just followed what people knew. They were going or coming, and it went around in circles, and that road brought me back to the house.

And, after a month of this, that's where they were, back at the house on Allison Street.

It was some two months before you found them?

BC: It was about a month, month and a half. I was there for a total of two and a half months because after I found them, I had to try to get back to Monrovia to go to the foreign affairs building to get their passports, well to the US Embassy, and try to check on their paperwork because their paperwork still wasn't good. I was here in the US, when the war started, but my parents had taken them to Ghana to try to get them out, and they were denied the visa, and I couldn't understand why.

So, with no luck in Ghana, they had to go back to Liberia.

When they first left the house in Buchanan, did they go south?

BC: They were displaced, and I don't know exactly where they went. But when I first got back and went to go find them, there was nobody there. I knew they were alive because people had seen them. I went all the way around the country, then I finally found them.

55

Jehuu

"LADY WIT A belly comin', *oh*."

This roadblock tingles. Something changed. All the energy is on the other side of the truck-barrier.

The screams start.

I smile, happy Odziki isn't shot, my teeth flash. Grandpa puts his hand over my face. Lines of refugees walk around us, between the tank and the ditch full of the dead. Steam rises from the road. My mouth is dry.

"Where that boy go? What's he do?" I ask past Grandpa's hand. Grandpa moves me through the checkpoint.

The officer from the table with all the papers moves us along. He looks past the tank at the boys whooping and laughing. His eyes narrow. This soldier wears a uniform, beret and baggy green and brown pants, sleeveless dark tee, small mustache. "Nah mind dem young blood. Keep moving, eyes down the road." He points, looks at Grandpa, waves, quick, quick, not even taking papers, not poking, or asking questions. "You too, old man. Move these peoples away." He pushes at our group, Grandma, Grandpa, cousins, Mardea, all them.

Screaming and laughing and rollicking goes on behind us. We have to walk close to the death ditch. They whisper to me, those bodies piled side by side, face down, face up. They smile through dead teeth, they growl at me, bloated fat-face, eyes bulging, like real people just dead. Oh, the bugs, all around, a black, living blanket. The smell is bad, waves come to my nose with the heat and steam.

From behind I hear the boy who tried to take Odziki's peanut butter. "See? I saying girl baby. I told all you. I told you it's a baby girl." He runs to the white truck and grabs a machete. Save me some girl.

Grandpa moves us quick down the road. Grandma hisses, "Ozidiki, you stupid. All them boys are crazy. They cut you, *eh*. For peanut butter." She shoos us with both hands.

I snatch a glance while Grandpa drags my arm. One look. What those boys doing?

A woman on her back in the dirt beside the road. Pinned down by boys, all kinds of boys, all kinds of dirty clothes. One boy on her neck, chokes her. Her arms windmill, up and down, side to side, snaky garden hoses. Another boy, a boy like me, stands over her with a big knife. Sun shines off the blade. His teeth glint between bloody lips, the sun synched with the metal of the machete. I turn to the road ahead, but not before I see him strike down.

The screams rip into my chest. They stay there for a long time.

.   .   .   .

We stop for a night at a refugee camp. I close my eyes, but there's no sleep. I'm sick of just walking then sleeping. I want to play, I want to chase the waves, play football. There's no ball. This is a Red Cross refugee camp, one of the better ones. There's water and a little food if you stand in line. A place for tents and someone checks on you. A fence to keep out bad animals and maybe soldiers looking for children to take to the war.

We try to rest in the big tent. Mardy is crying. Grandpa sings soft to her. He sings Banuwa lullaby.

Banuwa, Banuwa
Banuwa yo
A la no

171

Nehnio la no
Nehnia la no

Don't cry, Don't cry,
Pretty little girl don't cry
Don't cry, Don't cry
Pretty little girl don't cry

Your father off at the village
Your mothers out for a while
Your brothers down by the river
No need to sit and cry.

Sometimes we sleep in the bush, in a circle, our packs for pillows. We squeeze together, and try to stay off the ground, build a bed of grass or leaves. Grandma and Grandpa don't ever seem to sleep. Almost always when I'm awake, they are awake. We find a little food, maybe some water to share, then we walk to find a place to stay. Some neighbors or friends let us in their home; they share food. They let us get clean. Never thought I could like a bath.

But then the guns come, and we walk again. The war is like a beehive. You hear it, you feel it, and you move away from it, sometimes in a rush, waving your arms to not get stung.

Walking day after day when you're eight is boring, long days with nothing to do except move away from war. I close my eyes and see my football goals, the ones Grandpa brought home. I see the field scratched into the dirt. But I see Joseph too, first when he's alive playing, then when he's shot and bleeding. I wish I could say goodbye to him. To say things, to play one more time, football in the back yard.

Instead, I see his grave.

. . . .

We thought we'd find safety back at our house, our old lives. How long can a war go on? How many bullets are there? Back to football in the yard, my grandma's kitchen, my own bed, water, food, T.V., and church on Sundays. A roof over our heads.

The walk back home was full of checkpoints, dead left by the side of roads, the country burned up. What was once the constant smell of potash cooking fires in and around the streets was now a stench of pyres, dead disposed of to keep away vermin, insects, and disease.

Still no water, still food is hard to find every day. When we got home, the neighborhood was wrecked, streets destroyed, holes in everything from mortars and disrepair. Vegetation leveled by fire or trampled under-foot. It was the old neighborhood, but it was not the same. In the suburbs of Monrovia, soldiers looted everything. The old smells and sounds and feel of Grandma's house was replaced by shit and piss and death. In the walls, the ceilings. It was war smell. It stuck in your nose, your mouth, hung on clothes.

Somehow, the house was intact. Glass smashed, nothing valuable left, but standing, better than most houses. Everyone said it was God who kept it safe, God and Grandma Joanna. We fixed up what we could, Grandpa with his new limp, Grandma with her new sad eyes, me and Mardea, uncles, aunts, friends who we called brother and sister, all gaunt, trimmed and wretched by the years of walking, hiding, surviving. Allison Street, that place of community, was now a place of refuge, where people came to get away from war.

I was nine, but older, aged by the walk, Bigger, but not yet stronger, that would come with food and water and running. But I was the age when the soldiers come and take you, and that scared people. You see it in their eyes, the way they hovered over me and Mardea. We spent a lot of time inside.

The tank was gone, but its shadow was still there.

. . . .

Jehuu, why you sit there all the time?

I gaze onto the back yard, the place I used to kick football, score goals, sneak off into the mangroves. It was where I went when I missed mum most.

Now I only think about the bodies and the flies and the blood. About dogs who sniff at the dead before they take a bite. I think about the *pop pop pop* of guns all the time. I think about the woman at the bad checkpoint.

I sit back from the window, and I wait for something to happen, soldiers to come and take off my shirt, to look for Krahn ink. The guns are still outside. I wait for another bullet to find someone important to me.

The bullet does not pick and choose.

This neighborhood is no good, but I'm sick and tired of Walking Boy. "I jus' looking, Grandma."

"Come away from the window, *eh*?"

"Jus' looking."

.   .   .   .

Refuges come back when it seems safe, repatriate northern Liberia from Sierra Leone, eighty-thousand by boat, car, and their own two feet, refilling empty cities. Then it isn't safe and cities are shelled into rubble, no facilities, no infrastructure, no food, no water, no toilet. Imagine, just imagine, your city empties every six months, and refills again. That's all people know.

We came back to Allison Street in 1992. The house empty. Other houses destroyed, no resemblance of what used to be a neighborhood, debris of debris. Wood, plaster, metal, nothing of value, all that either was blown up or taken for the war. The ravaging of suburbs around Monrovia was absolute, except for a few houses here and there, random and scattered, like the violence, like the rest of the country.

Still not safe. When the guns come close, it's time to go back inside. Joseph's grave a reminder that bullets don't care where you are when they fly.

One day we're in the house, eating fish and nuts bought from market ladies who line the streets; they sell what they can scrounge from the countryside and abandoned places. Then we hear whoop from the front of the house.

I think of the boys at the checkpoint.

"It's me pap."

"You…that you, Bonita?"

"Yes, papa it's me."

We run to the front of the house, and there's Mum. After two harrowing years, a nine-year old boy needs to see his mama.

56

Bonita

So, you're in Buchanan, you finally found them, and you have to get them to the embassy in Monrovia?

BC: Jehuu and Mardea had to get visas and then blood tested at a local hospital to meet international travel requirements.

How was that travel, from your mom's house to the big city?

BC: It was maybe the most dangerous place in the world. Roads of mud and awful water, destroyed by mortars and war. Almost no way to go in cars or trucks or vans, anything that needs four wheels on the ground had to go slow, almost like walking. Road like a killing place if you weren't lucky and careful, the Tubman Road. Plenty of weapons, enough firepower and killers to fill the whole war.

Back and forth to Monrovia from the house on Allison Street. Eighty-eight-miles one-way. Between hiding on the floor of a van and showing papers at dangerous roadblocks, soldiers, all fidgety and antsy.

Paper work has to be the most frustrating thing there can be. The only thing I wanted was to finalize visas for the kids, but the paperwork was two weeks out still, so they told me. Outside the US embassy was chaos, people without hope or a place to be. Weapons on the streets, uniforms of soldiers, confusing and a mystery. The streets of the capital city were a bomb, waiting to explode.

57

Jehuu

YOU KIDS PACKED? *Ready to go?*

"Mama, we just got home." So tired of walking, so tired of not being at a home. So tired, I just want to sleep and play and not be hungry. I watch out the back window. No sounds, not even the birds that sit in the trees at the edge of the mangrove forest. Mama comes to me, strokes my head. My hair is tight so I can mop sweat easy and it doesn't soak my hair, like on the walk. She smells so good, like soap, like fresh air and mornings.

"We have to go Jehuu, have to get away. Get us to America. I have a home there."

America. That word, that idea gives me a chill. Wonderland, streets of gold, food, plenty of water. Me and mum look at the back yard, at Joseph's cross, falling down. The day we buried him comes back to me as gauzy memory, behind a heat mirage. I helped dig, a little. I didn't see him dropped in the hole, didn't see the dirt cover him. I wonder how he is in heaven, if he can look down at me. I look at the sky, wave a small hand down by my side. Mama sees it, and I feel her arm tense, pulling me close by my shoulder.

"You've seen a lot haven't you, Jerome?"

My old name. "I guess." I seen what I seen.

"I missed you in America. I worried every day. Do you miss Joseph?"

I want to cry but not in front of mum. Before, I cried all the time to her. Somebody hurts my feelings, I fall and scratch a knee, mean

177

kids in the neighborhood take my ball, a teacher takes my candy, my Skittles. I run to mama or Grandma and cry. I don't think I could cry for Skittles again.

She's right. I do miss Joseph. I can hardly remember his face. The blood in the front room, I do remember that. His gasp when the bullet hit him, a wet thump, and his breath is gone from his body. All that blood, but his face is a blur.

Mum is home and everything is better for now. Daddy still somewhere, no contact, no word. We think after the war we will see him again. Daddy is part of the war, in my head. I don't know what side because it doesn't matter. When you're nine years old, you know it's the side of good. If the war would just end, maybe we can see him, maybe we can own pictures of him. For now, there is so much to say, so much to ask and tell, so many stories.

Mama, we saw dead peoples, every day.

Mama, we got so hungry.

Mama, Grandpa got SHOT! Right in the leg.

Mama, what's America like? Is it cold? Is it hot?

Mama, how did you find us?

So much to say, so much to hear.

"We going soon kids. We going to America where I have a house just for you. No fighting, no war, no soldiers.

"WE going this time? We going? How Mum?"

So much to say, so much to do.

"Have to fly. It's way across the ocean. You can only get there by airplane."

"We going to fly? But Mama the airport in the city doesn't work. Nothing works."

So much to hear, so much to learn.

"Then we find another airport."

"Where?"

"In another place."

"How will we get to the airport?"

"Walk, ride, a car, or bus."

"Aaaawww…more walking? More soldiers? Mum you just got here!"

"To get to America, yes we have to walk to some airport that works. It's not safe here for kids. Not for anyone. Not with the war still here. Maybe never again."

"If we stay, anybody can come and take you, take this house. Anybody, any boy with a gun. Any boy can come and take me, take your sister, take you, Jehuu. They can steal you, give you a gun, make you a soldier. Anybody, any time."

So much to learn.

"Grandma and Grandpa will stop them like before."

"Not this time baby boy, baby girl. This time they take you. The soldiers. You saw them, on the roads. It's time to go."

"How? How will we go?"

"I have stuff to sell, to buy our way to Monrovia and the embassy. Grandma, dad, they know people to give us safe passage. We can trade, cigarettes, foods, clothes."

"Will we go see daddy?"

So much still to hear, so much still to learn.

"No, that will not be a safe place. We will try the Ivory Coast."

"When?"

"I have to get papers first."

58

Liberia

"An assemblage of reasonable beings bound together by a
common agreement as to the objects of their love."
—*Saint Augustine; The City of God*

SAINT AUGUSTINE TRIES to describe civilization, a community of
reliant peoples.

He takes for granted that the soul of a collected people will be
reasonable, and will love sensible, obvious things.

Like children.

In the United States, there are havens, uniformed officials to
petition, places to find morality and sanity. You go to the police and
find relief from danger (usually, not always), count on the military
for broader relief. Maybe the clergy, houses of worship for physical
and emotional sanctuary, a hospital where doctors heal.

In Liberia, during the Civil Wars those havens had inherent fault
lines, demons inside once-trusted institutions doing what demons
do. Relief from danger, death, mutilation, rape, horror was left to
the people who could do the least about it. The general population,
some two million, were reasonable, peaceable people; this is not a
warring country overflowing with violent people. It is a place of
religion, all kinds, and the people who practice holy, dutiful, peaceful lives.

But the warriors, those responsible for the wars and the savagery were all very bad, evil at their core no matter their excuses, their pitiful rationales, with not nearly enough noble actors.

Charles Taylor, Prince Johnson, ECOMOG, the Liberian military, one warlord after another, lined up without a scorecard, weaving words like patriot, national pride, and liberation into their civil war, meant to suggest righteousness, a jingoistic justification to commit atrocities, steal resources for personal comfort. Such opportunity wasted. Men like Tolbert, Doe, Taylor, soldiers from Nigeria in the name of peacekeeping, all had a chance to do good. They all failed in one way or another, succumbing to greed and brutality.

Women and children have always been the demarcation line of a civilization, a universally accepted understanding that the vulnerable need protection, deserve a chance at life, protected by the honorable and the strong. In Africa, in Liberia, in those civil wars, the vulnerable were prey, easy targets, a resource to carry out brutality and repression. The sick and elderly burned alive, women raped and enslaved as sex chattel, children weaponized and ruined, picked off from the herd as orphans, killed, starved, used as human sacrifices. Literally eaten alive by devils calling themselves men. Those not slaughtered, forced into hell, drugged, whipped, confused into killing. The countryside ravaged by pirates posing as liberators, a generation of animals, and crops, and every renewable resource gone, sold off to the highest bidders. Devoured like a field of wheat before biblical locusts.

No offspring, no crops, nobody to re-plant.

. . . .

Eighty-eight miles (140km) is a pain in the ass distance under the best of conditions. It's over an hour driving a fast car on fast roads. It's more if you travel through towns and villages, past stop lights and signs. It's forever on shattered streets, stuffed in the back of a mini-van, clutching papers, peering out windows trying to discern which AK47s are pointed at you, traveling over destroyed roads, so muddy sometimes you have to get out and push. It's hours on end.

Eighty-eight miles, the distance from the Caulcrick house in Buchanan to the United States embassy in Monrovia. For Bonita, that was the daily ritual, load the kids up, take them to the capital. The return trip just as harrowing. In Monrovia, wait in lines at government buildings, plead with officials for a single stamp on a single document, relentless red tape and denials. Then, return home, eighty-eight more miles, do it all again another day. If fortune smiles and you get clearance, be ready to go right away, so carry what you can on your back.

This was the life Bonita Caulcrick found when she returned to her beloved Liberia.

All Hail, Liberia, Hail!
All hail, Liberia, hail! (All hail!)
All hail, Liberia, hail! (All hail!)
In joy and gladness, With our hearts united,
We'll shout the freedom,
Of a race benighted.
Long live Liberia, happy land!
A home of glorious liberty, By God's command!
Liberian National Anthem (Part 2)

BOOK 2

A BOY FROM LIBERIA

Prologue

Jehuu, 2005

IT'S THE FIRST full practice in pads, blazing sun, hazy and hungover.

We sweat before we leave the locker room, guys leaking oil from the parties of night. Coaches smile, just a little, when they smell the exhaust. It stinks of late-night beer, pizza, testosterone-laced new-found freedom. Boys think they're men because mommy and daddy aren't watching, can do whatever they want, no consequences. Today will be a graduate course on what happens when you don't prepare for hard work under a hot sun. It will be pitiless and necessary. It will be fun to watch, for some.

Spartans don't puke! A battle cry against summer mornings in East Lansing on the campus of Michigan State University.

But this field is my home. I breathe grass, soak up sweat, alive when muscles scream for rest. One more step, one more rep. The grunting, spitting, heaving chests...someone will crash this morning. It won't be me. You don't crash and burn on your home field, someone else does.

A hundred times I've done this drill. Since eighth grade. High-step, lift knees so cleats clear the bags, pump arms, keep your head up, cover the nose of the ball. Nothing to it, my mind wanders between reps. Guys bent over, hands on knees, heads bowed, panting. Your helmet is heavier on mornings like this, your uniform tighter, your chest banded. The ones who didn't prepare getting their wake-up call a little too late. I smile at those guys. When it's my turn, I take the ball and run.

Get back in line, catch my breath, go again.

The practice field is churned up from the army of cleats pounding out two-a-days, no time for turf to recover and repair. Utilitarian freshman dorms slouch on the horizon, brick and mortar, boxy, squared corners, framed grids of cement sidewalks, tramped grass marks walkways between buildings. Low profile block-buildings remind me of another place. Construction crews work pneumatic tools and air-guns, prepare for opening day of the semester when fifty-thousand kids swarm campus. *Crack crack, pop pop,* echoes in the morning haze.

Hand-off exchange, accelerate and cut, ball-security drills, receiving out of the backfield, and now the bag drill. High knees, pump arms, get to the other side. Water break coming soon.

Run Jehuu, run.

Those buildings, a small city casting shadows on the misty horizon.

Churned turf, mud, and dust, torn up by pounding feet.

The smell of sweat, men pushed, afraid that their bodies will fail.

The *pop* and *crack*. The past.

Run Jehuu. Run!

．．．．

Sniper. Dah!

I frown inside my smoking hot helmet, confused. Makes no sense. I'm doing the bag drill. High knees, protect the ball. Shake my head, heavy and awkward. Helmet is a cave, dark, claustrophobic. The football field telescopes down to a pinprick of light, off in the distance. From behind my eyes, a flash. A whisper in my ear.

Run Jehuu. Run.

．．．．

Gunfire! Everyone down! Pop, crack, pop pop pop. Turf explodes at my feet, the ground jumps in clumps of sod. It's alive. Hot mists coalesce into shadows, shapes, buildings, and there it is, Africa. Liberia. A decayed city, buildings destroyed by war, glass from exploded windows lie in reflective sprinkles, asphalt streets shredded by mortars, trash everywhere. If you look closely, there's humanity, a foot, a hand, clothes that look empty but aren't.

Grandpa screams, *Ahhhhh. Hit!*

Run Jehuu. It's time to run. Grandma Joanne. A whisper on the wind.

Where? I am calm. I've run before.

To the other side Jehuu.

I run.

My sister and cousins scatter across the narrow road, race the bullet. We slide behind burned-out vehicles, between buildings. The other side. The dead in my path, churned-up earth, holes from exploded mortar shells. Bodies lying still, bloated from the heat. Insects invade black-blue flesh, looking for food and shelter. Insects in Liberia are the lucky, plenty of food. And the dogs, they eat well when they're not being eaten. Some bodies are still alive, writhing and stark. Those are the worse. Thick red fluid seeps into the dirt, puddles turn the mud scarlet. So much blood, like after a rain.

Lift knees, pump arms, keep your head up. If you trip on a body, a bullet will find you.

Run Jehuu, run.

. . . .

In Liberia, smells are distinct, the bush, the ocean, potash cooking fires, both sweaty and perfumed bodies, human waste. Everything is pungent and powerful. When I walked there for two years, there was constant blood and fear, decay and death. Liberia smelled bad. When I moved to Clymer, I'd smell something burning or rotting, and Liberia would flash in my mind, an involuntary strobe of memory.

At Michigan State, that summer work-out, it was the heat and the smell from sweaty men in soggy uniforms. The power tools, buildings in the horizon and especially the heat. With my ears ringing from fatigue and physical contact, I can't distinguish between the bang of a backfiring engine (or the whap of tool or the staccato *pop pop pop* of a nail-gun) and a weapon firing in a world a million miles away.

All of it together and next thing I know, I'm back in Liberia. It's happened before – sensory overload sends me back. Back to the country where I was born.

1

Clymer, New York

CLYMER, NEW YORK came into existence like a million other hamlets.

In February of 1821, almost certainly under a blanket of snow, 21,985 acres of well-watered hilly uplands were organized into Clymer, a bonafide registered entity of New York State with all the requisite benefits that come with that designation. Gardner Cleveland, a progenitor of the spanking new hamlet, and a revolutionary war soldier (Topham's State Troop Regimen out of Rhode Island, if it matters), was the man who, according to legend, named the New York crossroads town after a rowdy Pennsylvania patriot named George Clymer, who as it so happens, participated in the Stamp and Tea Acts and signed both the Declaration of Independence and the U.S. Constitution, one of only six men to do so. An auspicious baptism for this burgeoning agri-centered plot of pure Americana. It's not recorded if George Clymer inhabited, or even visited, his namesake township, but Garndner Cleveland spent his post-war life in Clymer fruitfully populating it with three children and thirty-four grandchildren.

. . . .

The contiguous United States was changing at a furious pace, six years removed from the War of 1812, James Monroe's Era of Good Feelings. The period of peace saw the country expand when

Spain sold Florida to the United States (cheap at five million dollars), the number of ratified states increased to twenty-four, and the Santa Fe Trail, connecting Missouri to New Mexico grew from a glorified, dangerous trader's footpath ,to a civilized, commercially viable conduit.

Clymer's expansion was no exception by enthusiasm, if not by scale. By 1822, eighteen families claimed parcels and a tight village formed around natural commerce: first store in 1823, grist mill in 1825, cattle business and school in 1831, a full-time physician in 1836 and so on.

Methodists and Dutch reformed churches practiced almost from the start, and a significant contingent of Amish settled there and still prosper to this day, a vital part of this corner of the world where time moves slowly. The population of Clymer in 1915 was 1,316 citizens and twenty-five aliens. The 2010 census report 1,698 souls (with not a single alien of note).

While the formal idea of Clymer was being laid down in the south-most corner of Western New York, James Monroe was being sworn in as the fifth President of the United States. A year later in 1822, a ship sailed into Cape Mesurado on the west coast of African, establishing the settlement of Christopolis, later named Monrovia, Liberia, one of only two country capitals named after a United States president, and eventual home, along with Clymer, NY, to Jehuu Caulcrick.

. . . .

Return to the route. Return to the route.
God's green Earth.

You drive to Clymer from almost anywhere and your GPS will encourage you to get back on track, back to the main road. When you're tucked this deep in the corner of New York state, you're closer to Indiana than Manhattan. Clymer is the edge of that edge, sharing a border with Pennsylvania. It's about halfway between Jamestown,

New York, and Erie, Pennsylvania, the two biggest markers on a map of that quarter.

Jamestown, New York is the big city nearest Clymer. It's about forty-thousand citizens stuffed into nine or so square miles, seventy-one miles south of Buffalo, New York, one-hundred-fifty-eight miles from Pittsburgh, one-forty-five from Cleveland, and some four-hundred miles from New York City. With more than one building over five stories, but not more than ten, Jamestown city limits are pretty small, not a Buffalo, or a Rochester, or a Syracuse for New York State comparisons. Clymer is to Jamestown as Jamestown is to a New York City Borough, that much smaller in size and scope. Not insignificant, however, Jamestown was once the furniture capital of the world, and boasts alumna like Lucille Ball, Robert Jackson, Roger Goodell, and, nearby, Jehuu Caulcrick.

Clymer is surrounded by woods, forest, plowed farm fields, and enough trees to supply oxygen to the northern hemisphere. Visitors can successfully navigate the main roads – there are two in and out of town from the four points of the compass – but not the nooks and crevices, the backroads, trails, and shortcuts. Not the tree stands, the make-out spots, the places to hide. You only know those places if you're a grid meter-reader, you plow snow, or you grew up there.

In Clymer, the school dominates the village, a single building with facilities unapologetically minimalist, brick and mortar, wood structures, built by craftsmen, parents and alumni of the school. You could walk the perimeter of the school and easily count your steps, K-12 in the same building. In the school parking lot of sixty or so stalls for faculty, staff, and students, you'll find more work trucks than you will sedans; this is a school with a specific policy on riding your horse to class. It's old brick, solid as a fallout shelter, like the people who send their kids there. It's where you'd go in case of a natural disaster. School colors are crimson and off-white. The playground for the elementary kids sits on the west end, with slides, swings, and climbing apparatus with hard edges. The downtown is as small as a downtown can get, with only one stoplight.

The school district owns thirteen busses, any more would be a waste of yellow paint; just not that many kids to move. The running track is cinder, circles the football field called *The Pasture of Disaster* (someone, maybe Jehuu's class, named it). Imagine coming from an urban city school to play in *The Pasture of Disaster*. The Pasture. Football goal posts look like somebody's plumbing, white posts propped up in the squared Y. There are mowed athletic fields, plenty of grass in Clymer. It's a place, when organized and managed by the right people, where you could build a young person into a strong citizen.

Jehuu went to this school, played football on *The Pasture of Disaster,* ran around that track. But he lived in a place removed, a town called Findley Lake.

. . . .

Leaving the school, take a left onto Browmell Road and drive straight into even deeper countryside, population density removed. Get ready for your GPS to redirect you. Proceed to the route, the navigator pleads, an endless loop begging the driver to return to some documented path, passing from trees to more trees and then into a forest. Narrow tracks open in the tree-lines, tributaries that your GPS would not recognize, the countryside is inundated with camps, cabins, and long rides between school bus-stops. This is not a short trip, Findley Lake to Clymer village, Jehuu did not walk to school from his house.

Return to the route.

Findlay Lake is further west than Clymer in New York, and best described as bucolic. A four-season resort called Peek-n-Peak is wrapped around a small, fully functional lake with fishing, water skiing, summer cabins, parks, camping, and snowmobiling. The lake sits at the base of the ski and golf resort, famous for small hills and a five-star golf course lined with condos and a resort hotel. It's difficult to reconcile the presence of a five-star resort tucked into the remote hills outside Clymer and Findley Lake; it pops up out of nowhere. This is where Jehuu grew up after Liberia. Findley Lake township splits the distance between Jamestown, New York and Erie, Pennsylvania. It's close enough to Erie that colleges (Mercyhurst College, Gannon University, and suburban universities like Allegheny and Edinboro) house their rowing teams on the pristine shores of the small lake. Summer homes line the lake, small fishing cottages and more ostentatious summer houses alike. Until the late 2000s, Findley Lake was a dry town. Jehuu grew up with access to resort living and resort people and a recreation lake.

. . . .

You might be able to dream up a path less likely to lead to a career in the National Football League than the one Jehuu took, but you'd have to stretch your imagination. Clymer isn't New York City; it isn't Buffalo (New York's second-largest city). Hell, it isn't even Jamestown, the anchor city in Chautauqua County. It's an agrarian hamlet where you'll come across a combine harvester and cow before a library. When Jehuu was there, it was also a little bit of football heaven. It was Hickory, Indiana. It was Alliance, Ohio. It was Green Bay, Wisconsin. A place where corn-fed tough kids figure out who they are through hard work and football, maybe not more than other small towns, but doubtless as concentrated and urgent. There is plenty of sweaty effort and "knock that other kid out of the box" character. Strength, muscle, and sinew, but small-scale in a big world of sports. There is nothing indicate there might be a Clymer High Pirate playing a sport for a living, it's just too small.

Jehuu was different that way. He's the exception to the rule that small schools can develop big-time talent.

Different in other ways too. He has verbal fillers that saturate his controlled speech, punctuate the stories he's told time and again. And everything like that is one of his go-to inclusive statements substituting for "etcetera". His eyes light up and memories take on a vivid life. It's part of the nature of an athlete, rehearsed cliché and platitudes. It's his routine, his go-to. But his story rings different, unique enough to grab headlines on a national stage, Michigan State, ESPN, the NFL, capturing his fascinating journey from a childhood spent in a tortured nation to a man who plays a game at an elite level. From a childhood running from danger and death to an adult running with a ball in his hands. A gem of a tale plucked from a roster of stories about athletes overcoming adversity, none of them remotely similar to his.

. . . .

Clymer had two Black families when Jehuu was there.

Jake Burkholder is four years younger than Jehuu, but age isn't the sort of barrier in small Clymer that it might be in a place where more than a dozen kids fill your age bracket. Jake's family – mom Nancy, dad Randy, and sister Taylor – and Bonita's brood, Jehuu and Mardea, are very close for obvious and non-obvious reasons.

Randy Burkholder is a Clymer Pirate alumnus, class of 1969. He met Nancy, from Erie, Pennsylvania at the Peek & Peak Resort, where enough Clymer relationships begin that it bears mentioning. They moved West for a spell, Colorado and Montana, until they realized they had all the West they could ever want right there in Western, New York. They moved back, bought a farm, and Nancy went to work at Clymer Central School, a new Pirate.

Bonita came to the area following a man and marriage and a better life, eventually, bringing Jehuu and Mardea with her.

It's more than probable that the Burkholders and Caulcricks represent two more Black families than live there today. That might sound like another world, impossible to imagine, but Clymer's neighbor school systems, Panama, Sherman, Westfield, and Ripley, are almost all white also. Some of the larger schools (large being two hundred or so students in a class) closer to population centers, had a few Black families, but you don't see true diversity until you get to Jamestown or Dunkirk, New York. Primarily white populations tend toward racism and bigotry, generations incapable of letting go of prejudice, of fear of the unknown and the different.

Jake is big, like Jehuu, an accomplished athlete at the high school and small college level. He grew up mostly oblivious to skin color. His dad was Clymer, born and raised, so maybe it was Clymer, or maybe it was the Caulcricks and Burkholders and how they handled themselves.

2

Jehuu

David and Joanna

RACISM IN CLYMER could be blatant, but it wasn't the lethal xeno-phobia I knew in Liberia.

Some of the same people who cheered for me on Saturdays, weren't comfortable around my family at church on Sundays. Teachers, school administrators, classmate parents who followed Clymer sports, who emptied the town for away football games, made sure I knew not to date their daughters. People did stuff behind my back, made snide remarks, did stupid things, but nobody was going to randomly kill me for having the wrong tattoo or last name. Every town, small or big, had pockets of it, whether it's discreet and a secret part of community approval, or outright, the product of fears of the unknown. Clymer was no different, and neither were the places I visited or played sports. One football game they kept calling me Yahoo over the loud speaker (every time I ripped off a big run or made a thunderous tackle). You tell me, is that brazen racism or lazy thinking?

But there's no denying my family was unique, a black family suddenly inhabiting a white place...a very white place. We came from near royalty in Liberia, my family held government positions, we had a history of respect and influence. That pedigree, and our brush with a violent, radical existence, sheltered us in a cocoon of ambivalence toward people who were ignorant and showed it.

Also, racism in the United States in the twenty-first century couldn't hold up to African bigotry. Someone might call you a name in passing at the store, keep you from getting a loan, from buying a house in a certain neighborhood, but no one was going to cut off your limbs because of the color of your skin or a tattoo on your arm. Racism in the United States can't compare to being murdered for simply being who you are.

. . . .

The formula is the Black kid comes to the rural town, drops in from nowhere into a world he doesn't understand and can't navigate. He suffers racism in some ways, shows his value as a human, and is eventually accepted.

That's only part of the story of my family in Clymer. It helped that I was big and fast, with an ability to slam other kids around on a football field and basketball court. That's a commodity in athletic sports communities. My sister is smart and beautiful. Those traits helped smooth transition from a Liberian refugee, to a valuable and respected citizen in the United States.

Clymer met us half way. For the most part, the townspeople didn't have a huge problem with Black people in their world. There's no escaping being the only black person in a room full of whites. Even when people aren't looking, they're looking.

It helped that we spoke a similar language, though mine was more accented, inflected. Liberian English is filled with idioms and references that don't easily translate into American English. Liberians are culturally used to making themselves understood by western countries. They practice the inflections and expressions with the idea and hope that they will visit the United States or the United Kingdom, the same way someone might mimic the lyrics of a pop song or dialogue of a television show. Think of British bands like the Beatles, cockney when they speak, and pure American English when they sing.

I had to tone it down when I went to school. The roughhousing. The loud personality. I brought that culture from Liberia. We played hard, we were loud, and we talked all the time, quick bursts of communication. There were probably worse places to bring that energy. Clymer kids are mostly physical – walk or bike where you want to go, bail hay, fix fences, and think nothing of it. Work, physical contact, wrestling, and roughhousing was okay, I just had to learn to pick my spots (like, maybe not in a classroom or church).

I was happy, grateful not to be walking around Liberia. Mum's experience with hospitality and Firestone executives paved a way for us to fit in, make friends.

And then of course there's football.

3

Clymer

"Though the palm tree in the jungle is big,
who knows how big its yield will be?"
—*Liberia saying*

THE SCRAPBOOK IS Giant.

It says so right on the faux leather cover, *Jehuu's Giant Scrap Book* (two words: scrap and book). Huge sheaths of black construction paper bound with metal rivets. Meticulously arranged newspaper articles of Jehuu's football and athletic career, from a freshman sensation at the smallest high school in New York State that hosts an interscholastic twelve-man football team, as a record-setting running back at Michigan State University, right up until he prepares for the NFL draft.

Faded, delicate newspaper articles from the Corry Dispatch, the Jamestown Post-Journal and the Buffalo News, in ascending order of circulation, glued to the pages. Jehuu's Giant Scrap Book was constructed by Mrs. Coach Bailey. The first page has the inscription in perfectly legible cursive, *For you Jehuu with much hope and best wishes for your future, thanks for the precious memories*, signed Mrs. Coach Bailey. On that signature page is a list of the Top Ten Greatest Football Players of all Time. In a testament to the fanaticism of Mrs. Coach Bailey, she has surveyed the entire history of the National

Football League and determined that Jehuu be ranked fifth, after Johnny Unitas and before O.J. Simpson (thankfully).

The scrapbook opens with a comprehensive description of the 1999 New York State Class D Football Championships as described by the Corry Journal, the home weekly for Clymer. It's the culmination of Jehuu's freshman year, the second year he ever touched a football. There is a New York State Section VI game program highlighting athletes from the year in southwestern New York. Jehuu is prominent here. Clymer head football Coach Howard McMullin says, "Nobody's interested in my players. We don't have real fast kids. We don't have what you'd call talent. We're a small farm community."

That was about to change.

. . . .

Jehuu was the new kid, a great athlete, and so popular right away.

Nancy Burkholder is a teacher at Clymer Central School. She noticed Jehuu the day he came in with his new backpack and started walking the halls. She took to him and his sister, became easy friends with the family. Having an advocate in the school helped Jehuu and Mardea make the transition from dirt roads and refugee shelters of Liberia to the sanitary halls of New York public education.

Jake was not yet in school, four years younger than Jehuu's nine, in a unique position to understand Jehuu in the United States. Both spent most of their school years looking across the playground, the classroom, the cafeteria, the line of scrimmage, at kids with white skin. The stands and bleachers, filled with white faces (except for their families).

The boys first connected when Jake managed middle school sports teams at Clymer and Jehuu played. They were both Pittsburgh Steeler fans, Jehuu taking to the black and gold while watching an American football game on a Liberian TV, and Jake following suit – there's as many Pittsburgh fans in Western New York as any other save the Buffalo Bills. The families vacationed together. Nancy braided Mardea's hair. The Caulcrick's helped on the Burkholder's farm, baled hay, ripped up drywall. When he got his driver's license, Jehuu drove a yellow Cadillac and farm truck owned by the Burkholders. They played video games in each other's basements. Jake says, "We knew Jehuu was from Africa; he used a lot of different words, rubbish bin for garbage can, boot for trunk, stuff like that. But he really sounded like he was from America, had no dialect at all."

Randy eventually sold the Clymer farm and cows and got a job at Cummins, the international engine producer, in a plant closer to Jamestown, and the Burkholders moved out of the hamlet of Clymer, population 1,600 or so, to the bustling metropolis of Lakewood, New York, thirty miles up the road, population 2,600-plus. Jake transferred from Clymer to Southwestern Central School in the eighth grade, same place where Jehuu would later coach. When Jake was a freshman on the Southwestern varsity football team, he played against Jehuu, a senior in Clymer. Both were big, raw athletes with size and speed. Jehuu's skills allowed him to reach the pros. Jake became a very good college player.

"I learned the confidence and the connection with teammates from Jehuu. He was always very connected; he had a singular goal, to be a good player. It helped having a talent like Jehuu to look up to. Obviously, a great football player, basketball too. Skill-wise he wasn't great, but nobody could keep up with him athletically. I guess he was sort of a big brother – playing basketball, hanging out, talking, and figuring out schools, colleges.

"I was lucky enough to go on several recruiting trips with him. We went to Michigan State to Nike camp. We were wined and dined; it was pretty awesome, that world. The best trip was Rutgers where we rode in Coach Schiano's candy apple red escalade. My family went with Bonita. Determining where Jehuu was going to play in college, we were pretty involved. My mom helped look at educational aspects of school; she was there to ask some questions that had nothing to do with football.

"It was the same at Syracuse and Maryland. We'd do trips over spring break; my mom and dad would pack up the mini-van, and off we'd go. It was a great commitment; we went as a big family.

4

Jehuu, Freshman

"Jehuu is a gifted athlete. You could tell he was going
to be a big kid. He's got a set of legs on him
that you wouldn't believe."
—*Coach McMullin*

FRESHMEN PLAY VARSITY football at Clymer.

This happens at large schools as well, when you get a superior younger athlete, but it's a way of the world at smaller schools. A football roster needs twenty to twenty-five players, minimum. With only fifty to sixty boys in an entire post-secondary school system, you need a pretty good capture rate to field a team. That's why it's so hard for New York State Class D schools to compete against bigger schools. The second-string cornerback at a Class A school is probably a junior or senior. At Clymer, it might be an eighth grader.

If six or seven kids from a junior and senior class don't play, get hurt, choose to play in the band, or would rather do anything other than grind out a football season, a roster gets thin fast, positions stay empty. There's pressure to be on the football team.

And Clymer football is hard.

. . . .

"Jehuu, come in, close the door." Coach Mac sits behind his sparse desk. I'm standing in the doorway.

"Oh. What's up coach?"

"Moving you to varsity. You'll start practices with us."

"Oh, uh., okay." I not fully sure what that means. I know all the kids on Junior Varsity, where I'm supposed to be. I know some of them on varsity.

"Might be a little different, but I think you're ready. What do you think?"

I have zero idea what to think. I'm starting to like football, getting the hang of it my second year, but varsity is a big move. Everyone's bigger, they seem more serious. I think about Saturday games, in front of the crowds. Maybe a night game under lights. The better (slightly) uniforms. Then I wonder what my mum will think. I decide she is not going to like it, her little Jehuu playing with the big guys. Maybe I don't tell her. Maybe Coach can break it to her. I think all this in a flash, but I say, "Oh, yeah, whatever you think Coach." Because that's what I was taught to say.

"I think we'll start you there, see how you handle it. Start at linebacker on defense, okay?"

"Yes sir, whatever you say." You might have to tell my mum though.

"Any questions?"

"Is there a playbook or something I could look at?"

"A what?" Coach frowns.

"Never mind."

"Oh, hang on. I think I have something." Coach digs through a drawer of his desk, comes out with one sheet of paper, not even front and back. I take it and look at the same plays as JV; slant 44, 30 trap, 38 pitch, belly 42, not much else.

Clymer football.

I started out playing linebacker, running back every now and then when we did offense. Then I had more carries and eventually became the starter.

Not everyone loved that idea.

. . . .

Something's not right. I can tell right away.

Stop short of my equipment locker to look around. Teammates in the dressing room, pulling on gear. Dirt, grass, sweat smells cover soap, shampoo and laundered school clothes; the transformation we all make from home to Pirate football. The locker room is an echo-chamber, industrial tile floor to ceiling, easier to mop and hose down, sounds bounce around, whispers are a shout.

I look over my shoulder at the guys sitting at their lockers. Nobody looks at me, but there's a vibe, faces turned to their stark metal cages. Usually I get poked by now, Hurry up kid, let's go! I frown into my own space. My equipment doesn't look right, doesn't smell right.

. . . .

The day started with me missing the athletics bus, the one that brings players to the school pre-season before school starts. Happens all the time, my sense of urgency for mornings and practice not nearly the same as the school bus driver's schedule. I missed it and not for the first time. Coach's wife came and picked me up. It's a simple thing, really, getting a special ride to practice.

Except when it's not.

When I finally get to school, I don't notice much, a few grumblings here and there. Words like spoiled, and favoritism seep through the buzz. It doesn't bother me, didn't bother anyone else when I was on the sideline, a substitute. But now I'm getting on the field, and it's made a few guys on the team jealous.

I reach into my pile of pads and uniform, everything is wet. My first thought is my stuff didn't dry overnight, still sweaty from yesterday's practice, or maybe from the washing machine at the school.

But sweat dries, and the field wasn't wet yesterday, and nobody else seems to have the same problem.

So why is my stuff soaked?

Then I realize what's wrong. The smell that's so different than the usual locker room stench. The way the guys are working so hard to ignore me. The half-laughs and muffled conversations ricocheting off the walls.

"Holy…someone pissed on my stuff." I say it as a matter of fact, as a wonder, like you might say, Hey, there's an elephant in the room. I don't register any other emotion, really, just that I solved a riddle.

Equipment.

Wet.

Smells like a bathroom.

Two plus two equals urine-soaked equipment.

Then, urine-soaked equipment means somebody pissed on it.

I look around the room to see if anyone has registered the fact along with me, if anyone is paying attention. It takes a minute, one that feels like an hour. I'm more confused than anything. I don't know what to do, so I slow-walk out of the locker room, head down, to coach's office.

· · · ·

When the upperclassmen pissed on my equipment and waited for me to grab and wear it for practice, I wasn't humiliated or enraged, or all that. It wasn't a racial thing to me. It was older guys bullying a kid who was different, who was probably taking the place of one of them on the team. But that wasn't something I completely understood.

· · · ·

Now, Coach is hot, his sense of right and wrong lit on fire, and coach doesn't get hot, ever.

"That's it. We're done. This season is over. That's not the way we do things, not the way anyone should do things."

My mind goes blank. Then I'm back in Liberia. I'm seven years old, walking on a dusty road, thirsty, and everything smells. Human smells, shit, piss, and decay. It's hot. Sweat covers my face, runs down my back. Not the righteous sweat of hard work and harder play, of summers filled with bike rides and scouring the nearby woods for deer and turtles, of chasing the neighbor's dog out of the yard, or Coach standing over me with a whistle making me do another sprint. (The other guys groan when he does that. Nobody knows that running is the easiest thing in the world for me. It's the walking that's hard.) This sweat comes from my anxious, nervous brain.

"Wait what? I just wanted to tell you that I can't put that stuff on for practice. Coach, I want to play. So does everyone else."

"Some want to piss on your stuff, Jehuu."

"Yeah, but not all of 'em. I want to run."

I don't want that taken away.

I want to run.

· · · ·

We played. I ran. And I tackled, and I kicked.

Coach made them see, played me in spots at first, showcased me to a team and a town not used to players like me. He put me in at defensive end one game early in the season. The other team's going in for a score, they run an option, and I time the pitch perfect, take the ball out of mid-air, and go the other way. Green grass and daylight the only thing in front of me for ninety-five yards. It felt like the first time when I started playing, nothing but the wind whistling through the earholes of my helmet, and my legs churning up turf.

There wasn't much doubt after that about me getting on the field. My soccer roots made me a strong kicker. Our senior punter came up to me and said, "Oh, I guess you're going to take my job now, too." I'm a freshman, what am I supposed to say? *Uh, yeah. I kick it farther than you. That's the idea, right?* A hard act to balance for me and for coach.

The pissing incident felt like hazing, petty jealousy, but if you don't believe there was some element of racism in it, you'd be naïve.

Freshman year we went to the New York State Class D title game. Class D in New York State means the school can't have more than five-hundred students in grades nine through twelve. We had ninety-four. It's as far into the post-season as Clymer has ever been. I rushed for 1,840 yards on 274 carries that year. It seemed easy – get the ball and run with it, and don't let anyone knock you down. It was fun. Once coach figured out I could run, it was a steady diet of me behind a huge experienced line.

Clymer football.

For my freshman campaign, twenty-three touchdowns, over seven-hundred yards in five post-season games, a ninety-yard fumble return, a ninety-yard kickoff return. I kicked another twenty-eight extra points for a season total of 188 points. I scored the over-time touchdown to beat Maple Grove in the State Section VI championship. Had 234 yds, three TDs in that game. Great stats for the season, but they didn't mean much to me; I was so new to football. Didn't have a reference point for good and bad, except the end zone.

They didn't know my name to start the season. They did after.

Coach Mac tells the newspaper, "Jehuu's got a heart of gold, but he also just wants to help his football team win and do the best he can."

5

Jehuu, Sophomore

AFTER MY FRESHMAN year I heard a lot of, "Okay you're good. But that doesn't mean a whole lot in Clymer."

No hero worship, no blowing smoke. No bigger high schools came knocking, no travel teams, or Nike reps sniffing around. Coach Mac wouldn't let them near me anyways.

But one thing that stuck with me. One day me and my boys are hanging around, playing video games, eating everything we could get our hands on, John Nickerson, me, and Austin White. The Three Musketeers we called ourselves without really knowing why, except there were three of us. Austin's older brother Joe played at Clymer, a great lineman. So, the trash talk starts. We're saying thing like, *Oh, we're going to be better than your teams were. We're gonna win a state title.* And then Joe says, "You better hope Jehuu hasn't peaked."

I was like, *C'mon! Peaked?* Then I was like, *Hang on, could he be right?* Big-time college athletes, pros, all have stories about dominating young, as freshmen or sophomores in high school. You hear those stories every day, take them for granted.

You don't hear about the ones who faded into the back of the film room, off the depth charts, except in the barrooms of dead dreams. You get to hear the stories of morning lifts, grinding out two-a-days, believing in yourself that turn into a state championship. Nobody talks about when all that work gets you nowhere. It's one of the shames of sports, that the scorers get the front page. Name the starting quarterback on the NFL champions. Now name his center. That quarterback, who gets the MVP, the trip to Disneyland, doesn't get to touch the ball unless the center gives it to him.

In Liberia, as a refugee you were less than an asterisks, you weren't even a statistic. You were a guess, a target, a ghost, one in a crowd of walkers, with your head down, your eyes strictly non-contact.

I got a taste of running with my head up at Clymer. It was something I could control. I felt like somebody, not a little kid lost in a crowd, helpless to contribute, to fight. When I ran a football, nobody stood on a white truck and lorded their false, stolen power over me. Nobody wielded a weapon I couldn't touch or told me where to go and what to do. Nobody smaller or lesser than me had a say.

Nobody told me I couldn't run.

. . . .

Coach Mac comes up to me, "Some schools are interested in you." He dumps a big box of letters in front of me – Cal, Stanford, Notre Dame, Pitt, Iowa, Syracuse, Maryland, some more from smaller schools. The yoke gets heavier, that weight that I already peaked, always there, pushing me down, like African heat.

It gets to a point where you just stop reading these letters. I didn't open most of them. Penn State offered me first, I didn't even know it. One of their coaches came to Clymer to visit with me. He says, "Well, what did you think of the offer?"

I said, "What? You didn't offer me."

He freaks. Makes a call, gets a fax, and there's the scholarship offer from Penn State. It goes like that. They find you.

. . . .

Keep moving. Away from the noise. Away from trouble.
That's what Liberia taught me.

Game two of the season. We're on the road in Ellicottville. A good team, a good rivalry. I take the ball into the line of scrimmage, 30-trap more than likely. I run into a pack of uniforms, our and theirs. A stalemate, but there's no whistle, the play doesn't end. So I keep churning, looking for another yard, get spun around, and cover up the ball. I try to back into another yard or two. It's a little strange to me that the defense isn't wrestling me down. I mean I'm right there in their grasp. Instead, they lift on my uniform, my shoulder pads, stand me up.

From around the end, behind the pile, a blur of white in my peripheral, home team colors, not ours. I barely have time to flinch when the white uniform launches at my knees. I'm on one leg, trying to twist away from the hit when I feel the knee bend inward, almost touches my other leg. I hear *pop*. Feels like I was shot; I wonder absently if it's anything like what grandpa felt when he was hit. I flash on grandma pulling a bullet from his leg in a smoking hot refugee tent.

I'd heard it all before, will hear it again throughout my career, and I guarantee you I'm not the only good player who's had it that way, Go get his knees. Not Tackle him low. Not Trip him up.

Go get his knees.

Ellicottville players came for my knees and got one.

Down on the churned-up turf, I breathe the cut grass and soil. It's not the same as Liberia. It's different. My mind comes back to football, inside my helmet, my teammates, the sideline, the stands. A referee stands over me, striped shirt, white stretch-pants, black socks. Finally, I get up, limp off the field.

The knee feels funny; I don't think much of it right away, but there's a grinding in it I can't shake off, no matter how I twist and massage it. I go in for a play, it pops and I come back out. In for a play, and it gives out when I lean on it.

Finally, Coach Mac says, "In or out, Jehuu. If it's bad, let's get it fixed." He could manage me in and out of the game (like they do in college), and we'd be a better team with me in, but Coach takes

213

care of his players. Another coach, another school might keep me in, maybe get the win, maybe ruin my knee for good.

In Clymer, we got each other's backs.

. . . .

On the bus ride home, I get ice for the knee. I can feel it tighten, the swelling like a watery cast.

"How is it?" Everyone stops by my seat and asks.

"Don't know. Feels tight. I'll be okay."

"Hope it's not shot, ACL or something."

"Thanks a lot."

Everyone stops and asks except Coach Mac. He's had other players injured, he knows you treat it like a normal part of the game. You don't worry the player, you don't panic. You keep composure, you do the process. Get it checked by a doctor, get the diagnosis and prognosis, do the rehab. Coach treats everyone the same, every situation with quiet confidence.

The team piles into a McDonald's for the ritual post-game meal. Twenty-two of us, in just-played uniforms, football pants and short sleeves. I limp in with the ice pack on my knee. We look like a TV commercial any fast food chain could use to sell another billion hamburgers, small town football team, hungry boys living the American Dream.

We sit down with our meals, the usual rehashing of the game, the Who's-dating-who, Where we meeting for video games, What did you get on the math test. We got our calories, we got our cokes lined with straws, we got our unused napkins. I don't take part, my worries getting the better of me.

If I can't run, then what?

Coach Mac is last through the line. He sits down with his meal, takes the straw out of his coke, pops the top, and takes a drink.

Some kid goes, "Hey Coach. No straw?"

Coach Mac, quiet like always says, "Don't need a straw, gets air in your drink. Don't know any man who uses a straw."

Twenty-two Clymer football player straws (and maybe a few more from regular patrons) squeak out of plastic lids and pile in the middle of tables with extra napkins and wrappers.

I smile into my own coke. Take the straw out and lay it on the table. Everything is going to work out.

We got Coach Mac.

. . . .

When my knee got busted up first quarter of the 2000 season, I had to sit out. No running. Walk, sit, walk some more. I was stagnant. My freedom to move, to react, to escape, was taken away.

Made my skin crawl.

It was a cheap shot, I have no doubt. Intended to hurt me, which I guess is part of the game, but not really. I blew up plenty of people in Class D football, wasn't all that hard, fill a hole, lower a shoulder, launch and watch them fall. All that physical potential I had exploding in small moments in time. Those instances of controlled, acceptable violence cumulate into a package of violent release.

But I never went for a knee, never for a head-shot, didn't need to. I guess other teams did.

But now I'm in Clymer sweats, watching the yards go to someone else, rooting for my guys like it's my job. But my skin crawls. I need to run. Patience is hard when all you want to do is run. But I did it, sat for four games, some six-hundred plus potential rushing yards left on the ground.

. . . .

Hardness is baked into Clymer football. There's toughness beat into us by Coach, by our legacy, by the league we play in. The biggest challenges we had were right in our little city, practices where we callused up pounding on each other. We always said we didn't care who we played – small schools, big schools, hell, we'd step on the field with a college team if coach asked, but we were going to bring the tough. You might be faster, stronger, more skilled, your playbook bigger, more resources, better equipment, but you would not be tougher. The school, the town, the rural nature of our daily existence – corn-fed is the way it's put around these parts – would not allow it. Clymer can only build so much football from the limited raw materials it has. It can, however, assemble tough in great big building blocks. Toughness is to Clymer as latex is to Liberia. Like latex, we patiently harvest it and ship it out into the world to be molded into usable products. I grew up, school-age, believing everybody had each other's back. If you need help, you get it. If you can help, you give it. Lives are intertwined in a smaller community. Farmers, workers, builders are always borrowing equipment. A tractor dies, borrow one. Need to finish a line of fence, call up the neighbors who pitch in. Cars, trucks, animals stuck in the snow, come help push. That brings people together.

And sport brings people together, too.

· · · ·

Fourth game, sophomore season.

I'm back, partly. Coach Mac lets me play defense, linebacker and safety, and kick. We're at another super small school, Panama High. Panama is as backwater as it gets, and a big rival, sharing a border with Clymer. You live here, you go to Clymer. You live a field over, and you go to Panama. That close.

Over the loudspeaker the announcer says, *Yahoo Carr*, every time I make a play. Tackle made by Yahoo Carr. Over and over again. I don't know if it's racist or a mistake, but it's a bad idea for the guy's home team.

Carr was my last name for most of my life in Clymer, the name of the man my mum married when she moved to the United States. We lived with him in Findlay Lake and took his name to start. Then later, mum went into Clymer school to make sure that our names were registered as Caulcrick when it was time for Mardea to get a driver's license. Most people knew me as a Carr in Clymer well before the name Caulcrick surfaced.

We open the game with a rare pass from Bennink to Smith (if your name ends in ink you probably played football at Clymer). Big gain, sets up the run the rest of the day.

We win 20-6. I block a punt. Get three huge sacks. Another dozen tackles. AJ, my back-field running partner, as dominant a runner in Class D that isn't me, picked up the slack on the offense. He runs for over five-hundred yards in the games I sit out. Behind that huge line, he kept us in the thick of the playoffs, in the papers, on the state rankings sheet.

Coach McMullin says, "Now that's Clymer Football. Our backs did a heck of a job. We haven't been able to use Jehuu, but hopefully we'll have him back next week."

Yeah, hopefully. Tackling is fun, but it's not running.

. . . .

The season sails along after my knee heals, and I can play both ways again. We make it to the New York State Section VI championship game at Ralph Wilson Stadium in Buffalo, November 2000. If we have a nemesis not named Panama, it's Maple Grove High School. Every year I played we battled them for supremacy of Class D.

We're 8-2, they're 9-1. We split wins during the season. In the championship, it's 6-0 in the first quarter, ground and pound, give no quarter, take no prisoners, whatever cliché you want. It's Clymer football. Maple Grove football, too.

A blind-side sack, fumble and 51-yard return by Stan Milecki for us changes the course of the game, a staple of Clymer football play, opportunity hustle combining into success. Me, AJ, Stan stuff them on defense. Then another blocked punt, then a timely interception by our senior leader, Jordan Bennink. We run the ball on offense, seems like a hundred times, no turnovers, pass twice. They get a field goal and nothing else. We win 6-3. I score the only touchdown of the game from one yard out after the second blocked punt.

Coach McMullin says, "We were lucky, weren't we? No turnovers, that's what we really worked at. That was a great win, Maple Grove is a great team, things just went our way."

Coach Mac, a man of few words.

Maple Grove is allowed to win in the regular season series, as long as we win the playoffs and advance. We got whacked at their place, 22-0 early in the year, they looked way better than us. But we're playing in the Far West Regional and they're not. There wasn't a score in this tug-of-war stalemate until the last eight minutes. I managed sixty-eight yards on eighteen carries, every one of them contested, earned.

· · · ·

There are over sixteen thousand high school football teams spread across the United States. It's impossible to compare apples to apples, except by student enrollment, so competition can be as varied as the populations these school serve.

Our far west state quarterfinal game was against the Red Jacket High School Indians. It's no contest. We win 50-8. It can't be easy for a team to be outmatched that much in a state quarterfinal game. Every section is different across the state, every class level. Class D, Section VI, where us, Maple Grove, Ellicottville, and Panama play, is a pressure-cooker. Much harder to win than other regions in the state.

218

There are four teams from our section that would beat that Red Jacket team. We were a two-loss team – to Ellicottville, who we beat first round of the playoffs, and Maple Grove. We hit our stride at the right time, played our brand of Clymer Pirate football; run the ball, make all the tackles, win the turn-over battle, make sure the ball rolls our way.

· · · ·

State semi-finals.

Goddamn Dolgeville. They figured out how to stop us. The game was brutal. We kept it close, 14-6 final, but we were on the wrong side of the final score. I had eighty-four yards; they bottled me up pretty good. AJ went for eighty-nine. Mostly we did nothing in the first half, down seven-nothing. We cut it to 7-6 in the fourth quarter, but ran out of time. After our only score, we never got the ball back. Couldn't get them off the field. Only two possessions in the second half, the one score and lost fumble on a kickoff. One hiccup in a game like that ends in tears on the sideline.

It was a great ride, though. The way the season started, no one expected us to be here. It felt like a step up.

Coach Mac told the newspaper, with his usual class, "I'm so proud of the kids. They had to come a long way, and they did."

6

Clymer

February in Western New York is dead-of-winter. Frozen winds run down the great lakes, from the tip of Michigan. They build momentum like an avalanche, and spin off the shores of Lake Erie at a place called Dunkirk, New York. From there, south to Lake Chautauqua, a weather locomotive pulled into a low-pressure conclave. Squalls, white-outs, lake-effect-snow, are the everyday vocabulary of local weather-folk. It's a tundra that forces people indoors, peeking out windows to see how much snow needs to be shoveled from walks and driveways.

High school football in Western New York is a memory, the record book re-written. Basketball season is in full swing. Jehuu, with his size and speed dominates the courts for the Clymer Pirates. The finer points and skill sets of the game elude him but don't keep him from banging around opponents and getting the job done. You don't want him guarding you.

No classes this holiday Friday. Saturday morning, the boys will head to the gym to referee little hoopers and continue Clymer-song, mentoring the young by example.

Jehuu sits at his house in Findlay Lake. A chest cold has him on the couch, under a blanket watching TV. Sideways rain will turn to sleet, then to snow, when the mercury inevitably slides, unable to hold against gravity and cold. There are no malls to cruise, no game rooms to haunt, no movie theaters, no hang-outs near Findlay Lake or Clymer. A normal Friday vacation day means seeing friends, video games at Austin's house, maybe riding out to Peak n Peek resort to hang at the indoor pool and look at girls.

But not today. Today this cold has set up shop in Jehuu's chest, coughing, sneezing, probably a fever. If his mom was here, she'd feel his forehead, but she's in Florida for the holiday. Jehuu has the house to himself. He likes the house to himself. He owns the couch and remote, juice boxes, snacks and whatever's on TV. Maybe he'll get out of the house tomorrow after little kid basketball.

But not today.

. . . .

The 2001 season for the Clymer Pirates football team was an extension of Jehuu's dominance on the gridiron. When you own a Humvee, you drive the Humvee. When you have two, pick one and never worry about getting where you're going. Jehuu and AJ Milecki, backfield running mates, are those vehicles. It's a pretty simple concept that doesn't escape Clymer Coach McMullin during the years Jehuu stomped the turf of Western New York. Jehuu's best friends are the starting linemen, Austin White and John Nickerson.

Being bigger, stronger, and faster will always cash in on the football field. In 2001, Jehuu hits 31 touchdowns, runs for as many yards as he wants, almost always without playing the second half of games. Coach McMullin pulls him in blowouts, a gentleman to the opposition, lessons in humility and respect for his student-athletes. He knows he has his hands on a hurricane of a football team, he can win games without leveling the trailer park.

This team has eleven wins against one loss on the way to another state semi-final. There they run into a running back named Mike Hart, the New York State Section V record-setter who, in real-life-is-stranger-than-fiction, ends up in a University of Michigan uniform across the state from Jehuu at Michigan State in East Lansing.

Accolades, scholarship offers pour in. Jehuu is memorialized in the media, and in the New York State record book.

Jehuu, the Runner – the natural, if unlikely, evolution of Jehuu, the Walker.

Jehuu, the Teammate – the manifestation of Jehuu, the Refugee.

Jehuu, the Young Man – negotiating a new, friendlier world of opportunity, grown from Jehuu, the spoiled Little Boy from the war-torn, brutal country of Liberia where he and his family beat improbable odds against survival.

Jehuu carries that sense of fortune, that he's alive, that his family is thriving in the United States. He'll be quoted anytime he's asked about how lucky he is, how blessed, how fortunate and thankful. He carries that sense of gratitude. But the lessons he learned in the brilliant chaos of Liberia wane in importance as his life in bucolic, embracing Clymer, moves steadily to the front. He starts to believe that now, finally, he has the world by the balls. Gone are the mortal questions, avoiding the bullet and the machete, avoiding the attention of a crazy child soldier with a gun or meeting a warlord. No more doubts that his life in Clymer is real, as the crash of thunder or the smell of roadside kill became innocuous stimuli that lose their power to take him back to a world where little boys starved, were summarily shot, or were kidnapped into a rebel army.

The doubts no longer plague him, Clymer teammates saying he probably peaked as an athlete his after his freshman year. He has no more of the doubt that crept in after the knee injury his sophomore year, that suspicion he couldn't quite shake about himself as an athlete that made him time and time again, tell people he had no interest in playing football past high school. Telling everyone that his vision for the future is a job in a cubicle, wearing a jacket and tie, playing for the company softball team, drinking beer with his mates on weekends.

He now has a feeling that he is immune to the vagaries of luck, misfortune, and bad decisions (pass left, run into a firefight, pass right, live another day).

Losing that doubt, letting his guard down, he almost lost it all.

7

Jehuu, Junior

NUMBER ONE RANKED team in New York State Class D.

Me and AJ in the backfield, the line almost completely intact – Jeremy Schenk, Garrett Willink, Shawn Blakeslee, John Nickerson, Travis White, Joel Neckers, my boy Austin White. We're huge for a small school, can pile up rushing yards, first downs, score at will.

We beat Westfield High 46-0. They get minus 25 yards of offense. We get 210 on the ground. Coach McMullin is a gentleman; we could have picked a score. I get 10 rushes for 93 yards and two scores. Piece of cake.

"We never stop working on the line," Coach says. "Every single day."

8

Clymer

THE KNOCK ON the door was one he shouldn't have answered.

Not if he'd been thinking, considered where his life was, where he'd come from, where he was going. But that wasn't something you do in Clymer. When the doorbell rings, you answer.

The saying is when opportunity knocks, you answer. All those sayings are part of the sports world, Where there's a will, there's a way; You miss a hundred percent of the shots you don't take, all that. But opportunities have no inherent moral designation.

"We're gonna do that thing today. I set it up." Abe says this, a friend from the area.

"The thing with the girl?"

"Yeah, we talked about it, Jehuu. Today, in Corry." AJ slips in the house behind Abe, takes off his jacket. Jehuu and AJ, the Clymer Humvees, two all-state level running backs and Abe, the hanger-on. AJ drops his coat on a chair and heads past the TV for the kitchen. Abe keeps his coat on, stands in the doorway. The three boys look from each other to the TV.

Abe Acherson is twenty-four years old. Jehuu and AJ are eighteen, adults by the letter of the law. Age differences don't mean much in Clymer. The school is a single building, kindergarten through twelfth grade. You mingle, in school, on sports teams, around town. To fill sports teams, the band, the school play, every class has to be involved, a numbers thing, so older kids and younger kids are automatically flung together. It's a productive situation when the older kids look out for the young. When they use their maturity to their advantage, it can get more complicated, less wholesome.

"Man, I'm sick." Jehuu pulls the couch-blanket over his knees. "Let's go tomorrow. Or next week."

"Has to be now," AJ says from the kitchen. "She's dropping the bag. Up in Corry."

AJ and Abe wear jeans and heavy work boots, jackets over hoodies. AJ has a shock of blonde hair framing his face.

Jehuu looks up from the TV remote, stops cycling channels, "Kidding me. I feel like crap. Can't you guys just go?"

Abe plops on the couch. "We need your mom's car."

"My mom's car?" Jehuu frowns.

"She's gone, right? On vacation?"

AJ stands in the kitchen door with a coke, "C'mon Jehuu, you said you would."

The plan is simple and moronic. Abe stole some pictures and e-mails off a young girl's computer, then sent her a message saying he'd expose them unless she paid him $2,800. "It's not even against the law," Abe said, when he told Jehuu and AJ about it. "She gave me the e-mail password. It's not like I hacked it. She just doesn't want to get in trouble."

Neither Abe, nor Jehuu, nor AJ look up the penalties for extortion, much less for unlawful use of computer, or theft by extortion, or criminal theft by extortion, or terroristic threats, or identity theft, or harassment by communication, or unlawful access to communications because that's exactly what they were doing. If they had taken a moment, they might have hesitated.

Or they might not have. Abe made it sound easy – $2,800 divided by three is roughly $900 each after expenses, gas for Jehuu's mom's car, and McDonald's big meals.

Nine hundred dollars is a lot of money. What $900 isn't, in Jehuu's case, is a half million dollars of an NCAA Division I football scholarship.

9

Jehuu

FIVE GAMES IN, and we're still ranked first.

We've given up six points total, four straight shut-outs. That's 188-6 if you're keeping score, and we were. The latest was Sherman High School, maybe the second smallest school next to us. 44-0. I had a buck-twelve on 11 carries. Haven't played a fourth quarter since game one. AJ hit 100 yards in the first half.

.   .   .   .

Next up is Forsestville.

Fifth straight shutout.

Now it's 224-6 for the season. Our starters ran 11 offensive plays and scored on six of them. Yeah, you read that right. Three TDs for me. It means we're getting ready for Maple Grove, staying fit, running our eight plays to perfection. Maple Grove, our biggest game every year. Mostly, I just want to stay healthy. I got a good dose of how much it sucks to sit and watch from my injury last year. I'm fully aware that things can change fast.

10

Clymer

"My mom's car?"

Jehuu is still under a blanket, watery eyes, stuffed nose. "I remember saying I'd help. I don't remember saying we'd use her car. "

Abe, now beside him, on the couch, frowns. AJ from the kitchen door shrugs, looks down at his coke.

"Why do we need her car? Use yours." Jehuu sits up, takes the blanket off his feet, peels his eyes from the TV.

"She knows my car. If she sees it in the parking lot…"

"I thought she didn't know who's doing this."

"Jehuu, she can't see my car." Abe sits there palms up, arguing.

Jehuu grimaces. This makes less sense the more he hears. "So what, she sees your car? What's she gonna do?"

"That's why I need you two there. In case she does something." He looks at his hands, "Just easier with a car she doesn't know. C'mon man. We talked about this."

AJ finishes the coke, "C'mon Jehuu. Let's get this over with. If you don't go, we can't do it. And you said you were in."

Jehuu turns off the TV. "Let me get some sweats."

11

Corry, Pennsylvania

THE MCDONALD'S IN Corry, Pennsylvania is almost empty.

So is the parking lot. The weather turned bad and maybe that's keeping people home, but with school out, the place should be busier. "How's it go again?" Jehuu asks, face down in a burger.

"She's drops the money, supposed to be in a bag, by the Salvation vArmy box." Abe looks out the window, food untouched.

"Then what?"

"Whaddya mean then what?"

"Then what's she do?"

Abe frowns. Looks at his hands, then at AJ. Looks at the unopened cheeseburger, the cold fries.

She drives away," AJ says. "What's the difference?"

This was a masterfully, monstrously, next-level bad idea. Jehuu knew it; AJ probably knew it too, but $900 feels like something, and really, they were just there to support Abe. The guy was convincing, that's something. They didn't hack the e-mail. They didn't send the note asking for cash. Barely knew the girl. Abe, older, smarter, a fast talker. Jehuu and AJ along for the ride, moral support, or maybe more if something weird happens, something physical, maybe?

So, President's Day 2002, three kids with a half-ass plan for making a few meaningless dollars, sit in the McDonald's in Corey, Pennsylvania. Jehuu, the one with the most to lose, the one who has come the farthest to be in this place, tells himself he's along for the ride, he's there for the free food, because his friend needed to borrow his mom's car, and he said he would.

But, honestly, he's there for some money too, isn't he?

He's forgotten the doubt, forgotten the luck and fortune and the opportunity all those people provided him.

He forgot himself.

12
Jehuu

Jehuu in Clymer

SECTION SEMI-FINALS AT *The Pasture of Pain.*

Our house. We moved to 9-0, beat Randolph, a big rival before I got to Clymer, not so much now. Final was 44-14. I hit for a 142 yards on 22 carries. AJ, 144 on 18.

Gentleman-Coach McMullin says to the paper, "They've worked hard this season."

True.

He says, "You don't know what to expect because every year is different. There's no such thing as a rebuilding year in high school. We're very fortunate to go to Ralph Wilson again."

Not true. We knew.

"It's all fun," I say to the same reporter.

13

Corry

A BLUE CHEVY Blazer pulls across the empty lot, adjacent to the McDonald's

It moves slowly to the Salvation Army drop box in the distance. A girl opens the driver door, jumps out, and sets a black duffel bag on the side of the box. She drives away.

"That's her." Abe sits up in the McDonald's. AJ slinks down in the booth beside him, the burgundy hood of his Clymer Pirates Football sweatshirt covers his face.

Jehuu looks up from his burger. "I don't see anybody else." There's no school and this place should be teeming with people, kids, parents, but there's nobody around, no cars in and out of the plaza, no one near the Salvation Army.

"Let's go while there's nobody around."

And that's when Jehuu should have known this was worse than just a bad idea. The signs were there; he didn't read them. Maybe he didn't want to, maybe he didn't choose to, but his awareness of danger has been stifled, that second sense he developed in Liberia, knowing when things are just plain wrong, dampened by success and privilege.

The three are up and out of the cold plastic booths at McDonald's, dump their garbage, pull their winter clothes tight. They walk across the parking lot.

14

Jehuu

Sectional championship, third in a row.

They almost got us this time. I get a lot of my football perseverance from Maple Grove High School. This game was such a test, a life lesson. They pushed me, pushed my whole team. There is no way Clymer Pirate football players from 2000-2003 aren't better people because of the games we had with Maple Grove. I get that now; I didn't then. Then I just wanted to beat them so bad.

A thousand Clymer fans, the whole town, crammed into a small section at Ralph Wilson Stadium, a fraction of a fraction of what the Buffalo Bills will play in front of any given Sunday, but a mob-scene for the smallest high school in the state. Our crowd is like a school of fish in a sea of seats. A good day to be a burglar in Clymer.

They witness a classic. Just high school football at its best. We come from behind with a 34-21 win. On to the next level, one step closer to a state championship. I had probably the best single game of my life, 152yards, two TDs, fumble return, strip-sack that was returned for another TD. That's 28 points. I had the world in front of me.

I didn't need $900.

15

Corry

UNDERCOVER COPS EMERGE from nowhere, from everywhere.

A platoon raining down on the Salvation Army parking lot. A ton of screeching steel squad cars hurtle at the three boys, guns are drawn.

Hands! Hands!

Jehuu has a moment to think about Liberia, about rebels shouting orders from behind drawn weapons, about running for his life. It's a moment, a flash that says *Run!* Then he shows his hands. He's gripped by the neck and slammed onto the hood of a patrol car.

"Got you!" A cop says into his ear.

Jehuu says nothing. The faces of his people, his family, his friends, parents of friends, teachers, most of Clymer, flash in front of him. Then it's colleges, letterhead from recruiting offers, notes from big-time coaching staffs, Penn State, Rutgers, Ohio State, Michigan State. Pictures of his life, what it was supposed to be, explode in a tight sequence of loss, then they evaporate into the wintry mist surrounding a McDonald's in Corey, Pennsylvania. Ghost images retreating into the bush.

This is it.

. . . .

That's Caulcrick and Milecki. We got Caulcrick and Milecki. The Clymer backfield. The cops at the Warren, Pennsylvania trooper station know these high school athletes from across the state border. The local rag covers their games.

What the hell are these kids doing here?

Going to jail, that's what.

This is a big deal. Extortion. Felony-level stuff that a junior in high school -fresh off a classic football campaign, and into a basketball season, a pillar of a small but close community with nothing but upside and bright future- should not experience first-hand. After Miranda, fingerprinting, phone calls, shackles and cuffs, Jehuu and AJ are put in a cell. Abe, the mastermind, is put in another close-by.

Abe is bawling, he knows he's in trouble, that he's dragged the boys into a mess, "Is Jehuu okay? He was sick."

Jehuu is interrogated. He knows enough, but not enough to help the police.

Whose idea was this?

"I don't know."

Did you send the blackmail note?

"No."

Were you planning to hurt the girl? Maybe kidnap her?

"No!"

Any idea how much trouble you're in?

"I don't know."

Jehuu still believes on some naïve level that he's not involved in this, was just along for a ride. That he can get out if he can just take a minute to think and get his story straight. He knows one thing, he's not going to cry.

At least he doesn't think so.

16

Jehuu

BIG NUMBERS IN the Western Regionals, the game that put us back into the New York State semi-finals.

I went for 256 yards and four TDs. The team moved to 11-0 with a 42-21 win over a Section V team. In the game, I scored my 31st touchdown of the year. These quarterfinals have been the easiest game of our annual march to a state championship. Our league is usually brutal competition, sectionals against Maple Grove is a war (not a real war, I know what that is), and the next level, the semis are rough too. AJ rushed for 91 and two scores.

"We just played well because the offensive line came in and clicked," I tell the newspaper. "I like this place."

Jeremy Schenk was the defensive player of the game. My musketeer Austin white had a sack.

17

Warren, Pennsylvania

YOU GET THAT one phone call.

The boys call AJ's mom, Marge. She hangs up. Jehuu's mom is in Florida. They are put in shackles, arms and legs, and paraded to the judge for a quick arraignment. Jehuu gets a taste of what slavery feels like. He shuffles to the courtroom in leg irons, hands cuffed tight in front of him, the more he twists in them, the tighter they get. He's hobbled, couldn't run if he wanted. The sound of the chains makes him think of the bullet-casings he waded through in Liberia, a hundred years ago. The shackles remind him of his Liberian countrymen tied up at roadblocks, those two years of walking up and down the West African coast. He gets a drink of water only when they allow it. No food. Nothing is in his control, not the heat or the cold. Not where his next meal will come from. Not the clothes he wears. A tin toilet in his cell, bars that block him in, better than any defense on the field.

He'll recognize this feeling again six years later when he's being showcased at the NFL Combine, where he'll be paraded half-naked in front of grown men looking to purchase his physical services. He won't forget the visions of the Warren, Pennsylvania jail and courthouse or the streets of Liberia again. Of how they both tried so very, very hard to keep him from running. Of how lucky he's been to escape that fate.

It's a long night at court. The boys are eventually released on recognizance. They get no sleep. Jehuu knows sleepless nights; he

237

just figured he was done with them. The next morning Jehuu shows up on time for little kid basketball at the Clymer gym, his job is to referee the pee wees, to call traveling and fouls, and show them sportsmanship and teamwork. To be a big brother. But he's tired and depressed. He knows that everyone knows. It might take an extra few days for Clymer to get some things – election results, the new movies, or mail, but news like this doesn't sit still. Everyone knows some version of what went down at the Corry McDonald's yesterday, the tin-cup telephone network is more efficient than any internet connection.

Coach Bailey runs the Saturday pee wee basketball league. He kicks the newly arraigned Clymer Pirates out of the gym.

Jehuu and AJ are also removed from the Clymer men's basketball team.

18

Jehuu

THE BUZZSAW.

That's what we ran into. If I'm a Bulldozer, Mike Hart is a Buzzsaw. He scores five touchdowns for Onondaga High School, and we lose in the Far West semifinals.

"He's like Barry Sanders," I tell the Jamestown Post-Journal.

Hart says about me, "He's a horse. He's real good...real strong and fast. He's the best back we've faced all year."

We gave up 63 total yards in our 11-game winning streak during the regular season. But in the semis, Hart gets 350 by himself, with his line.

It's not a game of one-on-one, no football game is, but the two of us stand out. The stats look that way. I got 229 yards on the ground, but I fumbled twice. It's a good game, we fight back to take the lead 20-19 after halftime. Feels like we finally have the game under some control, but after my fumbles, the game is pretty much decided. Another year ends in the Carrier Dome in Syracuse.

It was really a hell of a football game when you were playing in it, and when you look back at it. But right after the final horn, not so much. The loss hurt because we were ranked first all year in Class D. When people discredit Class D football, when they say the smallest class in New York State doesn't have much competition, I always point back to this game. Me and Hart get full rides to Big Ten schools. At Clymer, we believe we'll always be as tough as you on the field. You might be bigger, stronger, faster, better football players, but you won't be tougher. I'd take that team and go compete with any high school football team.

I bet Hart says the same about Onondaga.

19

Clymer

"Victim in Extortion Case Agrees to Plea Bargain Deal"
—*Jamestown Post-Journal headline from March 2002*

OTHER HEADLINES FROM that winter:
Three County Men Charged in E-mail Extortion Scheme
All Star Athletes Reputations Endangered Following Charges of Extortion
Case Against Three Area Men Moved to Another Court
Where a November ago the sports pages of these newspapers touted a football legacy in the making, they now opened above the fold with a story of crime and punishment. For the unknowing public, outside of Clymer, it's fodder ripe for speculation and judgment.

How much does anyone really know about that Caulcrick kid?

I heard he's like twenty-one years old?

How did he end up in Clymer? Is he hiding from something?

Didn't he come from Africa?

Why him? Why Clymer?

Is there racism in those judgments, overt or subdued? Yeah, there probably is. For Jehuu, the realization of the wrongness of this singularly stupid act settles in. When you're seventeen and arrested for the first time – no experience with the judicial system, no run-ins with police from your past – you have no real way to understand

241

what your future holds. You don't know the ramifications of your actions, except to know they will be bad.

On the other hand, when you've experienced justice as arbitrary and capricious, malicious and deadly as in Liberia during civil war, you understand that you probably won't die from this. You can consider hope.

Bonita goes to work to obtain a competent attorney. She laments that Jehuu has blown his chance at a scholarship. "It's gone," she says. "It's all gone so fast." Just like that, a snap of the fingers. It can all go away. If you have a hundred kids who run a football almost exactly the same, you're not going to put your money on the one that spent a day in handcuffs and shackles. Why bother? Go get another one off the football tree.

Jake Burkholder, an eighth grader playing in that Saturday morning pee-wee basketball league at the Clymer gym, sees his friend Jehuu walk into the gym. Jehuu's wearing orange snap-off sweat pants, close enough to prison garb, but Jake doesn't register that fact. He notices the tired, hassled look of him. He thinks, *He looks miserable, must have been up all night.* He doesn't know the half of it. He also doesn't notice when the coach running the league tells Jehuu to leave, that he's not welcome with these young kids, teaching them sportsmanship and teamwork.

Jake hears about the arrest, as does everyone in Clymer, as does everyone in Western New York, as will every college with a scholarship offer on the table for Jehuu. Jake knows Abe and AJ well. He doesn't know them as criminals; he knows them as older boys who he hangs with sometimes, who let him have the X-Box console, who buy him an ice cream cone. When he hears that the police officers showed excitement about nabbing two high-profile high school athletes like AJ and Jehuu, Jake thinks simply, I bet. That's what you see on Sports Center, you see players ruined.

The Burkholders will continue to support Jehuu, a mistake is a mistake. They go to the Erie courthouse with him to visit lawyers, for court appearances.

. . . .

The 2001 football season was an undeniable success for Jehuu. He rushed for 1,670 yards on 205 carries, more often than not with fewer than 11 touches in a game. Coach McMullin's style is conspicuous; he says of Clymer's record setting runner, "He had a nice season."

Classic Clymer humility and understatement.

Jehuu scored 33 touchdowns and 231 total points, that total boosted because Jehuu is the team's kicker; run the ball across the goal line for six, turn around and kick it through the uprights for one. He also bumped his career points to 514, best in Western New York. Career totals of 73 touchdowns on 4,398 yards. The Jamestown Post-Journal named him the area player of the year, the second time in three years. Newspaper sports reporter, Scott Kindberg gushed, "Quite a season for an exceptional young man, who remained remarkably grounded."

If he'd done the math, he might have stayed home on Friday of President's Day 2002. If he could picture the future, and weigh outcomes and compare possible paths of his life, he might have perched on that couch, ate his snacks, watched his TV, rested his cold, and hit the gym Saturday morning. If his mom had been home, if he hadn't wanted the free McDonald's cheeseburger, if anyone other than AJ had implored him to go, he would have shrugged off this crazy plan, recognized it for a fool's errand. If any of those things had been the case (turn left, death, turn right, life), he wouldn't have been shuffling in leg irons, presented to a judge, possibly exchanging a life of promise for the cold of a federal-level conviction marking his life. If someone who could fathom the future, the Burkholders, Coach Mac, anyone, had popped into the house to check on him that day, he would have dodged another bullet, to go with the thousands that already missed him, missed Jehuu, the Refugee. Instead, he embarrassed himself, his team, and he let down an entire town. He ignored the future and took the bait. President's Day 2002 came and went, and everything changed, at least for a while. The critics, the naysayers, the too-good-to-be-truers had their day.

. . . .

Victim in Extortion Case Agrees to Plea Bargain Deal, Clymer Students Could Face up to Five Years' Probation

That's the last one, the final headline. It's a win for AJ and Jehuu, no other way to play it. Tim Lucas, Jehuu's attorney does the negotiation, and it's a success. "The significance of this is he will earn a total expungement of his arrest and charge upon completion of the program. There was a lot of support from the town. I've never had a case with as many letters and phone calls of support as I've had with this case."

Abe gets $10,000 bail and looks eleven years in prison right in the face.

Jehuu calls every school that recruited him and tells them the story. A mature gesture.

For the Clymer boys, a bullet is dodged, charges dropped from felony to misdemeanor at their first arraignment, and a possible complete exoneration after completion of something called an Accelerated Rehabilitative Disposition Program. A path out of the mess, not a Liberian mess, a juris-prudence mess.

Clymer rules, that you have each other's backs, help when you can.

20

Clymer 2002

JEHUU'S SENIOR HIGH school football season starts.

Buffalo News sportswriter Bucky Gleason does a huge piece on him for the September 29th issue, and suddenly Jehuu's name is being mispronounced by a greater corner of New York State. Gleason gives readers a glimpse into the history of the Caulcricks. Lots of details, lots of drama.

Jehuu was, by his junior and senior year in high school and every metric, a man playing with boys. The fact played out in genetics, environment, and circumstance. He used those Blomo thighs and muscle to blow people up as a linebacker and bulldoze through arm tackles as a running back. He applied locomotive speed and eye-popping agility to chase down opposing speedsters and escape defensive backs who thought they'd line him up for a hit.

He played in the smallest division of high school sports in New York State. When he was in eighth grade, and as a freshman, he physically matched the other team's upper-class players. When he was a junior and senior, the script was flipped exponentially. He was facing freshman and sophomores with normal physical assets. The match-up was patently unfair.

Another indisputable fact was that Jehuu was older than almost all of his competitors. He had physical maturity on his side because of the two school years he lost wandering the Liberian country-side, more time to build size. Nutrition and mental setbacks aside, that life could only make him tougher, more resilient, more introspective (if, of course, you can pull all that off without going crazy).

The sentiment around the county where Jehuu played was here's this man playing with boys, beating up on eighth graders in Class D sports. The rumor had always been that he didn't have a birth certificate. Nobody knew how old he was, could be twenty, could be twenty-five. He sure looked that old. How is this fair? The sentiment, the fact, was distant, ignorant, opinionated, maybe racist.

He was, in fact, 19 years old, and whether it was because of Africa or Blomo (or Clymer and Coach Mac), he was more physical, more developed mentally than almost every other kid he met. But he wasn't 20, and he wasn't 25. He was a teenager who ended up being strong enough, fast-enough, football-enough to play Division I football against the best high schoolers in the world, and that should have told anyone everything they needed to know. This wasn't an adult playing against kids; it was an athletic specimen in their midst.

If his 19 years didn't quite square with every other major college recruit in the country, the raw data did – speed in the 40, bench press, instincts for finding the end zone. Plus, the phenomenon that he spent two years out of school, matriculating his way around a warred-up Liberia, instead of sitting in a classroom matriculating his way toward summer vacations and the next grade. He was older, yes, but he paid for that age and maturity by giving part of his youth to Liberia.

21

Jehuu, Senior

Undefeated to start the season, 3-0. I have eight touchdowns already, all those extra points kicked, around 500 yards rushing. Could be a lot more. Easy so far for us. I sit most of the second half of every game, Coach McMullin calling off the pillaging, displaying his customary sportsmanship. Coach is in his 32nd season. He has nothing to prove. There's no way for kids to understand, to appreciate that number, it's too big, too many years, thirty-two We just know to follow him. How many men has this guy built? A goal in my life is to be one of them, to never let him down.

Clymer is ranked number one in the state again. Class D. Still the smallest school in the state to field a complete football team.

Then comes the Maple Grove game. We lose the first game of the season and top ranking in the middle of tropical storm Isadore that rumbled all the way north from a Caribbean hurricane. I stand out, but it's not enough, 132 yards and our only score. What a game, what a mess. I tell the newspaper, "We can be beaten. Now it's a test to see if we can step up and be more ready to play football." It's a convenient cliché; belief, confidence, loyalty to the team, things I learned from Coach Mac.

The paper wants me to brag. You carried the team. You're headed for all-state. Where's the help from your teammates? I say, "Without the line blocking, I'm nothing. We have a thing here, if the line gives me five yards, I'll get you five more. I'm just so happy to be in Clymer. I love my friends, everything here. I wouldn't change a thing even if I could."

It's what I believe.

. . . .

State quarters-finals.

We play Lyons High School from Orchard Park, New York, where the Buffalo Bills play, almost a home game for them. The Clymer faithful take up familiar positions in the vast stands. I go for 144, my backfield mate John Shirley gets another 100. On defense Matt Bennink gets a huge pick early to finish the first quarter. We start the second half with a 20-play drive for 82 yards, and a score. They tie the score, and we do it exactly the same way, another 82 yards in another 20 plays. I have an 80-yard kickoff return to start the second half that breaks their heart. They never see the end-zone again. Out of 64 offensive plays, 61 are runs, 277 yards total on the ground. We win 28-6.

It's Clymer football!

. . . .

Clymer empties one last time in my high school career.

Fans swarm to the Carrier Dome in Syracuse, where the college football team plays. They watch us lose again in the state semi-finals. Again. Fourth straight trip there. To goddamn, Dolgeville.

Again.

I had a 187 yards on 27 carries and a touchdown. Austin got a sack. All said there were just too many football players on the other side of the ball. We went up first; I hit a 36-yard run. Then they score three straight times. The third quarter was a stalemate, no score. Then they put it away in the fourth. We gave them a nice chase but ran out of time. I scored the final touchdown with only four seconds left in the game. Those are the highlights.

Coach Mac tells the newspapers "The kids did a great job, and they left everything out on the field, and I'm really happy for them. We're such a small school and you saw what our depth is compared to theirs, that's why it's even more remarkable that we were here. But we were."

Coach Mac leaves me out of his remarks. That's why we were such a great team, why I think of him as a father figure.

The Dolgeville coach says, "You have to give credit to Caulcrick. What an awesome running back he is." That salved the hurt from the loss. A little.

I tell the reporter, "It was disappointing coming this far and losing again, but I still had a great time."

Losses should hurt, they don't have to hurt forever.

Game over.

High school career over, I graduate the following spring.

On to the next thing.

. . . .

My high school career ended with 6,500-plus yards and 712 points. It's kind of bittersweet, but not really. I'm on to a bigger stage, and besides, I still have track season where I'm the Class C/D defending champion in the shotput.

Coach Mac, my mentor, my father figure, my hero, tells the paper, the public, one last time, "He's been very good for us. We've had some real nice ballplayers here, and he's certainly added to the ingredients. I don't think he's reached his potential. We're going to find out. I know he has the ability...he has the tools. He's just starting to grow up."

22

Clymer

"Who moves to Clymer? How does Clymer…
get blessed like that? I felt really happy that I had the
opportunity to coach him."
—*Howard McMullin*

OBJECTIVELY, JEHUU WAS named one of Western New York's fifty greatest high school players.

It's an accolade that shines a light on Jehuu only slightly more than it does Clymer football and all that school stands for.

He officially gained 6,650 yards in his high school career, fourth highest total ever in New York State football, 101 touchdowns (also fourth place), thirty-four 100-yard games (third), 715 total points scored (third). All those yards came on basically one play; give it to Jehuu, from a few different formations. He rode that basic Clymer offense to rushing records and awards – league, class, section, Western, New York, then state, and eventually a full ride scholarship to Michigan State University. Those are the empirical, objective numbers, representative of him being fed the ball by a coach who knew a Humvee when he had one to drive, trusting Jehuu to run.

And run and run.

23

Jehuu

THE RECRUITING SEASON starts in earnest for me.

Coach Mac, me, and AJ hop in the Mac-mobile and head southeast. It's our recruiting visit at State College, Pennsylvania, home of the Nittany Lions. Penn State is probably the biggest football school closest to Clymer, lots of fans in the western New York area. It has a satellite campus just across the border near Erie, Penn State Behrend, that attracts a lot of local students and athletes. You can do two years at PSU Behrend and transfer to main campus pretty smoothly if you like, or you can stay for all four. Engineering school, similar to the big campus.

I used one of my recruiting visits to go to a game, talk to coaches, and see the facilities. We arrive mad early, coach parks a million miles from the stadium. *Easier to get out when the game's over,* he says.

Yeah, because that's what AJ and I are looking for in a trip to a Big Ten football contest. Getting back to Clymer.

Great seats, compliments of the Nittany Lions recruiting department. The game is wild and fun and momentous. It's Coach Paterno's hundredth win. Lots of pageantry, bells, and whistles. The love for this guy at State is something you can feel, like a grandfather in a rocking chair telling you stories.

Like Coach Mac.

Games over, pageantry's over. They do a huge affair on the field, pomp and fireworks. There's a few speeches, Coach Paterno gets on the microphone, deflects praise and the place goes wild.

When it's over, AJ and I get up to file out. Coach sits.

"We going, Coach?"

He looks us over. "Going to wait until it empties out. No lines."

AJ and I look around. There's a hundred-thousand people milling for the exits. Any idea how long it takes that many people to move anywhere?

By the time everyone's out, and we get back to the car, all the traffic will be right in front of us. *It'll be like we parked at the front door*, I think, but don't say, as I sit back down and grin at AJ.

24

Michigan State University

THE DRIVE FROM Clymer to Michigan State University campus, is about three-hundred-sixty miles.

That's about the same distance as Jehuu's two-year walk from his grandparents' house in Buchanan to the southern tip of Liberia and back. That route depended on where the food was, where the fighting wasn't, his first life in Liberia, the one where he was hungry, thirsty, hurt, cold, hot, too wet, too dry; never complete, always lacking.

The drive to Michigan State's campus was smooth asphalt to pristine athletics facilities, maintained with a fine eye for detailed cleanliness and entitled opulence, was the opposite of Liberia during the wars.

Michigan State University is old as hell, if you want to go all the way back to when it was the Agricultural College of the State of Michigan. 1855 is when it opened. It's younger than independent Liberia by eight years (1847), than Clymer by 34 years (1821), but not by much. It was one of the first institutions of higher education to teach the sciences of agriculture in the United States. Today, it's a behemoth with over $3 billion in endowments, an enrollment of over fifty thousand, employing some thirteen-thousand faculty and staff.

It's old, and it's big.

East Lansing, the town that hosts the institution, is described by Wikipedia as "a city directly east of Lansing, Michigan." Accurate, if not informative, probably because if not for MSU, there would be no need for another, directionally specific Lansing. The city of East Lancing boasts fifty-thousand souls, same as its university and is about the same size as Jamestown, New York, the metropolis closest to Clymer. You could empty Jamestown, East Lansing, or Michigan State into Jamestown, East Lansing, or Michigan State respectively, and precisely double one of their population.

Michigan State has its own river, the Red Cedar, 556 buildings (42 dedicated to athletics), 26 miles of roads, a hundred sidewalks, and a Superconducting Cyclotron laboratory – one more than Clymer, Jamestown and regular Lansing combined.

25

Jehuu

"Jehuu, Coach Stoutland on the phone for you."

Off the couch with a bounce, TV can wait. Mom holds the portable, hand on her hip, with that look. "How come you don't jump up and grab the phone when it rings? We know it's for you this time of night."

"I know. What's he sound like?"

"He sounds like Coach Stoutland." Now she makes that face, My crazy boy asking crazy questions.

"I mean happy or mad, what?"

"You done asking the silly questions? Take the phone." Mum maintains a pronounced Liberian lilt in her speech. She thrusts the phone toward me.

I take the phone and a big breath. Can't get comfortable talking to coaches at big schools. I'm just Jehuu, they are…well they are who they are.

"Hi, Coach."

"Jehuu! How we doin' today?"

"I'm good, coach."

"Good, good. Someone here wants a word with you."

"Um, okay. Who?" The line goes quiet.

Then, "Jehuu?"

"Yes sir." I think it's Coach Williams with some news. Hold my breath, they're taking my scholarship. I'm not good enough.

"Kind of name is Jehuu?" I don't recognize the voice, the tone is friendly, ball busting. "Kidding, man. Jehuu, this is TJ Duckett."

I'm stumped again, then it hits me like a brick. TJ Duckette, the huge, record-setting running back from Michigan State. My game is like his, he runs hard, bruises defenses.

"Uh, hi sir."

"Yeah, sir, okay. Anyway, welcome to Sparta."

One of the main reasons I chose Michigan State was because they showed a lot of their games in New York. I watched guys like Sedrick Irvin and Duckett run. They reminded me of me. And now, a guy I watched was calling me, welcoming me to school.

The college visit sealed it for me, though. It was awesome. While I was touring campus, I went to the stadium. As soon as I walked down the tunnel, AC/DC's "Thunder Struck" starts playing and the big screen says, *Welcome Future Spartan Jehuu Caulcrick, Clymer High School, Clymer, New York.*

I got chills, have to be pretty jaded not to. I went to the locker room and was the first one there, my family following with coaches. I look at a locker and the nameplate says, *Number 30, Jehuu Caulcrick.* I saw this jersey hanging in a locker. I tried on the jersey. My mother started crying. The deal was done.

After I committed to MSU, a coach from Michigan called me. I told him that I signed with Michigan State.

He hung up.

26

Michigan State

IN A SMART world, the college recruiting equation would be a practice in equity investment.

The time and effort spent coaxing an athlete to be part of your university football team measured against a level of production on the field in an investment portfolio to be graded at a time of reflection and accountability; What did we spend in time and money, and what did we profit for that expense? What can we measure? Yards, catches, interceptions, blocks, tackles; how many were there? Divide that number by how much was spent, and you have a valuation of your recruiting process, not to mention the money spent on facilities, equipment, coaching staff and support personnel.

The actual value of recruiting expense for a student-athlete is supposed to be the education, both academic and life lessons taught on the fields and courts, molding that student into a complete person better able to contribute to society. If that was ever the goal of college athletics, it's a long-forgotten idea.

College athletics is not an efficient world by many standards and certainly not as a cost-effective enterprise. Budgets are a joke, on the high side. Michigan State University hosts 25 NCAA Division I sports. Football and basketball bring in $70 million in revenue ($23 million for football). In 2019 Michigan State's operating budget of $108 million ranked 17th among public universities and seventh in the Big Ten. There are two countries with lower GDP's than MSU's annual athletics budget.

Power programs are almost identical in recruiting philosophies and tactics. College sports is big business, at least as big as any entertainment industry in the world. So colleges and coaches making millions in salary and endorsements have a pretty fat incentive to throw money at every player they can, see if it sticks, mortified by the idea of missing out on the next superstar, or losing them to a rival school. They're selective only in where the money goes, not how much is spent, and it isn't even real money; they print it on a tuition bill, put it on enrollment books, but it doesn't leave a pocket.

27

Jehuu 2003

My cell rings, The Michigan State Fight Song.

> Spartan teams are never beaten,
> All through the game they fight;
> Fight for the only colors:
> Green and White.
> Go right through for MSU,
> Watch the points keep growing,
> Spartan teams are bound to win,
> They're fighting with a vim!
> Rah! Rah! Rah!

I pull it out, sitting in costume, holding a script (annual school play, all hands-on deck at Clymer). It's Stoutland. Good, I have questions about my scholarship, about school, when it starts, all that. But hang on, coach never calls when it's school time, always at night, so he can talk to my mom too.

"Hey coach. What's up?"

Quiet. A sigh. Then, "Jay, glad I caught you." Another pause. "You alone, got a second?"

"Yeah, yeah." It barely sounds like coach, he never asks if I'm alone.

Coach Stoutland is the main coach recruiting me; he's my contact. I can get hold of Coach Williams if I want, but he's got a hundred other recruits to juggle other than the running back-slash-linebacker from Clymer, New York. Think about it, in basketball you get fifteen or so scholarships, baseball maybe twenty, thirty? In football you have twenty-two unique positions on the field, offense and defense, and that's without special teams. A team recruits three deep at each spot, and you start at sixty-six moving parts. NCAA Division one teams get eighty-eight scholarships. Coaches are shepherding over twenty new faces a year. Recruited positions are farmed out to assistants, head coaches coordinate and close deals. Stoutland is my guy.

"Jay, gonna come right out and say it, you'll be caught up soon enough by someone. We just got fired."

"We… what… Coach?" Did I get fired? Can they fire me? I don't even go to their school yet.

"Fired, we got fired. Coach Williams, me, the whole staff."

That's a pretty speechless moment for a recruit, for a kid in a costume getting ready to close out his senior year playing a part in the school play. "I…what does this mean? What do I do, what do you do?"

Coach breathes into the phone. He takes a few seconds to replay the speech he's probably given to more than one new Spartan. "Sorry, Jehuu. I get it. Confusing. Your next step is to get with your parents, maybe grab Coach Mac, and start to process this. You'll have an opportunity to drop your letter of intent. You can re-enter the recruiting pool. You can stay at State. Figure out what's best and make sure you take care of yourself."

We share some chat. I ask about where he'll end up, wondering about his future. I mentally shrug at everything he says. It's a regrouping, reassessing. Takes time to understand that plans have changed.

It won't be the last time.

. . . .

After the firing of my coaches, the Spartan ship started to empty like it was sinking in a storm, recruits bailing out on their commitment, rather than bail water, released from letters of intent by the NCAA. The recruiting hundred-yard dash was on, colleges counting scholarships and positions and depth charts, seeing what they had left to offer recruits, what positions needed upgrading with ex-Spartans.

I had options, but I'd worked so hard making this decision, and I was tired of the process. Being wanted feels great, but being somewhere ready to wear the colors, play the game, felt just as good. But you don't know what will happen, who the new coach will be, what their philosophy is, if you fit in. The school has to honor the signed contract/scholarship, but the new coach doesn't have to like it. If they don't want you there, you're not there, they find a way. I wanted to play. To run.

I had other official visits, so I took them. I had to. If MSU didn't work out, I needed a place to go to school, to play football and get an education. I checked recruiting sites, news releases. One name associated with MSU kept popping up, Kaleb Thornhill. The Thornhill family bleeds green and white; they are what a lot of people think of when they picture a Spartan Warrior from East Lansing.

Kaleb became my North Star. I decided, s much to make things easy for me, if he kept his commitment to Michigan State, so would I.

When coach Williams recruited me he told Spartan nation, "We think he's going to be a kid that's going to come in and help. He's a very physical runner. He can get done what a coach is looking for in the one-back offense. He can step on the other side of the ball as well. We really like him…he's mature enough to step in right away."

But Coach Williams was fired. That changed everything.

. . . .

On December 19, 2002 John L. Smith was named the new coach at Michigan State University, the school's twenty-third. I didn't know him from any other coach, except that he was pretty popular at Louisville, the job he left for MSU.

I was a pretty high recruit for the school. Was SuperPrep All-American, second-ranked fullback, the fifth-ranked by Rivals. com, fourth of top fifteen New York SuperPrep players, made the All-Eastern U. S. Team. When we had our first conversation, he told me a lot of the things I wanted to hear, put me at ease with my decision to stay in East Lansing. He told me I'd be a halfback, have the opportunity to compete for a role in the offense, coming right in, to play early. That's what I was looking forward to, what I wanted as a college football player. Get in and out of college, play football right away, run the ball.

But there were definitely mixed messages I had to sort through. Coach Smith tells the media, "We've got four or five running backs. Probably one of these guys will end up at running back. We'll keep the best one there and others will find a place to play because they are good athletes. They're good players, or we wouldn't have gone out and recruited them. Next year I will be able to tell you more about these guys. They all look good on paper. We'll have to wait a year from now. I'll be able to tell you who's good, and who isn't."

That's different than what he told me in person. Wait a year? Find out who's good and who isn't? Wasn't I recruited because they knew I was good enough to play? They sure made it sound that way, all the talk, all the promises. I already saw my name on a jersey, in a locker, on my recruiting visit. Caulcrick over a blocked-out 33. I was still working on the presumptions and promises of Coach Williams and Stoutland. I had to come to terms that I might not be Coach Smith's guy, that he didn't necessarily want me there, that I'd have to prove myself all over again. They couldn't pull my scholarship, but Smith's comments screamed defense. He wants me to play linebacker, not running back.

The other running backs recruited in my class -Sylvester Brown from Canton Mississippi, Cole Corey from Tecumseh Michigan, and Maurice Davis-Smith from Warren Ohio- all believed we'd get to run the ball. Some were undoubtedly heading to the defensive side of the ball, no getting around it. There's only so many carries in a game, in a season.

I liked linebacker, felt solid there, like I belonged. I like hitting people on defense.

But I love to run.

.　.　.　.

I graduated Clymer with twelve other seniors, four years in high school and a lifetime of memories over in a flash. Felt like yesterday I was being introduced to the school, the small town. Liberia was a world, a lifetime away. Like it happened to another person. The stories belonging to someone else.

Four days later, I went to Michigan State for summer workouts and back to school, two summer classes. It's the same with all in-coming Division I athletes, as much to start the process of becoming a college-level student as for coaches to see what you can do in the classroom, how much work your academics are going to be for you and for tutors. They've invested a lot of money in us as parts of the team, pieces of a huge profit center of entertainment. The last thing they want to worry about is a player becoming ineligible because they can't handle the course-work.

My real job was in the weight room, get bigger, stronger, faster in a way that made me competitive with the best college players in the country. School wasn't in session, but athletics is a year-round job, you work for that "free" scholarship. Football players shared campus with basketball, hockey, some women's sports. But you don't really see those other sports, all of us in our own shelled-off world. Doing our work.

My first actual practice was more than half a mess. Had to be on the field before the first whistle at one o'clock. It's 1:58 and I'm standing at the equipment room door with a pair of shoes that don't fit (goddamn shoes again making me late).

D-1 equipment rooms are like a Dick's store on XXXL steroids. My locker was jammed with MSU green and white gear, loaded with what I like to wear, undershirts, sweats, hoodies, girdle pads, everything my size.

Except the goddamn shoes.

For a guy used to hand-me-down shoulder pads and yellow practice gear, this was culture shock. In high school, if we wanted decent equipment, we bought it ourselves. I never went without good football gear, my mum made sure of that -pads, helmet, the whole wardrobe. But this was kid-in-the-candy-store stuff. Like Christmas all football season. You ask for it, it's there.

I was pretty sure I had my practice stuff dialed in, but here I am, first day in the equipment room, waiting. The young equipment guys, work-study, interns, are there doing a job, in no particular hurry to make sure the freshman gets taken care of. Having a good time of it. *What's the name? You sure those don't fit, try 'em on again. How do you pronounce the name again?*

Ha-freakin' ha. Finally, our head equipment guy shows up. We called him Mr. Nick. "Caulcrick, what the hell are you doing here?" Checks his watch, "It's 1:58. Aren't you supposed to be on the field?"

I'm in a panic, but try to be polite. "Yes, sir, but I can't wear these shoes. They're twelves."

"Jesus Christ Caulcrick, what size?"

"At least thirteen."

He throws a pair of thirteens at me. I sprint to the field where the whole team is lined up, stretching. A hundred and ten guys in tight formation. There's no sneaking into that scene.

Our strength coach sidles up to me. I'm sweating like I ran a mile. "What's up Caulcrick?"

"Sorry Coach, I had the wrong size shoes. Mr. Nick was out, and…"

"Hm." He scratches his chin, squats next to me on the turf. I keep my eyes on the captains up front, taking us through leg stretches. "What size did you end up with?"

"Thirteens." Okay, he seems nice, asking questions. I breathe easier.

"Yeah, huh. I have twelves."

"Uh huh." Uh oh.

"And if you're ever late again, I'm going to stuff the whole shoe up your ass. Got that?"

"Yessir."

First day.

. . . .

Summers in big programs are pre-season training camps. Players work the body – bigger, stronger, faster – and learn skills for your position, balls skills for backs and wide-outs, blocking, tackling techniques for linemen. Then comes actual practice where you put it together, specific units, offense, defense, special teams. The coordination of a football team, a hundred players being where they're supposed to be at any given moment of any given practice is a logistical marvel, a thousand moving parts. All pre-season I worked at running back, learning the position, watching my name on the depth chart.

I didn't really know anyone on the team. Usually, a recruiting class gets together some and you know some faces. A lot of the guys I committed with dropped out when Williams got fired. The only guy I really knew because I tracked him on the internet was Kaleb Thornhill. He kept his commitment, and I kept mine. We talked online, but I'd never met him. When most of the guys rescinded their commitment. Kaleb and John Masters stayed.

I came from the country, as small a place as you can get – rural, woodsy, farmland. The first days at Michigan State were a shock to my system. The locker room was full of all kinds of people, from everywhere, but even guys from the same place were different. Guys who talked about gangs in the hoods, guys who told hog-hunting stories, speaking a slang I could barely understand. City kids from

Florida, with big city cred. Country kids from Florida with deep southern twangs.

Big bodies, rock-hard muscles, eighteen-year-old guys that looked like thirty-year-old body builders. Guys that could pound the weights, earth-movers that made the ripped guys look small. Fast-twitch guys that didn't stand still. And as many black faces as white.

I could tell I was out of my element, big-fish-smallest-pond-ever put in the ocean. It made me wonder if I belonged. How couldn't it? So, I didn't talk much, kept to myself, took it all in. I said, "Huh?" and "What?" so many times those first few days, trying to figure out exactly what the hell was going on, that the whole locker room figured I was either slow or nuts.

Kaleb had a car, and he'd pack it with guys heading to and from practice, meals, dorms, and parties. One day, I'm going back to the dorm after practice, and he pulls up, "Hey, you want a ride?"

I can hear the guys in the car, "Man, don't get him. Dude's weird." I walk toward the car, think better of it and stop. Think better of that and walk to the car again. It goes like that, walk, stop, walk, stop, all the time saying to myself, *What the fuck's wrong with you?* Like somebody has my body on a joystick.

But day after day, in the weight room, in sprints, going hard in practices, picking up skills, figuring out the routine, I realized I was okay at this level, that I could compete and play. When you show up and you do the work, day in day out, teammates respond, they let you in. Wasn't long before my Liberian personality, blended with my Clymer roots, and I got comfortable, became the fun guy.

Eventually, all those different languages, that locker room full of slang and personality, merged into idioms and jargon, and shared experiences. I learned to speak Michigan State football.

On days off, we went to the college golf course, packed Kaleb's car with guys, clubs, and beer. Kaleb and I ended up best friends, roomed together all four years, inseparable on campus. He became the center of that core of teammates and friends I cultivated at

Clymer with Austin and Nickerson. Kaleb and I, two Musketeers I guess, rotating the third member depending on the day or year or what we were doing. Together for life events big and small, game day, parties, graduation, draft day, later in each other's weddings, that kind of friendship. It started day one at training camp and didn't stop.

. . . .

All pre-season and after training camp, I did running-back work. It looked like coach was going to keep me on offense. Then the first wrench got tossed into my college football experience.

First practice after training camp, coaches ask me to work a few reps with the defense. No big deal, just getting a look on that side of the ball. Coaches spun it, Oh yeah, you're so athletic you're gonna play two ways for us. We want you to learn linebacker. I look back at it, knowing college football the way I do, and… C'mon. Both ways? That doesn't happen at the D1 level. But there I was a freshman, not knowing enough, and I'm built to listen to coaches, to believe them and do what they say.

So, now on defense, I'm out there thinking Go go go. I'm a hundred percent into it, no real idea what I'm doing in drills but getting after it. I'm thinking, play both ways, I'm thinking, be the best player on the field. I'm diving at running backs, knocking down passes, playing like my hair is on fire.

I hear, "Yo, kid. Chill." I look over and Tyrelle Dorch, a senior running back is staring at me. "You better slow down with that."

I'm aware of the depth chart at running back, and Dorch is ahead of me. I know I'm not likely to climb to a starting position. This guy doesn't want to be shown up; he doesn't want me to make the offense look bad. I have a shot to play some linebacker, why not? Get on offense in the future. Both ways! I'm thinking, *Screw you. I'm on this side of the ball. I'm not here to make the offense look good.*

Before the second practice of the day, I'm in the running backs room. There's a knock on the door. The linebacker coach sticks his head in and says, "Hey, we need Jehuu."

I look at Dorsch. He says, "I told you!"

Next thing you know I'm with the linebackers. No more running back meetings. Dorsch knew what he was talking about.

. . . .

The end of training camp every year, around mid-August, they tell you who's going to redshirt. They say things like, *We like you; We want you to grow, learn, develop.* That was me, now on the linebacker depth chart. With Coach Smith, if you're a redshirt, you practice, work on the game, skill set, run scout team reps, but you don't travel. You sit in the stands at home games.

Me and Kaleb were lucky, we got to dress and travel. If enough guys fall through the cracks -get hurt or mess up with the school or the law- we'd get to play. They kept us in uniform because of how hard he and I practiced. We both got scout-team player of the week multiple times.

Traveling, dressing was good and bad because back then, one play and you use a year of eligibility. Toward the end of games, our equipment guy would come over and take our helmets, so if a coach forgot and tried to put us in, we couldn't play.

At the end of the season I was still at linebacker, doing what the coaches asked. It looked like where I'd stay, no running the ball anymore. People told me, you can transfer if you don't like it. I wanted to run the ball, but this was still football, and I was taught to be a team player. I said if they're going to make me a linebacker, I'll go ahead and be the best linebacker I can. It's a Coach Mac thing, a Clymer attitude. I was brought up, you start something you finish it.

End of the season every player meets with the head coach. I remember sitting in Coach Smith's office, and he says the usual, good season, you know you got stronger, learned the system, all that. Then he said, "But I'm not convinced you're not a running back. So we're gonna move you back."

I was so excited. I could have jumped up and hugged him. It was that good news, that good feeling in your chest. Like when you're told you're about to start, to play more, to be a bigger part of the team. It was never an issue at Clymer, obviously. But at this level, it was something special to know I was going to run the ball. I was so focused inside, on the trees and not the forest, that it didn't hit me that I was going to do this at one of the biggest college programs in the country, as high a level as you can get next to pro ball.

We went to the Alamo bowl that year. That was one of the toughest times for me. Leaving home to start college wasn't an issue for some reason, I got buried in the work. But going to that bowl game was tough. You're a young kid, the first time you're really away from your family on Christmas day. The coaches are there with their families, and you're on the field practicing, getting cussed at. It was a wow moment. That's when it really hit me that, you're in a business.

28

Jehuu 2004

I'M BACK ON offense in a major college program. Life is great.

And the perks! The access and excess of a D1 college player are amazing, a life you have to live to understand. I came from Clymer, New York, I played in equipment that guys played in twenty years ago. We stuffed pads into girdles, we had old helmets, we had to buy our own practice gear if we wanted anything good. I bought my own facemask because I wanted one that looked like a real football player. Every position should have gear, protective padding, specific to what that position does -big pads for linemen who hit more often in a smaller space, lighter pads for a running backs and wide receivers who have to be quicker, even smaller for a quarterback who has to throw. At Clymer we had the same helmets, shoulder pads, shoes, nothing special for different positions.

You get to college, and they ask you what kind of equipment you want, they go get it from the equipment room. What size pads, what helmet, facemask. What do you want to wear under the pads, loose, tight? I didn't even know, took me a week or so to tweak my practice stuff.

Then you walk into the State football facility, and you see the huge pictures of the greats, guys like TJ Duckette and Charles Rodgers. Pool tables in the locker room, player's lounge has big TVs, couches. Walk to your locker and you have eight different pairs of shoes, ten shirts, ten pair of shorts, socks folded. When you're done with it you throw it in a bag, down a laundry chute, and it's there again the next day.

The game speeds up. Everyone is fast, as fast as you. In high school, I'd choose between running away from the defense or running through it. Always told my linemen, You give me five, I'll give you five. That way we always have a first down. We got by on size and instinct.

In college, the coaching is all pre-snap reads. If its outside zone blocking, read the defensive end. If he's outside, you go inside; you know everyone will be accounted for and there's one defender you'll have to beat, a linebacker or safety.

I remember my best games against Notre Dame, one time it hit me, Wow their defense is so aggressive, the cutback is there. They over-pursue. That's good and bad for a running back. You get away with it the first time, and you're like, Oh shit, it's there all the time. But then they see something, so they fill with the backer. It's a constant chess game, setting up defenders for a move later in the game, the defense making you think you have something then closing a hole.

On campus it was awesome, I loved Michigan State and East Lansing. Downtown Grand River, right across the street from campus. The famous bars there, Rick's, PP's. You walk in and the DJ puts the fight song on, and everyone goes crazy. We had a nice mix of players. Kaleb and I were inseparable. As a freshman, you're walking around with your Michigan State sweats thinking you're something special. You get recognized as a football player, and some sports geeks know who you are. The best was just clinging to the football player mystique. When I went back to running back was when I started to get notoriety on campus. Linebackers win games, running backs get in Sport Illustrated.

. . . .

Near the end of the season during my sophomore year (academically, a football freshman after a redshirt year), Wisconsin came into our house, Spartan Stadium nicknamed The Woodshed, agricultural/beat-down entendre reference understood. They're undefeated, ranked fifth in the country. It's a night game, and ESPN College Game Day crew is set up. Brent Musburger is on the network call. When you play a night game there's just a special feeling in the air, and we didn't have many back then.

Football is a sport of repetition, preparation, the same thing over and over again. When the time comes to perform, everything is dialed in. When the situation changes -different weather, a change in a starter, a wrinkle in the game plan- you can react using instinct and talent. When you play day games all the time, that schedule, that preparation becomes habit. Alarm clock set. Wake at the same time, leave the room so you're not late to team meals. Home games you don't have to look for the training, film or meeting rooms because you know them in your sleep. For road games, you lose a little advantage. You have to plan for where you're going, things get rushed, or you get to places too early, and you're bored. Routine is changed, your mind changes, your stomach changes, your energy levels change. *Did I eat enough to get me to the game with a full stomach? Did I eat too much and I'll be bogged down? Where's my locker? Is all my stuff there? Do I have the right cleats for this grass or turf?* You have to use energy to do things that come naturally in your home.

Night games throw you off balance a little more. But we don't think about that when you're a player, that's the coaches' job. For a player it's just such a cool feeling. The day before the game during walk-throughs, ESPN comes to your practice, and you're like, Holy shit, there's Herbstreit, Reece Davis, look around for Corso. The crowd is electric after a whole day of tailgating. You're just in awe of this.

So, Wisconsin in town for the national game of the week. If they win, they go to the Rose Bowl. If we win, we bust that dream in the mouth. Their staff makes the mistake of leaving a wheelbarrow full of roses outside their locker room (or maybe someone on our staff did that, the psychology of firing up a college athlete isn't all that sophisticated). We see the roses on the walk back to the locker room after warm-ups. If Wisconsin put them there, it wasn't especially intelligent to bring flowers to a woodshed. If it was our staff, the ploy worked. Coach fires us up, we go crazy, the locker room starts shaking, looking at those roses.

Blood boils.

. . . .

Zebra 32. Get used the that call.

That's the play that starts my party, my special career at State (also, the play where I almost get my quarterback killed, more on that later). Single back formation, inside zone run. I take the handoff, hit the hole, already a crowd of defenders there, interior linemen and a filling backer. I look outside, see light, bounce-cut, and start running downhill. Jim Leonard, their outside linebacker got sucked in, but he adjusts and comes at me. His angle isn't good; it's a race. He catches me sidelong, on the hip. I throw a stiff-arm, shed him like a Panama High School eighth-grader. On the sideline, a Sport Illustrated photographer snaps a shutter, the moment of contact. *Click, click, click.* With the touch of a finger on a camera I'm semi-famous.

Daylight, that finish line end zone that looks the same if you're in eighth grade at Clymer High School or at The Woodshed in front of a hundred thousand fans in green and white. I see it, but don't cross it, this time. I get shoe-string tackled by a safety or a corner I didn't see.

Run Jehuu run.

I get up, hear the crowd go nuts, my name on the public address game-call, *Caulcrick on the carry for a FIRST DOWN!*

I was a big dude for a running back, six foot, two hundred forty-five pounds. My linemen were bigger, around six-eight, three hundred pounds. They pick me up like I'm a bag of sticks, like a toothpick, smack me on the back, on my helmet. Adrenaline fireworks explode inside the offense, the fans. Charges sent into the stands, bounce back, alternating currents of electric fused consciousness, purpose, anticipated victory.

We win 49-14. I go for a hundred-forty-six yards and a TD. Felt like high school again. The game slowed down; I saw holes and cuts and that beautiful finish line.

That was my coming out game, a message to the coaching staff, to the rest of the conference, but mostly to myself, that I belonged, that I could have success. It was a realization that I found the right place at the right time. I understand the quirks of circumstance as much as anyone – luck, timing, chance choices that turn out right. Liberia taught me that. On that first play, Zebra 32, my linemen had to block the play. I had to see the plugged hole and have enough instinct to bounce it outside. Jim Leonard had to be fooled by the move and duck inside. The photographer had to be on that side of the field, on that yard line to snap the perfect picture. Fortune smiles, you have to appreciate it and take advantage.

The bullet doesn't pick and choose.

Sports Illustrated featured the game that week. John Biever took the picture for the article, me stiff-arming Jim Leonard. Sports Illustrated, with a circulation of a zillion, all over the world. College football fans see my picture and read my name. Instant celebrity. I was like, *Holy shit, I think I've just carved a name for myself.*

29

Jehuu 2005

DREW STANTON IS back at quarterback after being injured.

The college is pushing hard for him as a Heisman candidate, so our offense changes. We go pass-oriented, so he can be showcased, switched from ground and pound, thunder and lightning, to a three-back rotation. Running backs work more on pass-catching and pass-protection packages. Deondre Cobb transfers in. Jason Teague rounds out the backfield.

As a running back, it changes your mindset, your preparation, but you work hard, do your job. For the season, I managed seven rushing touchdowns, led the team, caught seventeen passes, but just didn't get the ball a whole lot.

. . . .

Zebra 32.

We're playing at Notre Dame. First play, I'm getting the ball.

In football, the first eight or ten offensive plays are scripted, the opening act of a play. The choreography for Notre Dame was designed from scouting reports and film study, rehearsed practice week until the starting offense was sick of it. The plan for Notre Dame was to establish the power run game, then play-action for Drew. We went over it maybe a hundred times. I knew the sequence like I knew my way to Clymer from Findlay Lake. You practice this opening sequence, that first play, so everything is easy, especially in front of a hostile crowd.

And you practice it so there's no way you can screw it up.

And here we are running Zebra 32 again, a play I know in my sleep, the same play I busted freshman year against Wisconsin. I'm getting the ball, first offensive play of the game. They don't know it. Sixty-thousand fans in the stadium and another million at home watching don't know it. NBC sports is doing the game, and they don't know it. Alex Flanagan, the sideline reporter might know but isn't saying anything (I hope).

But I know it, and my teammates know it.

Zebra 32, inside zone run to the right. Lift the left arm, take the direct hand-off, make a linebacker miss, let the legs take over. The first play-by-play call on TV will say my name. The first announcement on the stadium public address system; *Caulcrick on the carry, the next words for a gain of...*

We win the coin toss, receive the opening kick. A decent return puts us on the right hash, in front of our bench, the script in motion. The offensive gathers around the coaching staff on the sideline for final instructions. (But really what is there new to say? Zebra 32 has been drummed into us since Monday). We do the sideline thing so defenses don't know which personnel will be in for the first play, pretty standard strategy. I'm on the outside of the circle, stretching, jumping, leg lifts, pumping myself up for the first play; Zebra 32, Zebra 32, inside zone run, right side. The officials place the ball, the play clock cranks, and we run onto the field to a massive roar, thousands of full-throated cheers, all of it for the Notre Dame defense. Hostile environment.

We huddle again on the field, twelve yards behind the ball. Drew repeats the play, I'm not listening, don't need to. It's Zebra 32. Run it a hundred times. First play, Zebra 32. I'm on national TV; I'm getting the ball first play of the game. Establish the run. Zebra 32, Zebra 32.

Single back, I set with the team, try not to let my eyes, feet, or a lean, give anything away to the defense. Linebackers look into the backfield to see if anybody tips the play. Remember the snap count. Don't jump. Check the defense alignment. Inside linebacker should be easy to pin-block. Have to beat the end, maybe a safety. Drew's under center. *Green 18, green 18, set hit! Boom!*

I explode right.

Drew turns left.

His eyes go big, like a cartoon. I have a moment to think, *Oh shit.* He has the same moment to think the same *Oh shit.* He tucks the ball and gets dropped.

Tackled for an eleven-yard loss, the Notre Dame PA shouts.

Michigan State looks rattled by the crowd early, the television broadcast.

Time out!, our coaching staff.

You need to calm the fuck down, my offensive coordinator.

What happened?

We were still in Zebra, but with the ball on the right hash there was no reason to run it to the short side. The play is automatically switched to go left, wide side of the field. We practiced from this hash mark. The play becomes Zebra 33. Drew even said it in the huddle, but I was so fired up I didn't listen. I ran Zebra 32. The rest of the team ran Zebra 33. Now we're second down and twenty-one to go, on the road. The stadium is rocking; we're stuffed back in front of their student section.

That's when I start thinking, *Okay, I need to become a better student of the game.* I learned the importance of studying and understanding your craft as an athlete. What it means to really focus, to be immersed in details that give you the best chance to succeed.

Or at least run the right play.

. . . .

Coaches Williams and Stoutland, my first contact points for Sparta, were only there two years before I got to Michigan State. They went 16-17 overall record, 6-15 in conference. Not good enough.

Coach Smith wouldn't fare much better, a little over two years officially before he became a lame-duck coach midway through my sophomore season. We went 22-26 with him, 12-20 in the Big Ten.

30

Jehuu 2006

Jehuu at Michigan State

MY JUNIOR YEAR in 2006 started out a little rough in pre-season.

I carried a sloppy left shoulder over from high school. It would pop out, and I'd pop it back in. It was always loose after that, like a stripped gear. Freshman year in college, after my redshirt, when I went back to offense, I tore my labrum at the beginning of spring ball. The sloppy shoulder stayed loose. But I had that precious opportunity to run, and I couldn't blow it, so I played all of spring ball with a torn labrum. The day after spring ball, in early April, I had surgery.

I also had a minor tear in my meniscus, got scoped right before the 2006 season, a bunch of bone chips taken out. I was grounded for a week but didn't lose any real time. Injuries are a part of college football. I don't think people understand their real impact on us players. This isn't pro ball; we're really just kids, playing the game at that high level. Bodies and minds still sorting things out – sleep, diet, physical risks, pounding the shit out of each other every day in camp, on the practice field, loaded with testosterone and a lack of fully developed impulse control. It's a daily, organized version of Lord of The Flies. Coaches play you off each other physically. Someone gets hurt, you plug in the next recruit. Eighty-eight of us pounding on each other, looking for an edge to get noticed, to get in the game.

If you're a coach and you get the Lamborghini, you're not going to drive it fast? The Land Rover? You're not going to drive it up the side of a building? A body that can run through a brick wall, you're not going to take it for a test drive? Maybe drive it off a cliff? Coaches push the envelope of safety; players accept the risk.

Injuries are part of that. Expected.

· · · ·

We had a rotation for running backs to start the season between me and Javon Ringer, thunder (me) and lightning (him). Of course, he thought he was the bruising back, and I thought I was the elusive scat-back, that competitive arrogance of a division one athlete. We roomed together on the road and at home. (That was another thing I didn't think made sense. For home games, we stayed in a hotel right down the road from my bed, sitting empty in my apartment.)

Javon and I have a great relationship, I couldn't have been happier to share a backfield with him. We used to play rock, scissors, paper to see who would start the game. That's how close we were to the same running back, the same skill set, closer than people think.

All that mattered to us was if we won the game, that makes for some tight ties in football, that idea of sacrifice for the greater good.

Thunder and Lightning were responsible for seventy-three touchdowns in our careers at MSU, the most by any running back tandem.

. . . .

When you're a freshman at State, you have to stay in dorms.

The college wants you to get acclimated to student life. Sophomore year you can have an apartment on campus, to keep football players close. After that, you're either going to make it or not, and they let you stay wherever. We had an apartment, about ten minutes from campus. I had wheels so getting to classes and practices was easy.

I also had a shit-ton of parking tickets. I asked them to go back and look after I left, and I spent like $2,700 on parking tickets when it was all done.

Junior year season was a rollercoaster. I'm busted up a little, but we're going in ranked top twenty. There was a big ad campaign for Stanton for Heisman, lots of media time and effort spent on that. I remember thinking, *Drew's my guy, but I'm trying to eat too.* I don't think it affected the locker room, and Drew didn't hold it over anyone's head, but it was there, affected practices, game plans, things we worked on, what was asked of every position. Running backs want to run, not block or slip into flats for passes. Linemen want to block runs; they want to get downfield and flatten smaller linebackers, secondary positions, not spend all day backing up and catching big fast rushers. Linemen are much more exposed in a passing game than a running game.

To start, we didn't see it in the coaching staff, in decisions they made, in any favoritism. We started out 3-0, kept our national ranking.

And then came Notre Dame. Again.

. . . .

Another night game, ESPN Game Day on campus (sound familiar?). Tailgating, parties, national TV audience. The night before Javon and I are in the hotel room, we see the weather forecast. Rain and more rain. Thirty mph gusts. *Yeah, we're going to run the shit out of the ball.* Morning of game day and the forecast is spot on. It's pouring. When you watch game film of that day, you see wet camera lenses, stuff blowing around on the field. When you're a 245-pound lion, this is catnip.

The scripted first eight plays were what we thought the whole game was going to be, establish the run, too hard to throw in this weather. First play of the game I hit it big, almost break it, one shoe-string tackle away from breaking it for like seventy yards. Same as the Wisconsin run. Get up, jump around, get excited, and everything like that. Second play, we run it. Next play run it. Next play run it. We stay on the ground and take a 31-14 lead into the half. We know we're running; they know we're running, and they still can't slow us down.

That half I go seven rushes for seventy-some yards, no touchdowns, but me and Javon are into it. Our line is into it. Linemen like to plow; they like to move forward and get their hands on people running downhill. They like to round a corner and get a little d-back in their sights and get on the highlight film destroying someone downfield. They love launching off the ball, instead of pass-protecting when you're backpedaling and catching rushers, and the only time you make ESPN plays of the week is when someone makes you look like a slob and kills your quarterback. No lineman ever suffered by missing a run-block.

It's still raining, the field is sloppy, the ball is slippery.

The game should be easy from here. If we can handle four or five possessions, maybe three, three-and-a-half yards a play, eight more first downs, sustain a drive or two, we win going away. My line opened holes all first half; I'm pounding the ball. Javon has fifty yards to my seventy. How can we lose?

Then the second half happened.

. . . .

To this day, I have never been given a solid explanation for the second half of that game. I know a lot of people were pissed at how it went down. Best anyone can guess is it was a signature game for us, making it a showcase for Drew Stanton's Heisman bid. We're up a ton, the game looks to be in hand, so why not let a national audience see what he can do? Get him some media. Not much else makes sense. College Game Day is on campus, ABC and Brent Musburger on the national prime-time telecast. Someone, maybe the coaching staff, thinks, *Let's figure out how we can get Drew some national attention, some buzz.* No fault of Drew, he runs the plays the coaches call. He's in the huddle saying, *What the fuck are we doing?* He was in that mindset of let's win this game.

So he ends up throwing twenty-two passes in a rainstorm. He runs another nineteen times (he's the feature of forty-one of our offensive plays). Total offense for Drew is a 167 yards. Javon and I go for 224 total, 22 carries and four catches.

On the sideline, teammates are coming up, "Hey Choo Choo, are you hurt?"

"No."

"Why aren't you in?"

"I have no idea."

I paced the sideline. Stood next to coach and was ignored. Took my helmet off, put it back on. Stood in offensive huddles, cheered and pouted. All you want to do is help, to be part of a solution to the miserable outcome you can see staring you in the face. All you want to do is RUN and make things better, for all these people you care about.

Nothing. The game, the situation, the future, my future, was completely out of my control. There's nothing I can imagine worse than standing still when running is the best option.

Final is 40 for them 37 for us. Outscored 26-6 in the second half, the lone TD is a 30-yard run by me where I bust through a huge hole, break two tackles, and run away from a safety. That's my only carry of the half. I sit and watch Drew run and throw the rest of the game. I finish the game with eight carries for a 111 yards and one score.

Maybe, it's bad coaching, maybe trying to be too cute by half, they know we're going to run, let's mix them up. Maybe it's the Stanton for Heisman thing, pressure on the staff to get him a trophy. Whatever it was, it was a mistake, a mess.

And whatever it was, though we didn't know it at the time, it was the end of the season for us, the end of any more talk about a Heisman in East Lansing.

And it cost a bunch of coaches their jobs.

. . . .

"Choo-Choo, you gotta do media."

Game's over. I'm pissed, sitting at my locker. Confused, demoralized, so frustrated. I keep coming back to, Gimme the ball! I can do this! I really wanted to win that game.

"No. I don't want to."

"Hey, Jehuu, you gotta do it." Louie is our media guy. His job is to wrangle the psyche of a few dozen teenagers, through the happy, the angry, the excited, the vindictive, the pissed-off, and get them to do things like post-game media pressers.

"Who wants me to talk? I didn't play the second half. Grab Drew."

"Jay, look, you know this. They ask for you, you show up. It's the deal. The good, the bad, you gotta be the same person."

John Lewandowski, Louie, is ten years into the job at State, another five before that in the business, fifteen total, so he knows the drill. Part of his job is to get emotional Type A teenagers to talk to a national audience in a rational, understandable, reasonable way.

It's not lost on me, the similarities, in context, but not degree of intensity, between college football and the life of the Liberian child soldier. There's living, training, coordination of movement and effort together. There's the idea of family, camaraderie. There's trust, there's loyalty. There's courage and cowardice. There are leaders triggering you to do something physical. Both ways there's testosterone aimed at an enemy, there's the high of physical confrontation, the lows of failure. The kids of Liberia are filled with ideas of invincibility, built on black magic, smoke, and mirrors. They're filled with chemicals that wash over the brain, fire it up like an engine being fed gas. The part that recognizes humanity, is numbed if it's had a chance to develop at all.

In football, we're fed confidence and preparation and ways to build muscle and fitness. We're taught how to harness and use adrenaline. Imagine every college football player, thousands and thousands, built not for Saturday games, but rather for killing and maiming. Imagine the efficiency. The power, the capability.

Imagine twenty-five thousand Liberian children, steered to play a game, rather than sling an AK47, rather than patrol the countryside and kill and maim and rape. Switch those two lives in your heads, see how it feels.

It feels like me.

"Yeah, okay, I'll do it. Where's the microphone?"

Louie looks at me a little sideways. Like he doesn't trust me. Good reason for that. I'm still smoking hot, thinking, I'm gonna go in and just mother-eff this coaching staff. I'm thinking scorched earth, take my anger, my frustration and put it into answers to questions I know I'm going to get.

And, oh yes, there will be swearing.

And literally as I'm walking, I think about what my mom would think if that came out on ESPN? What would Clymer think? I take a few deep breaths, deflate. I'm just gonna go out and be the guy that Coach Mac taught me to be. We win as a team, we lose as a team. All these things came through my head last second, and cooled me off.

Reporter, "Are you hurt?"

Me, "No I'm not hurt." (I said this more than once in the interview).

Reporter, "Why didn't you get back in?"

Me, "I don't know."

The snarkiest thing I said was, *I'm not wearing the headset on the sidelines. So I don't know what's being said.*

The next day Mike Valenti from Michigan State radio sports show goes on a famously crazy rant. Yells at his microphone for eighteen minutes, goes hoarse. *What happened? Where was Jehuu?* The Michigan State paper the next day asked *Jay-WHO?* Mr. Musburger questioned the decision not to play me on ABC's broadcast. When ESPN did their pre-game feature on me and my story, they mention this game.

It was absolutely heart-breaking. We were 3-0 coming in, headed for 4-0, a team identity, a cushion in the standings, another win against a local and historical rival. To this day, I never got any definitive answer on the game strategy that left me out.

Later in the year, Coach Smith gets fired. Right in the middle of the season. They let him finish the year, but he was gone after.

Hand me the ball five more times, in a driving rainstorm at Notre Dame, win that game and he probably keeps his job. Losing it cost him a Big Ten coaching position.

My second college coach.

. . . .

Our 2006 season was up and down, mostly down after Notre Dame. But the job, the scholarship, was still football, practices, meals, meetings, film study, training room for rehab, ice baths, miles of tape and gallons of Icy-Hot. You don't stop; there really isn't time during the season. Reflect too long and the next game stares you in the face, and you're not ready.

We start 3-0, riding a high. We go in and lose the Notre Dame game in a season-breaker. We lose three more in a row, go to 3-4. Losing starts to seem easier than winning. The season slips away right in front of our eyes. You'd think skill, effort, preparedness would dictate performance, but it's amazing how the mood, the psyche of a team shows up on the field. More than people think. We're on a sinking ship; we know it and can do almost nothing to stop the slide into the depths, sunk in the noise, the buzz, Coach Smith in the hot seat.

Northwestern is our eighth game. It's a brutal place to play. After playing in front of about half a million fans total in five straight games, football at Northwestern's Ryan Field feels like an after-thought, something to do on weekends, not like The Woodshed, The Horseshoe (Ohio State), The Big House (Michigan). It lulls you to sleep, but this is still a Big Ten football team, perfectly capable of beating the shit out of you.

The same things I saw in our three-game, post-Notre Dame losing streak starts out at Northwestern. We just spent a month losing games, to Illinois by a field goal, a close one to nationally ranked Michigan, pounded at Ohio State when they're number one in the country. Now we're 3-4, and Northwestern is smoking us at their glorified high school stadium.

We're down 24-3 at the half. They explode to start the third quarter, and before we blink, before we decide we're even football players – Spartans for Christ's sake – the score is 38-3. They're cruis-ing toward sixty points. We're stuck on three. One field goal in three quarters, nothing since the first drive of the game. The lethargy, the laziness, the sleep we brought from the second half of Notre Dame is a living thing, a shitty meal we keep eating, a plague. Nobody can shake it loose.

There's twenty-some minutes left in the game. If we can somehow score a point a minute the rest of the game we'd still lose by double-digits. First drive of the fourth quarter, Drew throws a pick, another offensive possession goes up in flames. The air is sucked from our sideline, there isn't enough oxygen to breathe. Northwestern? It's impossible to imagine the walk to the locker room after the final horn, the atmosphere as we clean up, the trip back to East Lansing, Sunday film and rehab, walks to class starting Monday. How do you even prepare for your next game when you're 3-5 and hammered by Northwestern?

And then something happens.

Football happens.

Someone yells, *Let's fucking GO!* I think it's Drew. Somehow, it takes. We decide, as a collective of proud athletes staring at a catastrophe, that enough is goddamn enough.

We get the ball back after a four-and-out by them. We're moving the ball. It's almost all passing now, playing catch-up. Get first downs, stop the clock. We run play action from the twenty-yard line going in. My job is to chip-block and get into the flat. If the ball is caught by a wide receiver, see if I can get in on a downfield block, but be careful. I don't need to come back to the sideline with a yellow flag for a clip. I fake the handoff, pretend for a second I have the ball. From the flat, I glance into the backfield. Drew still has the ball, biding time for someone to break open; line is doing a great job. Now, my job is to get into a scramble drill. If Drew is flushed left, I drag. If he goes right, and he almost always goes right, I run a wheel up the sideline.

And there it is! Drew is in my back pocket running right. I spin from the flat and head up field. The linebacker is there, but he doesn't get a shot on me, he's flat-footed. If Drew sees me, this is six; there's nobody in front of me. I stick a hand in the air, I'm free, open field. Drew sees the hand and drops the ball into the slot. My head screams, Make sure you catch it!

288

Paydirt! I'm in the end zone. Touchdown catch for Thunder. And this feels like something, a start. Momentum. Like breaking the surface of the water, sucking air.

38-10. Three minutes left in the third. They should be able to salt away the game up twenty-eight, but we have life.

They drive it down to their own red zone. Forty seconds left in the third. A score here and we go back down five touchdowns with a quarter to play. All the momentum is tossed out and the mountain is Everest. No way to climb it, air and margins too thin.

Sometimes if you can't do it yourself, momentum and belief have a way of scoring for you. Kaleb becomes our momentum, picks them off in the end zone. His first of the season and maybe one of the bigger ones in Spartan history. Their drive ends, and we get the ball back still down four touchdowns.

But not five.

We drive down and score again, 38-17. Chipping away at the total. We stop them, and they stop us on back-to-back possessions and the clock moves into fast forward. Running out of game.

We go three and out and punt. Not good. Their defense is still wrecking us. They get the ball back and gain no yards. Our defense starts to wreck them back. We block their punt, carry the ball in for a score. 38-24, with 11:40 left in the game. Everest shrinks. Oxygen returns to Sparta. The avalanche continues, finally in our favor. With eight minutes left, Drew runs the option perfectly. Score and extra point, 38-31.

3:43 left in the game. Drew throws a touchdown after a great scramble. It's 38-all. That clock that was moving so fast to start the quarter feels frozen now. They have the ball, driving for a potential winning score, but nobody on our sidelines believes they'll get it. It's an amazing transformation. The intense dread of making a mistake, the fear of failure, anxiety, panic, alarm, has turned into a rowdy confidence. It came from nowhere, out of thin air.

But it came from everywhere too, the preparation, all the practices, the games we played together, the pride ground into us by our coaches. We are, after all, great athletes. We play the game at a level experienced by very. TV pundits, talking heads, like to tell you who sucks and who's great, but we're all pretty goddamn good, or we wouldn't be here.

I end up the leading rusher for the game with just 39 yards (two catches for another 29 yards). Drew throws for 294, two TDs and a pick. It's our defense that did the work to win the game. Stop after stop. Timely turn-overs. I was so happy for Thornhill, getting that huge pick. He was excited I caught a TD pass to spark the comeback.

Three minutes left and we get another interception. Go down the field and kick the game winning 28-yard field goal with 18 seconds left, bookending three-pointers to start and finish the greatest comeback in the history of college football (not just Michigan State, all of the sport, a hundred-plus years of keeping score). There's thirty-five or so of us in the complete annals of the game that can say we won that game.

I'm one.

The next week we go to Indiana, and we're favored by enough that the game shouldn't be hard to win.

. . . .

I hate John Mellencamp. Not his fault, he's probably a cool guy.

Indiana football is known as a step-child Big 10 program. They don't feature it at the school, it's all basketball. They rarely sell out. A bigger program like Michigan State can usually swoop in on any given Saturday and quietly walk out with a win. Their home field advantage is negligible.

But you can fill a stadium in Bloomington, Indiana when John Mellencamp is playing before the game. Also their coach passed away earlier in the year, and this was their first home game since the death. The place was sold out and rowdy. That many people just don't go to Indiana University football games. It was a perfect storm.

We're completely lulled asleep, again, learned exactly no lessons from the week before. All that momentum wasted. This should have told me something about this team. Indiana was a perfect chance to stay on the roll from the Northwestern miracle. A perfect chance to get over five-hundred, keep momentum, closer to a bowl bid. I swear to God I look on the sideline and one of my teammates is sleeping. That's when I know we're in for a long haul.

We get our doors blown off. Indiana takes their momentum from Cougar-Mellencamp and uses it to thrash us.

The week after Indiana is one I want to forget. We do our usual film on Sunday. Monday is our day off. On Tuesday, we see on the ticker Michigan State University fires head coach, but he will finish out the rest of the year. That's never a good way to learn your life is about to change in a significant way. Nobody told us, we had to find out on the news. Lots of guys in the locker room are confused, furious, insulted.

Coach Smith calls a meeting. He says things like, *Let's finish out the season on a high note. Show people what kind of team we are. Have some pride*, all the things you have to say when you're still coaching a Big Ten football team and want another job someday. But it rings false, like it's too much effort to even say, the definition of going through the motions. The game is hard enough at this level when you're totally focused, mentally prepared, into every rep of every drill, every film session. It takes up all your energy; there isn't always a lot left to compete. You use adrenaline and mental tricks to get up for Saturday. You tell yourself how important games are, you set goals, a winning season, a bowl game. When that's over, it's hard to reset. When coach was fired, the season sunk all the way to the bottom of the ocean. We couldn't revive what we had at Northwestern. There were no more Let's fucking GO moments because the answer always came back, What for? Go where?

We would go on to lose the last four games of the season, a couple we were in and a couple we weren't. A loss to Purdue by two, Penn State by four. There was no room for error, no level of perseverance to match the Northwestern effort.

Smith getting fired was no fun for me. I admired coach; he was a great man, still is. He was honest and loyal, and that isn't a good recipe for being a Big Ten head football coach. College sports are the ultimate expression of the American way. You win or you get fired, no matter how good a person you are. I bought into Coach Smith's system wholeheartedly.

In 2008, I was at the combine, working out for the Rams, and ran into Coach Smith. I asked him point blank why he didn't fire his offensive coordinator, especially after the Notre Dame game, and survive to coach another year.

Coach said, "Jehuu, you tell me how I can preach family to you one day, and fire a brother or cousin the next. How do I take food off their table by my own hand?"

"Coach, you know half your staff was using MSU to get to their next job. Climb the ladder to their own head job. Maybe take your job someday?"

"Of course I know," he said. "And I'll ask you again, so what?"

31
Jehuu 2007

"I visited Jehuu at Michigan State when I was a freshman at John Carrol, during a spring break. He was a celebrity, mostly because he was good, but he had that outgoing personality. I remember he lived with Thornhill, a couple other guys. So, I went from a DIII school football player where no one really cares to the head of lines at clubs, people stop you on the street, you're given stuff. We did lots of hanging out at the house and people came over because it was more of a headache going out and possibly getting jammed up."
—*Jake Burkholder*

SENIOR YEAR, MY fifth at State.

Totally different year, mindset, recharged. I'm voted captain with Kaleb, Pete Clifford, and Travis Key. Pete, Kaleb, and I all came in together. Travis was a walk-on, earned a scholarship. We were chosen by the team, a really cool feeling.

New coach, Mark Dantonio. Coach Treadwell is our offensive coordinator. Pat Narduzzi on defense. All first-year coaches at State, though Coach D was here as an assistant a few years before for Nick Saban.

I missed playing for Nick Saban by two years. He did a five-year shift in East Lansing and managed a winning record when we hadn't had one since 1990. He left for LSU.

Coach D and his staff will preside over one of the best eras at Michigan State, a twelve-year run; three Big Ten championships, beat Michigan eight times, school record thirteen wins in 2013 (finished 3rd in the nation), five trips to the Rose Bowl.

It started with my senior year, and I was his first captain. Proud to be part of that.

. . . .

First game of senior year at UAB. Their quarterback is Sam Hunt, the country singer. This game is special for a number of reasons. It's my senior year opener, the last opener I have in college, special enough for my family, my whole family, to come. It was the first time a lot of them attended a live football game. I had to get my hands on thirty-four tickets, more than I've ever had to get. It was so special coming out of the tunnel, just seeing my family sitting behind the team bench.

I rushed ten times for almost a hundred yards and four TDs, the first three of the game, one a 42-yard sprint. We had almost three-hundred on the ground as a team, our offensive line overmatched them. First game of the year and we scored 55 points. Coach D told me, "You need to have your family come every game, if you're gonna play like that." I got a Big Ten Co-Offensive Player of the Week award.

I liked the team, the chemistry, the idea that I had some control as a captain. Kaleb and I decided this was going to be a special season. The offense was solid, the coaching staff was in place, we knew this was the beginning of something for the college. We had a book we went through every day in training camp, the second to the last page of the book was *Pull the Weeds*. You can't have the energy sucked from what you're doing. We used it as a mantra.

. . . .

We went 7-5 my senior year, were in every game, all five losses by one score. Finally, back to winning more than losing, competitive every time we walked onto the field. It felt good, just football, and none of the other stuff. We went to Orlando for the Champs Bowl on December 28th. It was my first post-season trip since my true freshman season. We lost to Cincinnati, but what the hell, it was Florida over Spring break.

. . . .

I had a very good senior season, was finally allowed to run, like at Clymer, like on the roads of Liberia. Finished the season with 872 yards on 222 carriers, more than double my previous high. I've been asked a lot about the experience. One question always pops up, who's the best defender I faced that year. The hardest hit I ever got was by A.J. Hawk at Ohio State. I wanted to run into him; I'm thinking, *Let me see what this guy is about – what's the hype?* It wasn't hype. He is probably the toughest guy I ever went up against.

Coach D didn't mind giving me and Javon the ball. Pretty good results. My feet carried me to the goal line twenty-one times, a single season record at State. I led the Big Ten in scoring, 9.7 points a game, was honorable mention All-Conference.

For my career, I had 240 points, seventh most in MSU history, 532 rushing attempts, seventh most all time, 2,395 yards was tenth all time, and the stat I love the most, thirty-nine touchdowns, the highest at the time of my graduation, now second behind Lorenzo White. Scoring was my thing, finding the end zone. Every touchdown tweaking a memory of that eighth grader taking the ball for the first time and scampering until someone told him to stop.

There was never a time when I considered becoming a professional athlete, up until I was. American kids dream of playing center field for the Yankees, winning the Super Bowl, a gold medal. I didn't picture a life in sports of any kind. I wanted to wear a jacket and tie and long pants, grind out a work week doing whatever guys in ties and long pants do, push paper across a desk, take lunch breaks, spreadsheets, memos, meetings in conference rooms. Happy hour Friday night, bullshit about clients buying my widgets, company softball team one night a week, pick-up ball in the park, weekends on the golf course. Answer the bell with a hangover Monday morning like everyone else.

But I had value on a football field, so that's where I ended up.

32

Jehuu 2008

"A bird is in the air, but its mind is on the ground."
– *Liberian saying*

THE COMBINE IS a meat market. An absolute mind-fuck.

Just a crazy three days. The first day you run, lift, jump. But that's just part of it, the rest is all mental. They bring you in and ask all of these absurd questions. They asked me if I owned a gun. I said no. Couple questions later they asked, "So do you store your gun in a proper place at home?"

I'm said, "No I don't have a gun. Pretty sure I mentioned that." Don't know if they're trying to trip you up, like you're on trial? I guess they kind of are.

You get a number. I believe I was running back number five. You go to all these different meetings, and then you meet with every team's doctor. They look at your college injury list, and they look at your body to see if they find something they don't like. Every single team doctor, thirty-plus exams. Rooms are set up. You just walk in, go into the next place, talk to them. They tug on your injured body parts; every doctor yanked at my shoulder. It's weird and repetitive, a little disarming. A cattle-call. If they're happy with it, you're good to go. I was on a roll, no red marks, no alarms.

Until I got to the second to last doctor.

I'm leaving the exam, and they're like, "Maybe we need to go see an MRI on this shoulder." The same shoulder twenty other doctors said was okay. I had to go get an MRI. Jump on a shuttle from the stadium to the hospital with a bunch of other red marks. I got there at like 8:30 p.m. and didn't leave the hospital until about 2:30 in the morning. Then, I had to wake up the next morning to go run, jump, do drills again.

You're split into different groups; you do the workouts with your positions, get tested for speed, agility, vertical leap, bench, shuttle run. All of it.

I've never been speed dating, but I've seen it on TV. The next part is like that. You sit at a table; it's a cocktail party except there's no alcohol. Team scouts take turns coming to your table. They talk, ask their questions, and leave. Next scout drops in. The whole time, in the back of your mind, you're so self-conscious, wondering who's looking at you, what they think. The idea is to have good posture, always smile, handle your yes-sirs, pay attention to your manners because you don't know who's watching you. When you look back at it, the process is pretty obnoxious.

Keep in mind, this is a gigantic stadium filled with the best conditioned, biggest, strongest, fastest athletes in the world. Guys have been training for these tests; it's all they've done since the end of their college seasons. Everywhere you turn you run into guys you banged heads with in games, seen on TV, read about, or marveled at their stats. Everywhere you turn there's another fantastic stat for physicality going up on a board, brute strength, speed like you can't believe, Olympic-level performances.

After the power interview session, you have these cards for all your appointments for the next day. It's a little more efficient; these are all the teams that want to have a formal sit down with you, talks with the general manager, the owner, the head coach. I think at the combine I had four meetings with four different teams. You go in and talk to them, and they ask you different questions about your background. Some of them have you go to the board and draw up your favorite run play; what are you thinking? What's the blocking scheme? Is it a zone scheme, man scheme? What's your footwork? What are you looking at? So they really just try to focus on your football IQ, what you know, if you'll be able to pick up an offense. I trained for this with my agent in Indianapolis. We had all the physical training, the bench press, the lifting, the running, and everything else. We also had these interview training sessions. We practiced the infamous Wunderlich test.

Then comes the day that brings me back to Africa, the things I went through on my walk.

There's the session where you're in nothing but your compression shorts (you've seen that famous shot of a lumpy Tom Brady, it's like that). You go in the Bod Pod, get your body fat measured. Then you go to this stage, all these scouts sitting there looking at you with their pens and pads. You get on the scale, you go up there and spread your arms so they can see your wingspan, turn around so they can see your back; it's modern-day slavery with the owners sitting there, writing down everything. It's a crazy experience. I was like, Holy shit. But that's how it's done. I can't compare it to what a slave might have gone through, but there's no way to get that picture of a white slave owner checking the teeth of an African slave out of your head when you stand there. I understand I'm standing there of my own free will, trying to get a job that will potentially pay me millions of dollars, but it doesn't sweep that vision from my head.

33

Liberia

"African chiefs were the ones waging war on each other
and capturing their own people and selling them. If
anyone should apologize, it should be the African chiefs.
We still have those traitors here even today."
—*Ugandan President Yoweri Museveni, 1998*

SLAVERY IN AFRICA is ingrained into the culture, a bigoted caste system.

There is a natural expectation that one group of people will force submission on another. The difference between African bondage and western slavery is grounded in bigotry and racism.

Slavery in Europe was a chattel proposition. Slaves as a piece of property, no rights or humane elements are part of the equation. Human beings owned and used, like a horse or tractor. The slavery is an ownership and tool contract, no recognition that there is a human being on the other end of the indenture. Chattel slavery was for life, as were the children and grandchildren of the property, horse and cow, foal and calf.

In Africa, slavery is more of a barter or business transaction. A person might be enslaved in order to pay off a debt or pay for a crime. Slaves in Africa lost the protection of their family and their place in society, but eventually they or their children might become part of their master's family and earn their freedom. The service of the slave recognized as the currency, not the body and soul.

The African slave market was small-scale, a back and forth condition between tribes as one dominated another, a currency filling a need. It wasn't enough to supply the growing worldwide demand, especially from outsiders such as Arabs and Europeans. As that market grew, warfare, raids to get slaves, and kidnapping increased. The currency became more valuable, and the stronger tribal leaders had no compunctions about selling off their brethren. Europeans wanted Africans to work the land they owned on Caribbean islands and in America. Africans were valuable for their experience with farming, as much as their availability. About ninety-percent of Africans transported west had initially been enslaved by other Africans.

· · · ·

When the American Colonization Society dumped thousands of freed American slaves on the shores of Western Africa, the Americo-Liberian population stood at three percent in the Mesurado area. These freed citizens, fresh off experiences of being enslaved by their fellow man, did the same in their new world, enslaving others as soon as the opportunity presented itself, failing to recognize the hypocrisy. There was no empathy for the indigenous population; there was only basic septic human behavior, one sort of person dominating another sort of person based on arbitrary characteristics, like skin color and who held the best weapons at the time. Tribal Liberians were virtually, if not actually, enslaved by non-ethnic settlers, a transplanted educated elite who considered the Congo natives primitive heathens. The Americo-Liberians took on the characters of the slave masters from where they came. They superimposed political, economic and social systems over existing indigenous structures. Native Africans were limited to nominal positions of no social significance, little financial opportunity.

As Liberia grew into a new and enlightened future, the resentments from subjugation festered and fermented into toxic civil wars. Liberia became a petri dish for rebellion. The oppressed, mainly the Congo, reacted by clinging to and following false prophets, men like Charles Taylor, heavily armed con artists and charlatans craving power and riches, and not much else. Another kind of slavery emerged in the sham guise of rebel armies and soldiering. Children came under the yoke of service without representation or control as thousands were simply taken from orphanages, off the street, or wrested from their parents' arms to do the bidding of strongmen and warlords.

34

Jehuu

BEFORE THE DRAFT, I went away, got an agent, trained, went to the combine, worked out there.

After the combine, teams flew me to visits. All very encouraging. I thought for sure I was going to go to Pittsburgh. I met with coach Tomlin, met with their running back coach Kirby Wilson, and we had a great conversation. I grew up a life-long Steelers fan, and they were very impressed with the knowledge I had about old Steelers teams. We watched some film, and they asked questions. I answered, and it was just an all-around good visit. So, I had a pretty good feeling. I'd worked out for them at the combine, and when they flew me back in for another visit, I was like, Oh, there's a possibility.

It's a very strange, unique position to be in. Colleges come get you. If you're not projected top ten or twenty in the draft, the pros, you almost always have to go to them. Very strange transition. But I guess that's most life situations, right? You go interview, trying to impress an employer.

. . . .

The prefix on my cell read *seven-one-six*. Local call. The phone rang at approximately the same time the Buffalo Bills are set to make their selection in the fourth round of the 2008 NFL draft. I'm watching the draft on TV at my mum's house. I'm sure I'm being picked by the Buffalo Bills, my hometown team. They're calling to tell me so. My head rushes. I'm about to be drafted, to play more football, getting paid to do it.

The gang at my mum's house bristles. "Shhh. The TV." I lean in, waiting to hear Paul Tagliabue mispronounce my name.

Except he doesn't. He doesn't mispronounce my name. He doesn't say my name at all. No highlights on the ESPN draft show. NFL Films made a documentary of my family's story, our escape from Liberia to Clymer, for the draft. Looks like they didn't need to. Not a word about me from Chris Berman, no circling the wagon around Jehuu. No tremendous upside from Mel Kiper. Tagliabu might as well have said, Jehuu Caulcrick will not be the fifth-round pick for the Buffalo Bills.

I look at my friends, at my college teammates Kaleb Thornhill and John Masters, (neither had declared for the draft, they were there for support). I look over the table of snacks, the cooler of beer and soft drinks.

· · · ·

Round one of the draft a bunch of friends went and played golf at Peek and Peak Golf Course, in my hometown Findlay Lake, ignoring the minute-by-minute stress of watching your future unfold with every choice that's not you.

Round two was a maybe, so I paid more attention, tuning in to the TV, getting updates on my phone.

Round three came and went.

Round four, nothing.

The recalibration works fast, almost desperate, the seven stages of grief in fast-forward.

Now they're finishing round five and y name is still uncalled.

Then the phone rings. *What the hell?* I look at my phone again, the prefix is 716, Western New York.

Someone got it wrong (denial)!

What the HELL again (anger)?

Maybe someone else will draft me (bargaining).

Okay, I'm not getting drafted, done playing football, not getting paid (depression. This one didn't last long, a blip on my mental state).

Free agent path or maybe that businessman dream (testing and acceptance).

I answer the phone, still looking at the TV where the Bills just drafted someone named Xavier Omon with the hundred-seventy-ninth pick, a running back nobody ever heard of from Northwest Missouri State of the Mid-America Intercollegiate Athletics Association, NCAA Division II.

Seriously.

The call is the Bills, like I thought. They explain their strategy, which includes not drafting me. Xavier fucking Omon? Invite me in as a free agent. I'll get eighteen such calls in the coming days, and that feeling of being not-good-enough, that doubt, slinks into the back of my brain and rents a small space.

.   .   .   .

My plan was to graduate from MSU, go to a bowl game, NFL Combine, team visits and workouts, draft, find a team, sign a contract, head to my new home with a few more dollars in my pocket..

The wrench goes in when your name isn't called. Then you enter the system with all the other guys not picked to go to pro ball, looking for a job. Guys disperse into different attitudes and territory and hopes and dreams. You play the game of being an athlete – confidence, dominance, physicality, skill, knowledge. You sort out the locker room with the beasts, the bullies, the quiet corners, the flamboyance and false pride. Most athletes can tell who's full of shit and who can back it up. But it's a good idea to temper your opinions and assessments at the pro level. These aren't high school sophomores, nor are they the hundredth man on a hundred-man roster. These are, presumably, the best athletes in the world, the strongest, the fastest, the most violent collection. Big, fast, big and fast. There's the poisers, the heroes, the good guys, and the bad guys, like everywhere else in life. They're just harder to finger in this crowd of helmets, pads, testosterone.

But the politics in the NFL are like anywhere else, the risk, reward, the accountability. Coaches and scouts and owners don't like to look stupid. If you're a high pick, a name the fans know, you're gonna get your chance to play. You're gonna get my chance, too. When ESPN talking heads tout a pick, teams listen to all that. If a top pick is still available, are you gonna take the risk of getting someone like me ahead of that? Take the heat from fans? Take the risk I don't pan out and have that come back on you?

They try to get the mental picture from the Combine, but there's no way for them to know what's in my heart, in my bones. They know my past, a little. They get my test results –Wunderlick, arm-span, forty-time, bench press. They have no idea who I hung with in high school, what kind of teammate I am, my dedication to a cause, my level of perseverance, how long I can go without water or food or shelter. How I can listen to gunfire and not even blink. How I've seen dead bodies in the street, and they haven't. Tell me that's not an attribute you want on your team.

Go ahead, run a tenth of a second faster than me. Push a barbell up one more time. Jump higher. But if you want a man who's seen the world in its most raw form, and has chosen to rise, to roar, to soar, and you want them to run through a wall, or a street filled with bullet shell casings and sniper fire, you're gonna want me.

But they don't. They don't see. Forces, the market pushes and pulls and makes them take the guy that's less risk politically. It's easier.

35

Jehuu, New York Jets

- March 2008: Signed as a free agent
- August 30th, 2008: Waived after final cuts
- August 31st, 2008: Signed to practice squad
- December 23rd, 2008: Waived from practice squad
- December 26th, 2008: Signed practice squad
- December 27th, 2008: Waived from practice squad
- December 27th, 2008: Signed futures contract
- September 5th, 2009: Released final cuts
- September 6th, 2009: Signed practice squad contract
- Released outright prior to 2009 season opener

"When he went to the Jets, Jehuu invited my whole family for a visit. We're in downtown New Jersey. Next thing we know a limo shows up, and we go through Harlem and into Manhattan. Maybe a club? Maybe a nice place for dinner? Nah, not Jehuu. We went into Walmart to find the video game Rock Band. So me, my sister, and family stayed up all night playing. Such a simple, family-oriented guy. Took us to the Jets practice facility, showed us Brett Favre's locker."
—*Jake Burkholder*

THE JETS WAS my first contract. It wasn't my last.

Teams have a bunch of options to keep players under their control, develop them, see if they'll fit their system, without having to pay them full-on money. Practice team is one way, they sign and re-sign players to those all the time. You'd be amazed how many athletes are knocking around the league under these types of deals, from all over the college football landscape. (Not a lot with my Big Ten pedigree, not a lot with school records.) Most don't become full-time players, but there are a ton of them working.

I was cut, waived, re-signed, and released as many times as I can count in my professional football life. I got onto one fifty-three-man roster contract, but mostly my career was trying to prove myself. It was three years of bouncing around, moving from here to there, taking a new job, constant movement. Like Liberia, except I did it on planes, in hotel rooms, and at the finest facilities in the world of sports. The stressors and set-backs couldn't compare to Liberia, or living in small-town Clymer, or even the ups and downs of my seasons in East Lansing, but without a set contract, a welcoming home to play football, there's always that feeling that life can change in an instant, that someone else controls your fate.

But, believe me, I wasn't complaining.

I was a free agent in the summer of 2008, and then the Jets put me on waivers end of the summer, then signed me to a practice squad contract. Anyone would rather be making full-roster-contract-coin, dressing Sundays, a starter's-injury away from multiple snaps, but I was happy to just be in the process of being a professional athlete, playing football for a living. The Jets had a great running back room with a ton of classic players. I was learning from guys like Tony Richardson, sixteen years in the league, Thomas Jones, Leon Washington, Jessie Chatman, all those guys, great dudes. That was really cool.

· · · ·

Practice squad players run that week's opponent's plays to prep the roster guys for game day, both offense and defense. Coaches keep practice squad guys involved in case they have to bring you up, put you on the game-day roster. Kind of like the college red-shirt, you're part of the team, you do everything. You go to all of the meetings, all of the practices, then to the game, you just can't play. But you have to be ready, that's the crazy part. You learn the game plan, because maybe in practice Tony Richards gets hurt and you have to be elevated, so you have to know what's going on. You're in those meetings, preparing, and then you have practice squad meetings and coaches are like, So today this is what we are doing. You're going to be playing this guy (from the other team). I'd act like the other team's running back, try to run like him, power game, cut-backs, whatever it takes.

I was under a practice squad salary contract, pretty good money. Around Christmas time guys in position groups will buy each other gifts. There were five or six of us in the running backs room including a few coaches. I thought I was cool, got all of them like a two-hundred-dollar gift card for Finish Line or Footlocker or something like that. I'm thinking, *Yeah that's a lot of money I'm putting in there, taking care of my people.* I go into the pre-game meeting before the Christmas day game, and go *boom boom boom, Merry Christmas, guys. Merry Christmas.* I get a bunch of smiles, sideways looks, *Thanks man, thanks.*

And then here comes Thomas Jones, twelve-year vet, starting running back, ahead of me on the chart. He's like Merry Christmas y'all and he drops a Breitling watch on everyone, including me! One to everybody in the room.

Wake-up call Jehuu, this is the big time.

. . . .

Practice squad contracts only last a year. The Jets wanted me back, so I re-signed with them. It's called a futures contract, and it's for three years. You sign and go right into off-season workouts, right at the Jets facility, January through July.

All the Jets facilities are in Jersey, same with the Giants. (The Buffalo Bills are the only NFL team in New York State.) I lived in Florin Park in Jersey. People picture the stadiums and weight rooms and training spaces and cold tubs sitting empty when the seasons end, but they're used all year by players to work out on their bodies, minds, lifting weights, studying film, playbooks. We get paid to become better football players. July they let you loose, my first real off-season. I had really good friends on that team, Dustin Keller, tight end from Purdue, first-round pick, Erik Ainge, his uncle was Danny Ainge, got us tickets when the Celtics won the title, another nice perk of professional sports, the network of friends and families gets you places you never thought possible.

. . . .

Pre-season 2008 we travel to Cleveland for a game. We do Saturday walk-throughs, pre-game routines, prep for the game. I have a shot of playing a few packages, very excited to be on the team, playing in the NFL. A year ago I was at Michigan State, nursing a dead shoulder, meeting a new coach, wondering how my senior year was going to go. Now I'm still in green, but there's a few more dollars in my pockets, and I'm in my hotel room, getting some rest before the game the next day.

Chad Pennington is our quarterback, at least he is when I go to bed. But when I wake up, my phone is buzzing, like twenty-five or thirty messages, every single one some version of, *You guys just got Brett Favre!* I flip on ESPN SportsCenter, and it's all over the news, a blockbuster trade, Favre to the Jets. We all meet at breakfast with looks like what's going on. Pennington is on a flight from Cleveland to Miami; he was traded, told in the middle of the night. They literally woke him up in the hotel room. He was packed and out the door before the sun came up.

We're in warm-ups on the field at Cleveland Stadium. We have only back-up quarterbacks dressed. It starts lightning, so we head back to the locker room to wait it out. Someone says Favre's in the building. He busts into the locker room and goes around introducing himself. I'm at my locker trying to be cool, as if I'm not anxious to meet him, just another football player in a locker room. Rehearsing what I'm going to say, *Hey Brett, welcome to the team,* something like that. He's two lockers down, talking to some guys. I'm pumping up, talking to myself. He gets to my space, puts his hand out. I grab on, knowing he's famous, knowing he knows he's famous, knowing he's met a million guys in a million locker rooms. He says, *How you doin'. I'm Brett Favre,* all Mississippi syrup.

I look up from the hand and say, "I know", in like this timid little voice.

That's what I say, *I know.* Jesus!

He ends up being a really cool guy, likes to pull pranks, treats everyone the same. As down-home as he sounds and acts in interviews.

. . . .

I had a really good training camp, created some buzz. The last game of the pre-season I play great, run hard, pick up all my blocking assignments. Blow open some holes, and a guy named Danny Woodhead runs through them. Going into the locker room after the game and Tony Richardson, the vet, comes up and says, *Dude you blocked your ass off this game. I just hope you didn't block Danny into a roster spot over you.*

Oh shit. Here we go again, same as my linebacker experience freshman year at Michigan State. Didn't know the drill, didn't see the squirrely path onto the playing field. Should have whiffed a few blocks. I went out and tried my best and sprung Woodhead for a few long runs, the only way I really knew how to do things.

And he got the full-on roster spot. I stayed on the practice squad.

36

Jehuu, Tampa Bay Buccaneers

- December 29th, 2009: Signed practice squad contract
- January 11th, 2010: Released

LABOR DAY WEEKEND in New Jersey, Jets summer camp is over.

Season coming soon. Final weekend before cuts and I'm sure I'm good to go. At least I think so, the Jets haven't said anything to me or my agent. Some buddies and I go up to the Jersey Shore for the weekend. While we're there I get a call, *Hey Jay, it's Mike Tannenbaum,* Jets general manager at the time. *Come on down, we want you to sign your contract.* I drive from the Jersey Shore back to the Jets' offices. I'm in the outer office waiting and waiting. This is a twenty-minute transaction. And I'm still waiting.

Starting to feel like bad news.

All the guys are coming in, signing, and leaving. Another half hour goes by, so I reach out to my agent. "Hey, what is going on? I've been here for like an hour and a half now."

He says, "Uh, let me see."

One of the team scouts comes in and says, "We'll be right with you. Something big came up, and we're just making some final arrangements here." So stew for a while longer, wondering what's going on, wondering if I get a roster spot or a practice squad contract, maybe let go altogether. If I'm cut, that puts me back in the process of showing for teams, wanting to be wanted.

They finally bring me in and drop the bomb, the one I could see coming. *Some things have changed, Jehuu. We had to make a trade and some roster moves so we won't be able to keep you.* Etcetera, etcetera.

I'm like *oh, okay,* what else is there to say? I'm back to free agency again, that circle of confusion and indecision. I have my agent get some workouts from teams when my name hits the wire. Some teams fly me in. Nothing fits, nobody needs my exact set of skills. It's late in the season to find a place on a roster, but my rights get picked up by Tampa Bay; they offer me a contract.

In the back of my mind, ever since I left Michigan State, is the idea that I won't play football. It's the daydream I had as a kid, getting the office job. Football was a blast in high school, fun in college, both venues taught me a lot about life. It's less fun in the pros, the lessons come in finance and politics. Haven't loved that. Walking away wouldn't be the end of the world, like for most guys in my position. I got my friends and family, relationships I value more than the idea of being a professional athlete.

But the money! The perks! Playing on Sundays, moving through a world that so few people get to see. That clutched at me, held tight, whispered in my ear, *C'mon Jehuu, go get another contract. Go play football, bash up against guys, then get on the charter flight and sip the champagne.*

I get to Tampa and I just didn't like it there, the vibe. Fact is, I absolutely hated it, the culture was fucked, the place didn't fit my eye, my ear, my life. I spend a year with them under a practice squad contract. They want to extend it. I shut down the voice that says to quit, and sit in my hotel room, wonder what to do next. Do I sign? Do I bolt? More free agency? Go home and look for a job?

One of my old college teammates is on the team, he says it's great there, Tampa is the place to be. "Dude this is awesome," he says, "You'll be in Tampa, we can be roommates." I was going to sign. But the whole time, in my head I'm thinking, *I don't want to be here.*

I call my agent, "I don't want to be in Tampa anymore. Is there any way we can go somewhere else? Do they own my rights?"

"No they don't." I'm relieved. "Let me reach out to other teams."

At the time, I was so young, dumb, thinking I was in a position to dictate my future. So many people would kill for that opportunity, to be wanted by a pro football team, to have a contract on the table, to say *Hell yes I'll sign whatever.* And here I am saying, *No I'm not signing.* All because of a feeling I had.

The next day my agent calls. "Hey, I'm in contact with a team, they like you. Whatever you do, do not go into the Bucs facility. If they have you there they'll find ways to keep you, make you sign. Then they'll own your rights, you won't be able to sign with this other team."

So, now I'm holed up in my hotel room, waiting for one specific phone call, ignoring the other ones. The Bucks are calling, *Hey, you going to come down and sign your contract?* I'm hitting Ignore on my cell over and over again, stalling.

37

Jehuu, San Francisco 49ers

- January 12th, 2010: Signed a futures contract
- October 12th, 2010: Released
- October 20th, 2010: Signed practice squad contract
- November 20th, 2010: Released

FINALLY MY AGENT calls, "San Francisco wants you."

The offensive coordinator at San Francisco was Jimmy Raye, my running back coach when I was with the Jets. He played at Michigan State in the early 70s, coached all through the NFL. I know he'll take care of me because he was a former Spartan; we had a good relationship, he liked me.

Okay, perfect.

I'm on the next flight out of Tampa. I fly back home to New York. San Francisco overnights a contract, I sign it, send it back, and just like that, I'm a 49er. January 2009. In March, I head west for the first day of off-season workouts.

My time in San Francisco felt like there was some momentum building for my pro career. Mike Singletary was the head coach. I was excited to play for him, an old-school ball coach. Dude was a legend. The stories about him as a hard-nosed player informed his coaching style. I expected a physical training camp, an environment where my size and speed might stand out.

That turned out to be less true than I'd hoped. The NFL is a business. Not even the likes of Mike Singletary can survive that part of it.

. . . .

In March I'm in San Francisco for pre-season workouts. Make no mistake, the NFL is a year-long job, especially for the guys trying to break onto full-time rosters. The 49ers put me up in a nice extended-stay hotel. My job is to get bigger, stronger and faster, smarter about playing the game in their system, running their plays. I appreciate the opportunity; guys are out there paying gym memberships, watching the NFL all the time, and here I am set up in some of the best facilities in the world, getting paid for it.

At the end of the year, after mandatory camps, summer practices, pre-season games, I get asked to sign on to the practice squad. Kind of like with the Jets, but the 49ers don't want anyone grabbing me off waivers. That can happen without their approval if you're on a practice squad roster only, so they offered me what's called an active roster contract. That tied me to the team, gave me more money. I loved it. I had a great off-season, was in an offense I loved with Jimmy Ray. Plus, he advocated for me. If you're not a top draft guy, you need someone in the ear of the head coach, of the front office, to keep your name in front of them.

It's surprising how important that is, a coach who has your back, talks you up in contract negotiations, saves a roster spot for you, gives you advice on how to stay on the team, has a football philosophy that requires your specific talents. At that level, everyone is so close in ability, size, speed. The difference between a 4.3 forty-yard dash, and a 4.5 sounds like a lot when they talk about it on draft day, but players know that it's more important to know where to go at the right time on the field, how to pull off a blocking scheme, pass protection packages. Hell, it's even showing up for stuff on time, being squared away, attention to details. If you get a coach who looks at forty times, you're never going to get the best team. All the pieces need to fit, and there's a million moving parts. Belechick is so good at putting the pieces in place, he's won a bunch of Super Bowls. Not only knowing what job needs to be done on the field at the time and place, and not only getting everyone in the right place at the right time to do the right job but finding people with that specific skill set to be in that place at that time (and squeezing them into a salary cap). He doesn't need the fastest, the strongest. He looks for the smartest, the players who buy into the system, who know how to be in the right place at the right time.

My talents were comparable to almost all the running backs I competed with for a job in the NFL. Maybe a half step slower, maybe not. Maybe better hands, vision, a sense of the game. Maybe not. I wasn't a marquee name.

But I'd put my work ethic, my comradery as a teammate and understanding of the systems, up against anybody I played with or against. My life experiences and the coaches I played under molded me into that kind of player who happened to have NFL-level talent.

That set of soft skills buys you nothing in the NFL if the head coach and general manager don't see it or value it. Or they think they can teach it to just anyone.

. . . .

Mike Singletary got hired in San Francisco to replace Mike Nolan halfway through the 2008 season. He was an assistant in San Francisco before that. He took over end of October as the interim head coach, turned the team around, and the media loved it, tough coach makes all the right moves. At that time, I was in a New York Jets uniform. Jimmy Raye moved from the Jets running backs coach to the 49ers offensive coordinator.

I sign with the 49ers in January of 2010 after my Jets practice squad contract ends, escaping Tampa to reunite with Coach Raye. I work and travel with the team all that season. Coach Raye is my mentor and my patron. He watches out for me, and I start to get comfortable, feel like I have a place in his offense. I knew he'd advocate for me, knew I could go to him with problems, issues. But Singletary wasn't much of a head coach, very full of himself, disorganized, just didn't match up to what a head coach needs to be. I figured he wasn't long for the job.

Before we go to London for the game against Denver (only our second win the first half of the season), Raye gets fired. I knew something had to happen, with all the losing, and Singletary saw Coach Raye as the weakest link, the easiest to sacrifice. I didn't like that, of course. Coach Raye was praised the year before because of what he did with the offense after a bunch of injuries. Now he's getting tossed out to save Singletary's job.

I reach out to Coach Raye before we leave for London, tell him how much I appreciate his support, all that. I felt like he set me up to be successful in San Francisco, gave me reps, got me on the field, left me with an opportunity to showcase what I can do for a team. I was grateful. But the last thing he said to me was, "Be careful there, Jehuu. I'm not there to protect you, and I don't have any idea what direction they want to go."

That got me thinking. I said my goodbyes, but something as ominous as that can't be ignored.

In October 2010 we fly directly from the Carolina Panthers game to London to play the Denver Broncos for the NFL's annual game in Wembley Stadium. It's a treat for guys like me who get to travel but probably won't play; still have to be game-ready being active on the roster, but game-day prep is a lighter version of what the starters have to go through. A chance to fly overseas and check out a different culture, on the tab of the 49ers.

We're 1-6. Tension seeps into everything the team does, roster players, starters, practice squad. San Francisco is used to winning. Fans won't stand for all this losing. Neither will ownership.

British fans don't have a real clue what was happening, prompted by the Jumbotron on how to respond to what happens on the field. Big pass play, CHEER! flashes on the screen. The crowd cheers. When the cameras pan the crowd, the big screen says, WAVE YOUR FLAG! We watch where the cameras go by the crowd response, who's waving which team flag. The delay between the play on the field and the response is funny, as fans get instructions on how to act.

The NFL put us up for ten days or so, a plush resort just thirty miles outside the city. One of my best memories of the NFL. A bunch of us hook up with this gypsy cab driver one night on a trip into downtown London. He chauffeurs us around all week. Gets us when we call, drops us off at the resort safely every night. Keeps us out of the touristy spots, leads us to the best pubs and clubs. Our own personal driver and chaperone. He makes sure we stay out of the bad parts of the city. Lots of that there, soccer hooligans who'd love to take out an American footballer.

. . . .

Just back from London I feel pretty good. It's our bye week, the NFL giving you a week off after international travel. I'm to and from practice, meetings, film, the weight room. I feel part of this team, like I belong. I got an apartment, got a bunch of furniture, my vehicle, putting down a few roots in the area.

Early November I go to a bar, meet a nice girl, take down a phone number, plan a date. A professional football player, doing what we do.

Tuesday of bye week is a day off, but I go into the complex for a workout. I'm at my locker, toweling off in my wears when one of our scouts comes up, "Hey Jehuu, coach wants to see you."

I shrug, "Okay, let me throw on some clothes."

"Nah", he says, "Now."

"Now? In my draws?"

"Yeah. Throw on a towel."

Good news or bad news?

Obviously it's bad. *Hey, we're releasing you, going in a different direction*, etcetera etcetera. You don't listen much past, We're letting you go, it's all the same I n the end, the usual speech when they have a player they like better than you.

319

I shrug, "Okay". Go down to the locker room to finally put on some clothes, and my stuff is already packed, in a bag, ready to go. Like the equipment guys were waiting for me to move away from the locker. It's probably why they call you out in your underwear, so you're not in their gear when you leave the building.

Keep moving Jehuu, keep moving.

38

Jehuu, Buffalo Bills

Jehuu on the Buffalo Bills

- November 20th, 2010: Picked up off waivers from San Francisco 49ers.
- November 20th, 2010: Signed to practice squad contract.
- November 28th, 2010: Signed to full 53-man contract
- September 3rd, 2011: Cut from full roster.

MY AGENT CALLS, four o'clock in the afternoon, "Did you get a call yet?"

I'm in San Francisco with an apartment full of furniture, my truck, all my clothes and things, no family on the West Coast, a phone number for a girl, and no job.

"What? No, I haven't heard a thing. Should I?"

"Hang on," he clicks off the phone.

Hang on? To what? What am I hanging on to? Five minutes later the prefix on my phone is seven-one-six. Just like March of '08. Seven-one-six. Buffalo area. *Holy shit.* It's either someone from home who heard about me being put on the waiver wire, or it's…

A country drawl on the other side of the line, "Hello. Is this Jehuu?"

"Yes, sir. It is." I can't figure who's calling, can't place that drawl.

"Son, this is Buddy Nix from the Buffalo Bills." Buddy Nix is the General Manager of the Bills, I know that right away. My head thumps, the way it does when you score a touchdown, the way mine did when Coach Smith put me back on offense at Michigan State.

"Oh, hey Mr. Nix. What's up?" *What's up?* I have a way with words around important people.

"Jehuu, we'd like to bring you home." He says the word I was hoping to hear.

I pause for less than a heartbeat, "Yes, sir. I'd like to come home."

· · · ·

Back to Western New York.

Mr. Nix's call was at 4 p.m. west coast. They got me on a flight at 7:30 p.m. out of San Francisco airport. That's less than three hours to end one chapter and start another, the logistics of changing direction that fast dazzles me. There's no one to call to help me pull off the move.

But I have a number on a piece of paper.

I call the girl I met the night before, barely know her name. She answers on the second ring. "Hey, you know how we were going to have dinner tonight? Well, change of plans, I just got fired."

Instead of asking her to a dinner we talked about the night before, I see if she'll drive me to the airport. It's about as awkward a conversation as you can have, and my good luck, she agrees. I pack a quick carry-on bag and she picks me up. On the ride to SFO, I say, "By the way, these are the keys to my apartment, and these are my car keys. Could you pack my stuff up because the moving company is coming to get it?"

She agrees to that too, this girl I don't even know. She has access to everything in my apartment, to the truck I've been driving around town, to everything I own in California. The situation is pretty surreal.

I fly through the night, one layover. Arrive at Buffalo airport at 6 a.m. (3 a.m. my time), go right to the Bills practice facility. By 7:30 a.m., I'm in uniform getting ready for practice. A week later the starting fullback gets hurt, and I'm signed to the full fifty-three-man roster. The life of an NFL practice squad player –one day you're in London watching the Jumbotron tell the fans when to cheer, the next you're in San Francisco running dummy plays from the opposing team, the next week you're across the country on the sidelines in full uniform in Buffalo, New York. It was the best break I ever got in the NFL. Fortunately cut from San Francisco, fortunately brought onto a roster in my home state, got there when another player in my exact position was injured.

Ready to run!

The whims of people who control your fate, the luck, the consequences of perseverance aren't lost on me. The number of twists and turns in my life, both my lives, so vastly different as to not be the life of the same person, that bring me to places, with the right people at the right time, can't be luck, can't be chance only.

Has to be God-sent, fate, providence.

. . . .

I play professional football for one season with the Bills.

In some short yardage packages, the back-up fullback. Ryan Fitzpatrick is our quarterback; he's popular and hot at the beginning of the season. We're winning games. There is no other place in the league like Buffalo when you're winning games. The atmosphere of that corner of New York State changes. The air is lighter, easier to breathe, the coming winter months not nearly so ominous. I remember that from my Clymer life, and now I get to be part of it.

Fred Jackson takes me under his wing. I've been lucky as a pro, had a few mentors that spent time with me, showed me some ropes. With the Jets, it was Tony Richardson, seventeen-year vet, a fullback. He's a Jimmy Raye player, like me. He showed me a lot, helped me think like a professional athlete.

Fred is that mentor on the Bills, shows me how to play the game, how to recover from a shitty practice, how to act, what to expect. Football is a lot easier when there are no surprises, from on-field play calls, to contract stuff, to understanding what your coaches want from you. Jackson had a great feel for the locker room and the staff. He used to tell me all the time about his journey, in and out of rosters, try-outs, locker rooms.

When they brought in C.J. Spiller to replace him, the way he handled it sent me a message that I'll use for the rest of my life. He took the whole thing as a positive in his career, a challenge. He basically said, *Okay, now my agenda is all set, my job description is defined. My every rep in the weight room, the training room, the locker room, and on the field is to make my coaches know that I'm a great option in the offense. That they can hand me the ball and get what the team needs. That I am far too valuable to blink at when it comes contract time.*

Fred Jackson is a consummate Buffalo Bill. Coaches couldn't get rid of him, too valuable. Played eight seasons with the Bills,

2007-2014, 10,000 yards, 350 receptions, made it to the playoffs after that brutal Buffalo drought.

As important, especially in Buffalo, fans loved him, loved his effort, his dedication. You say his name to a real Bills fan and their eyes light up; they remember him running downhill, hard first-down yards, stiff-arms, staying in-bounds, picking up a blitz with abandon and disregard for his personal well-being. He was a great model to show an interest in me as a football player, as a person.

I was in the running backs room with some of the most professional guys to ever play the game, guys who bled perseverance and longevity. They were hard workers. For every guy with preternatural talent I played with and against (Duckett, Javon, Mike Hart, Spiller, Marshawn Lynch), I got to spend valuable time with guys like Frank Gore in San Francisco, Richardson in New York, and Jackson in Buffalo.

You think those guys can't teach you something? In a sport where the average career is 3.3 years, a running back is 2.57. Tony Richardson, sixteen years, Fred Jackson, ten plus, Frank Gore is probably still running (sixteen). I think of myself as a player like them, just not with all the breaks you need to be a full-time professional football player, some of the talent, missing the "right place at the right time" piece.

When anyone thinks of those guys, they see toughness. Every team they played on tried to find a better player, a better runner, and couldn't. The ones that did, ended up with guys who lasted 2.57 years, while these guys kept making rosters. Guys like that can teach you everything these is to know about playing in the NFL?

. . . .

I play special teams for the Bills, great to be on the field. I'm the off-returner on kickoffs. A kick falls short or they kick away from our big threat (in this case it's C.J. Spiller, a speed demon), I get to run the ball.

My big play was against the Jets, my old team. I knew the coach there; I knew all those guys on the team. I'm shooting the shit with them before the game, and they're saying, *Oh, you're on kick return? Get ready for one.*

Sure enough, first quarter it's a bloop kick to me, they're trying to keep it away from C.J., they take their chances kicking it to me. Made 'em pay with a big return.

The Bills special teams coach comes up to me after the season, "Jehuu, you ended up top five in the league for kick returns." He's smiling.

"What the hell?"

"Yeah, average. Two returns, 36 yards."

I laugh at him, "How 'bout we don't mention the two, just the average."

39
Jehuu

September 2011 the Bills cut me, and I stopped loving football.. That was enough for me.

The Green Bay Packers call that Fall, the one where I take the game off for the first time since eighth grade. I see the Wisconsin area code, and I guess right. I knew they were interested. They want me to come in and work out. I call my agent, and we hash a few things out. I've been in professional football for five years. The process, the practice squads, the uncertainty, in and out of contracts, cuts and waivers, it was more than I wanted to take on. The game within the game was too daunting this time.

I decline their offer, go back to the first tee box with a few beers in a cooler and don't really regret the decision not to play.

But the guys, the locker rooms, all that. You'll hear a hundred guys say they miss it. It's a cliché. But they're clichés for a reason. Because more often than not, they're true.

It's a hard thing to be a professional athlete, all that ability wrapped up in pride and physical arrogance, and you get a call from someone who wants you, YOU, not somebody else. They want to pay you good money, and you tell them no. You've had enough. Especially when you're only twenty-six years old. I get why guys keep coming back.

But, nah, not for me. Every second I touched a football past 2007 was one touch I never expected to get. Not when I first ran the ball at Clymer High School as an eighth grader. Not when I played for a state championship in 2005. Not when I caught a 35-yarder and beat Northwestern. Not when I got my diploma from Michigan State. I felt I'd run the course of trying to be a professional athlete.

And certainly not when I kicked a soccer ball into a mango forest in Western Africa and got lost. Every snap I played was a bonus in an improbable life, one I respected and cherished. Quitting the game wasn't all that hard.

40

Liberia

THE PATTERN WAS predictable, but only as seen in a historical context.

When you were in the middle of it, it was perfectly acceptable, naturally occurring, unless you had perspective, unless you could truly see.

It mirrored African history in general, Liberia more specifically, the phenomenon of rebellion, the unfulfilled promise of liberation. As Liberian history swept horrific from Tolbert to Doe, Doe to Taylor, so did Taylor's rebels mutate from emancipators, to skeptics, to murderers and rapists. It was the same in village after village as Taylor's army moved from north to south, making their way down and across Liberia, mountains to the coast, toward inevitable conflict with government forces and combatant warlords in and around Monrovia. That pattern repeated itself over months and miles until there was no other way to view the coming of Taylor's rebels than scorched earth and piled bodies.

How many stories of liberation were followed by atrocity? How many times was relief at the lifting of the hand of the tyrant Doe transformed into the fist of Taylor and his soldiers, his Small Boys Unit.

In that path was the town of Harbel, home of the Firestone rubber plantation.

41

A Child Soldier

"Taylor was like an eagle. He'd come at you with his claws
hidden, until he wanted to take them out."
— *Michael Mulbah Sr. Liberian Warlord*

TODAY, GHOST TAKES the coke but no Heroin and no jungle juice.

His senses are peaked – he smells the other boys like they are him, he sees through canvas sides of the tent, he hears the heavy boots of the officers shuffle in mud. When handed the needle, he squirts out the smack. When the bottle is passed to him, he pours out the juice. He snorts once, one line only. His body craves more, always more, but he resists, dulls his cravings and let the cocaine take hold of his senses.

Cocaine perks his ears, widens his sight, tingles his fingers, and hardens his back. Sounds print loud in his ears, the world brightens until he has to squint down the clarity. The heroin sometimes makes you crazy, the juice makes you slow and blurry, a soft warm blanket over the brain. He smells the rot of bodies and decay of the bush. Oil leaking from a car, an old station wagon with wood panels and rust where metal should be, the sweat on his cadre, Wonlay who is Chaos, Gabriel now Bug, Dawood, who they call Crow, all the others. Ghost knows all the names, both born-names from before, and magic-names. Names can be power. Knowing them all is a weapon.

"Point weapons to the outside," he calls down the line. "Tell them." The patrol grumbles but obeys.

"Do that," says the Command Sargent riding up front in the truck, sitting on top of the cab facing backwards toward his troops. He sends Ghost a look, a message, *I'm the boss here. I give the orders.* But he says, "Yes, you all, *eh.* Point guns to the outside. Be ready for the ambush."

Ghost knows weapons get heavy, a raised weapon droops in the arms of the smaller boys. AKs are hard, bulky, and heavy for the new recruits, when the truck hits a hole and bounces, anything can happen with a live weapon. Fingers twitch when you're full of the heroin, the juice and the lust, when you're lazy and crazy. When you point your AK outside the truck, and the finger spasms, nobody inside gets shot. It takes longer to raise a weapon and shoot than to lower one; he'll have more time to react if one of the boys goes crazy. It's happened before, boys settle a grudge, boys see things that aren't there.

"Stay wake all you," says Command Sargent because he needs to say something. "Watch out for the ambush!" Ghost knows there's no ambush; the truck moves too fast along the potted road. He keeps his face impassive as he scans the faces of his patrol. Boys snicker. The air passing over Ghost's body as the truck barrels along would feel good if it wasn't filled with foul smells, insects, heavy heat, potash fires in the bush beside the dusty road, decay, sweat, shit, bad breath, and fear. The reek leaks off the boys in the truck bed, fourteen of them, about six too many. The Liberian heat is on top of them, held down by a cloud cover. The patrol passes close enough to the coast to feel fish and beach, smells foreign to Ghost from the mountains.

They are headed for Firestone and the start of Operation Octopus.

All hail, Liberia, hail! (All hail!)
All hail, Liberia, hail! (All hail!)
In union strong success is sure. We cannot fail!
With God above, Our rights to prove, We will o'er all prevail, We will o'er all prevail!
With heart and hand our country's cause defending, We'll meet the foe with valor unpretending.
Long live Liberia, happy land! A home of glorious liberty, By God's command!
A home of glorious liberty, By God's command!

Liberian National Anthem (Part 3)

BOOK 3
TWO BOYS, ONE HERE, ONE THERE

Prologue

Liberia 1992

THERE WAS NO more reason for war, except in the minds and egos of a few bad actors.

The assassination of Samuel Doe in September of 1990 should have ended the second Liberian Civil War. His despotic reign was, after all, the driving force for the birth of Taylor's NPFL and Johnson's ULIMO armies. A nation has the right to protect its people from a tyrant, and the world tends to embrace violence for liberation.

When Doe was removed, Amos Sawyer was installed as the interim president of Liberia, until fair elections could be mounted. His claim to the position wasn't built on blood. He had a legitimacy that Taylor and Johnson didn't. He was voted into office by 35 different leaders representing seven political parties and eleven interest groups. His ratification should have quelled the violence, placated the masses, began at least the semblance of an era of governmental normalcy. Liberia should have paused and began to spend its resources on rebuilding. It should have rejoiced that the efforts of the rebellion was successful. Taylor and all the other warring factions should have worked on peace instead of war.

They didn't.

Ghost

Civil war has gnashed at Liberia now for what feels like forever in spasms of carnage.

Everything is scattered and loose. There's no reason to what we do, no schedule to the time or place of our violence. We just kill people here, rape girls there, burn down a house, leave the next one, a misty haze of ruined bodies and blood and bullets and drugs.

Kill, sleep, take the needle. Kill, sleep again.

What's it like for people trying to live a life, eat, drink, rest in peace? They don't know who drops bombs, government or rebels. They don't see which warlord sends murderers to their neighborhood. Is it Mosquito or his absurd arch-enemy Mosquito-killer? Is it Chuck Norris or maybe Rambo? They don't know Krahn soldiers from Kru, Bassa separatists from Mano warriors. This guerilla war, revolution, is a deadly match, back and forth, back and forth. People just try to see a path to tomorrow; they don't know war, so they don't take sides. Who has time or energy? When white trucks come, filled with wild eyes and black fingers turned white on triggers, they hide like everyone else. We might as well be them. They, us.

The bullet doesn't pick and choose.

But October blooms different. The start of Fall was all training, hard days of starvation and muscles burning from work. March, run, shoot, run some more. In and out of the creeks and rivers around the plantation. Into the ocean, hold weapons high. Fire AKs into the vast sea, run and fire again.

Waste of bullets.

After training came relaxing, a calm before a storm, an eye of a hurricane. You could feel it if you knew where to touch. Early one morning, with the African sun touching the horizon, hazy and hungover, the troops gather up. My troops pour out sweat before we even load weapons onto backs, AKs, mortars, extra ammo. Boys leak noxious oil from a solid week of parties, of lazy days playing football in Firestone fields, of chase and knock-foot, of cleaning weapons while music plays and food is easy, plenty jungle juice and weed.

Now, with eyes rubbed red, faces slack, arms drooping under weapons, we gather in force. All the Small Boys Units united in the same place, aimed at the same target. We flick bugs off scabbed skin, adjust charms, tug at wet clothes. Officers smile, pass needles, and blow and jungle juice. They are friendly. *Yes, Suh! Thank you, Suh!*

Pile into trucks, stinking of alcohol and sweat. Heat dampens any breeze that might blow us clean. We're dropped at the edge water of swamps that border the city, Monrovia. A fetid haze rises off the bog and mixes with human waste to create a lurid mist. Today, will be a graduate course on kids exercising the ambition of bad men. It will be pitiless and sadistic and unnecessary.

Small Boys Unit fight today. *Warriors of Liberia!* A battle cry for an October morning. *Dat city, it's yours, eh!*

This field is home. I suck the menace from the air, take it into my lungs, and hold it there to eat me from the inside. I soak up sweat. I'm alive when muscles scream for rest. One more step, one more scar.

You don't die when you're home, someone else does.

. . . .

Officers tell us it will be easy, in their camos and berets, faces painted tight with green horror.

They lie.

I see when they hunch up, hearing a gun *pop*. The corners of mouths quiver. Eyes bounce from the far side of the swamp, back to this side where we form into our squads. Their hands jump when something flicks in the swamp, a splash before the slushy mire settles. The way they slap at mosquitos too hard. They cover us with white paste and face paint. Crust forms around mouths and noses as they share false talismans in loud voices.

They tell us that this battle will be easy, that the city is ready for us to walk in and take – houses, riches, money, and women. Mostly, they tell us that once this assault is over, we will eat every single day, and have all the jungle juice we can drink. We have plenty of drugs, more jungle juice mixed with gunpowder, more needles full of sick-looking, cut-up heroin, snort-powder. Hunger is a more powerful motivator than glory, thirst even better. Boys will run through brick walls if thirsty enough, through a swamp for a sip of water.

One man chants with his troops, a warlord hymn. Another burns crosses into young skin with a branding iron heated by a cook-fire, the boys barely feel the torch, so amped up; but they smell the scorched meat of their own flesh. It smells like food.

Another, a warlord called Butt-Naked sacrifices a little girl he dragged to the swamp. She lies on her little belly, and they cut her open from the back. They squat and each takes a piece of her heart. They've done this before many battles, tradition, black magic for today's battle.

Young and strong and fearless and numb, the Small Boys Unit. But many of us will die this morning, despite what officers tell us.

This I know.

The capital is on the horizon, past the marshland. No buildings where the troops stage, it's all swamp. No people live in swamps. But animals do – terrifying beasts, prehistoric, scales and stingers, and teeth. The swamp churns and sizzles. The skyline of Monrovia looks close, but it's not. This will be a long run.

We stand in a thicket of brush taller than us. Transport trucks are gone. Somewhere a few weapons *pop pop pop*, nervous ticks of trigger fingers. From across the swamp, glints of steel in the rising sun. People know we're here, the forces protecting the city; government, ECOMOG. A thousand kids swarm, dance, nervous feet. A boy pees in the brush, another staggers to his knees in the heat. *Crack crack, pop pop*, echoes in the morning haze.

· · · ·

A hundred times I've done this drill. Been doing it since I was twelve and taken from my father's Jeep on the roadside out of the Wuteve mountains. High-step, lift your knees so plastic sandals clear the water, pump arms, keep your head up, hold your weapon in front, finger on the trigger guard, ready to drop the nose and fire. Nothing to it, your mind goes to another place. It's a running assault, this time through swamps. Heroin and coke are a warm-up. I look at boys bent over, hands on knees, heads bowed, panting. The ones who didn't prepare. Eyes roll back in their heads, they lick lips, let out whoops and cries, twitch and scratch.

High knees, pump arms, get to the other side.

Run Hope, run.

Those buildings, a city of riches.

The churned swamp, torn and broiling.

The smell of sweat, men pushed, boys afraid that their bodies will fail.

The *pop* and *crack* of guns, of human sinew.

Run Ghost.

Run!

Liberia

Here's Ghost. Ammo bands cinched around slim, scarred shoulders. He breathes through his nose, mouth closed against riotous bugs that swarm the swamp. The swamp is deep-murky, filled to bursting from the annual run-up to monsoon season in Liberia.

Clymer

Here's Jehuu at a low desk in an American third grade classroom (kindergarten was a Liberian school, first and second grade was the African bush or a refugee camp). Halloween is a few weeks away, then Thanksgiving, the start of winter, first snow, Christmas. Liberia is far away, but not so far he can't remember. Kids here are not the kids he left. For starters, these kids are all white, all of them. Dressed in warm clothes, the seasons tell them what to wear. Not like Liberia, where people wear mostly the same because it's so, so hot all the time.

Liberia

Here's Hope running through a swamp. Side-by-side with Small Boys Unit, attacking Monrovia, dodging death on the first day of a military assault, playing a part in something called Operation Octopus. How did he get here, Hope from the Wuteve mountains?

Here's Ghost and ten-thousand kids who should be in a classroom, learning their letters, their sums. Instead, they're the first, most expendable wave in the opening salvo of a hundred-twenty-day siege of the capital city of Liberia.

The manic savagery of these child soldiers will haunt Liberians and Western Africa to the present day.

Clymer

Here's Jehuu when the school bell rings. He leaps from his desk, grabs his pack and jacket from the coat closet just off the main classroom, bolts for the door.

"Slow down, Jehuu. We don't run inside."

He frowns, wipes his mouth with his sleeve. Feet dance in place. "Sorry, Mrs. Raven."

"It's okay. Just remember, you're in school now." His teacher smiles to show she understands. Mrs. Raven is Jehuu's first experience with American education. He says he tormented her that first year, when he tried so hard to calm down, to walk instead of run. She would more than likely agree.

School, right. The boy fast walks to the door, turns the corner into the hallway. His feet spin on the cold smooth tile as he darts into the light.

Liberia

Here's Ghost, the ersatz conqueror of Monrovia. The riches of victory forgotten. He's one of the only children to clear the swamp and enter the city. He snuck by the ECOMOG barricades at night, a real Ghost. He sits by the Ducor Hotel, bathed in swamp water, cement dust, and sadness. He wonders at a world filled with destruction, filled with death. He lets explosions wash over him, the noise drowning out thought, the carnage burying memories, creating a new reality for him, exhaustion, mental anguish he'll never relinquish. He knows from now until he ends, he'll wake every morning of his life and the first thing that will happen is he'll remember.

Clymer

Here's Jehuu at his new home. He bursts into the house like a bolt of lightning, knob barely turning before he kicks in the door. Backpack soars up the stairs, hits the second-floor landing. He pumps his fist on his way to the kitchen, a whirlwind, yanks on the refrigerator door, pulls a bottle of cold water off the inside shelf, slams the door shut, twists the top, tips it to his lips, never slowing momentum through the house. Cold liquid washes his throat, something unthinkable only two short months ago when water was as scarce as a soft bed. He crashes out the back door onto the porch, boots a soccer ball into the yard, flinging the empty bottle aside.

He chases life onto the freshly cut grass.

1

Liberia

BONITA CAULCRICK MAKES her daily journey to and from the American embassy in Monrovia.

When she and the kids arrive, lines at government buildings stretch around blocks; she's not the only parent scrambling for survival. She pleads with officials for a single stamp on a single document, only to receive endless red tape and denials. When buildings close for the day, the return trip to the house on Allison Street is just as harrowing.

Bonita brought some supplies from the United States to bribe and barter, a suitcase full of jeans and clothes. Grandma Joanna and Grandpa David do what they can to make her and the kids safe. They provide food and drink to exchange for anything their daughter and grandchildren might need, some currency to buy what can be bought. They secure passage from warlords known to the family. When their bus or van is pulled over, Bonita, Jehuu, and Mardea present their bona-fides and hope they are honored, hope they are presenting to sympathetic eyes. On more than one trip, the children travel alone, handed over to a friendly warlord and escorted to Monrovia to meet their mother.

But that eighty-eight-mile gauntlet affords opportunity for a lot of roadblocks and checkpoints, unscheduled and fluctuating, a moving target. Pop-up extortion, robbery, rape, and random slaughter is a constant condition of travel in Liberia. Moving north from Buchanan to Monrovia takes you through Kpelle, Do, Gola and Vai tribal territory. While those aren't the most notoriously dangerous clans in Liberia – that distinction belongs to the Kru and Krahn, and ECOMOG peacekeeping forces from Nigeria – any coordinated group with weapons and an attitude could be dangerous in and around the capital city. Anywhere two or more vehicles can move in and block a stretch of road, out of sight of the warring factions, is an opportunity to steal from travelers, settle old scores.

2

Bonita

Once you caught up with the kids at your mother's house, you went from Buchanan to Monrovia.

BC: Yes, I went to Monrovia to do the paperwork and come back and get them. But there were like thirty-five checkpoints within eighty-eight miles going from Buchanan to Monrovia. At every checkpoint, you had to stop, and get everybody out of this minivan that had probably ten or eleven people packed in it, and they take you to this room and search you, and then they interrogate you.

Did you say they had to be sponsored by a warlord to get through checkpoints?

BC: It was such a hassle to go to Monrovia to get them, so my mom was gonna bring them. She brought them to one of the warlords that she knew was a friend of the family that was able to get them to me.

Do you know how crazy that sounds to the average person? You had to hand your kids off to a warlord for a period of time?

BC: I know. It was a crazy place and a crazy time. We were desperate to get out of Liberia.

3

Jehuu

RIDING IS BETTER than walking.

We are small enough to sit on laps sometimes, so people don't mind letting us in their vans and trucks. Mardea and me want to ride with mum, but this time she is already in Monrovia. This time grandma puts us in a van with a man that looks mean, but he smiles at us, at Mardy more than me. He gives me Skittles. Mardea gets some berries.

"You kids stay with Tello here. Do not wander from the van. Do you understand?"

I look at Mardea. She squints at my candy. She will try to steal them, I know, so I stuff a handful in my mouth. Twist the top of the pack, put the rest in the pocket of my red shorts. I make a face full of candy at her. She scowls, and grandma grabs my arm hard. "Jehuu, did you hear me?"

I nod and rub my arm. Mardea smiles. Tello shakes a head full of Rasta braids.

4

Bonita

So, a warlord brought your kids to Monrovia?

BC: Yes. When they brought them to me, I was still working on getting them their paperwork because the embassy wasn't letting me just pack them up and take them until the paperwork was done here. So, they wanted me to come back to the States alone, send for the kids. I refused to do that because I hadn't heard from them for two years. And now that I found them I couldn't just walk away again. So, I told the embassy, "I found my children. You don't believe I'm here to rescue my own kids, even though they're listed on my own paperwork. If you check the paperwork, you'll see their names and ages. If you don't let me, take them, I'll leave them here, and you can take care of them. When you think the paperwork is complete, I'll send the plane tickets for them."

So, I said bye, and I'm walking away, and they're like, "Ma'am, come back."

I said, "Okay, but what do you want to do?"

They said, "Well, give us two weeks to call the United States and have them tell us everything is good."

I told them, "I'll give you one week." When I came back with them, they said it still wasn't good, so I said, now I'm staying here with you. I'm staying right in the embassy because I have nowhere else to go. I don't even know if I have a job to go back to because I've been here two and a half months. So they said, okay, let's see what we can do. They called and then it took another full day, and they finally granted me the visas.

I said, Okay now we can go.

5
Jehuu

WE LEFT GRANDMUM and grandpa back in the house on Allison Street, and met mum in the big city.

Mum says we're going to America. It doesn't look like it. It looks like we're going to sit in big, hot rooms and wait, forever. I'd rather be moving, running.

I lived in this city until I was six years old, when I moved to Firestone to live with mum and Thomah, then to Buchanan with Grandma and Grandpa and all those people. Seems like a long time ago. The smell of people too close, mixed with petrol and sewage, the smell that fills the air now, is different to me. I used to like the city. I don't know, *eh*? Before, people moved slow, going places, they smile and nod and rub a small boy's prickly head. Now, I'm nine years old, there's only hunched people who hurry and peer at you, scared faces. Nobody talks at you, nobody rubs your head.

We're back in the United States embassy. I've been here a lot, know how to get to the place myself. Turn here, up this road, left at the bombed-out store. Drive on clogged roads toward Antoinette Tubman Football Stadium, home of our Liberian footballers. There's no football now, no roadside stands of melon and casaba. Nobody sells cups of water or jewelry or good-luck charms. Everyone goes somewhere else.

The embassy is clean and cool. Mum and the man argue. She stands with her arms held out and palms up. "This my third time coming back tomorrow. Maybe there is no tomorrow for people. I'll leave them here, oh. They're safer with you because they are United States Citizens. I did the paperwork. I have it right here! Everybody leaves this city, why not my children? They might die out there in the world." Mama walks away from the man, me and Mardea hold hands, standing by a desk.

Mardy looks at me. "Where is she going," she whispers. "Is Mama leaving us?"

"No, she's not leaving," I say. "We just found her." But I'm not so sure, she looks like someone who goes away.

"Wait, lady! Come back here and get these children." The man stands beside his desk looking at us. He's plenty worried now. "Come back and we'll get you on your way."

Only then does Mama turn back. The man in the tie is sweating, his hands twitch. I watch close; Mama puts on her Mum-face, one hand on her jutted hip, her chin it stuck out, hair tossed., her face is shiny with sweat and worry. The man in the tie and brown shoes looks small.

"Okay, but what do you want to do?" she says. "Figure what to do. I'm not bringing them back to that place." With her other hand, mum fans herself with papers. The man in the tie flinches. Mum now like grandma, a Big Jue.

"Well, give us two weeks to call the United States and have them tell us everything is good. You can't be leaving these children." The man goes behind his desk and sits, but he doesn't help us. We just want to be going, get on a plane and leave. Why can't he understand? Why can't he sign papers? We're tired of walking all the time to the city and back. To refugee camps, through checkpoints, roadblocks.

6

Bonita

So what happens next? You finally get your paperwork in order.

BC: Finally, the man signs us on. He doesn't know what to do with the children, so he signs us on. It was that easy for him. They said, now you have to go, do all your medical for the kids.

Monrovia was still relatively civilized at that time? By October it was a very bad place.

BC: You could get around Monrovia a little bit. I remember the doctor's office was close to the executive mansion. It was close to Sinkor on the main road. It was one of the few places that was doing travel exams.

7

Jehuu

I HAVE A sucker.

It's red and candy-sweet. Mardea has one too, hers is green. I wonder if I'd like green better. I frown at her, "Can I try?"

She looks at me. Shakes her head. "This one's mine and I don't want your mouth on it. Just eat yours."

We're in a waiting room. Going to see a doctor. Mum says he won't poke us with a needle, just look in our ears and eyes and throat. I'm not so sure. Doctors are not something I know since the war started. We stood in some lines at refugee camps, outside tents, and peoples checked our hair and scabs and bruises. Been a long time since I waited to see a doctor in a building.

Mum sits beside us, she was writing on papers, but now she's reading. I go back to work on my sucker, legs swinging under the high chair.

There were no suckers on the long walk. There was barely water some days. You had to learn how to find food, and make it last. Odziki's peanut butter jar was with us for almost a whole week. Every night we found a place to drop blankets, sometimes in a camp tent, behind the red cross, some times in a bush clearing. Once or twice I slept in a tree, if I could find a branch wide enough. Any time we could get off the ground, we did. There's bugs and snakes on the ground.

"Kids, come sit close to me." Mum holds the paper away from her, like it's hot. She huffs once, shoulders move up and down. Her

353

foot taps the floor in a patter rhythm. Her eyes look puffy. "Come close Jehuu, Mardea." We're already close, but her eyes, her voice make us slip in tight next to her. "Your papa. In Sierra Leone. He's been killed."

Just like that. I try to see his face, his clothes or body in my mind. It's hard because I was so young when he had to leave, and when we had to get rid of all his pictures. I can't see a face, it's just a feel in my brain that was there, and now it's gone. Mardea holds my hand. Mum cries softly into her hands, right there in the waiting room. Right there is where my father is finally, totally gone.

8

Bonita

That's when you found out the kid's father was assassinated?

BC: Sitting in the doctor's office was when I found a newspaper. It says five-hundred Liberians killed in Sierra Leone. So, I took the paper, and I don't know why, but I was scanning down the names. They had two-hundred-fifty of the five-hundred names, the other half were not identified. At the end of this column, there was the name Jerome. Then you had to go to the top of the column to continue, and they had his last name. I was like, Oh my God.

Did you tell the kids?

BC: Yes. I don't know why I was looking for that except I remember somebody saying they saw him in Sierra Leone. And then I told the kids and ooh, yeah, while we were waiting in a doctor's office for them to get their medical exam for travel.

9

Jehuu

LEAVING MONROVIA IS a relief, even though I just found out that my dad is dead.

I haven't seen him in years, can barely remember him, but it's still losing a dad you expected to see again someday, something promised. There's a sadness that touches the edges of my mind; it weaves with and expands the blanket of loss that covers me.

But there isn't time to think, to remember. We have to move on, before something bad happens, before the war catches us.

The Ivory Coast airport is another walk. This time, mum holds my hand and whispers in my ear. We are stronger for our two years on the road, older. We know how to find water and food, beg or buy when possible. We cover more miles in a day, but we're so tired in the mind, oh. Knowing my dad is dead takes energy.

These roads we walk to escape Liberia go north, away from the ocean. No more sea-smells mixed with dead and decay and potash fires. Emerging from mangroves into the vast prairies and barren foothills is eye-opening, a horizon to see, an enormity to the world, stretching into infinity. Nowhere to hide, nothing borders roads, no bush, no trees. If cars, trucks, or soldier convoys come, we have to shrink to the side of the road and hope, hope they are in a rush to be someplace else, no time to see us, ask questions, see papers. Always the white pick-up trucks with soldiers, always the children with dead, red eyes, excited and alive, or dreamy asleep. They wear their costumes to disguise –in case they are held to account for what they do in the war – long coats, dresses, and scarves. Almost funny, the clothes, painted bodies, hats, and jewelry, but also there are blood stains. Where they come from? They are dried brick color, crusty, flaking off skin and shirts and pants.

I worry my little statue in my hands, keep it hidden. I remember the glassy, dirty boy who wanted Odziki's peanut butter. I don't want them to know I have anything worth taking. I want to be small, invisible.

I don't want to be a soldier anymore.

A clock ticks, a race you have to win. The closer we get to the coast, to the airport across the border, the more nervous we are, hoping they don't latch on you by the side of a road or stop the car you hitched, shoot the tires, shoot the doors.

We come to the line at the Sierra Leone border. Cars, people, trucks, old men, old women. Kids like me along the road. Not one able-bodied man or woman, all being used up. Mum is different; she is young and pretty and vital. We have to be careful no one notices her. Cars packed with suitcases, bags, some dragging a goat or sheep, some animals in cages on top. Lines that are days long to get to the border with hot, thirsty, hungry people coated in sweat and fear. Nowhere to bathroom except the side of the road. Nowhere to put your stuff, nowhere to lay your head.

10

Bonita

When the kids finally cleared, did you go straight to the Ivory Coast, or did you go back to Buchanan to your parents?

BC: From there, we got our paperwork, and we left, and we went to the Ivory Coast. We had to travel by road. This time it was even harder to go that direction because there were all these refugees just waiting to go to that place. We had to wait for transportation at night. Then we had to cross checkpoints going in that direction. This was August, right around Jehuu's birthday.

Where did you stay in the Ivory Coast?

BC: I stayed at a hotel.

What about Monrovia when you were waiting for the paperwork? Did you have a place?

BC: In Monrovia, I stayed with a friend in one of our houses. My family had a house right there in Paynesville. It was next to the football stadium, where we stayed before we went to Firestone.

How long was the trip to Ivory Coast?

BC: Taylor's forces were focused heavily on Monrovia, in the southern part of the country. That left a hole in the northern checkpoints and border guards, that we slipped through. We traveled on the road, and it took us like a week, just the three of us. And the cars would just stop, and everybody would rest up and then get going again. After the kids left, my mom tried to come say goodbye, but she couldn't get there. She had to turn around and go back. Mom and pop got out, but it was later. They wanted to stay in Liberia, but things got so bad they had to go.

We found out later that Taylor's forces spent the month softening up the suburbs of Monrovia, in Buchanan, especially from their southern base in Harbel, Paynesville, where we used to live with Thomah. He launched other attacks from Gbarna, his capital through Chocolate City, from the north down into New Georgia and Logan Town. A lot of raids had to pass right by Allison Street, trying to squeeze Monrovia into the Atlantic Ocean in the west.

You realize you got out just in time. Another few weeks and it wouldn't have worked.

BC: Yes. We got out just in time. In Ivory Coast, we had to wait for a flight for quite a while because we got here, in the U.S., on September 5th.

11

Liberia

THE INVASION OF Southeast Liberia by Taylor's NPFL was a practice in cluster-fucking a country.

If was one of the most tragic and homicidal parades in the history of mankind with murder, rape, and torture. As rebels, government forces, and opportunistic well-armed warlords competed for prized real estate in and around Monrovia, they took turns perpetrating horrific atrocities on Liberians who had nothing to do with the war, the innocent, the citizens who were supposed to benefit from rebellion. People, property, valuables, and resources were up for grabs. There were no good guys, no place to turn for safety, much less justice; right and wrong are immaterial when you're running for your life, a band-aid on a gunshot wound.

Rebels take control of a Monrovian suburb. They rape, kill, and purge it of rivals. They take what they can carry and burn the rest. Government forces retake the same suburb, purge more, punish rebel sympathizers, burn the rest. The cycle repeats itself daily. If you aren't in one army or the other, you're either "recruited and trained", or you become a refugee.

In order to survive this revolving massacre, you have to become very good at recognizing who's coming down the street looking for spoils. People who last in the neighborhoods keep different colored clothes handy, prepared to change colors and sides in an instant. Men kept removable tattoos for both the Krahn and Bassa tribes, they switch ink to placate whoever comes with rifles and machetes.

Survival instincts kick in for the vast majority of Liberians, creating ways to survive day by day.

. . . .

Survival is a strict and unapologetic task-master. It doesn't allow mistakes. Anger is smothered by fear, righteousness by pissing in your pants in the face of extinction. Outrage is a luxury. Complicated theories of morality and fairness are untaught chapters in the book of life, ignored in the face of hunger and thirst. This was the fate of Liberians for their civil wars. Nowhere was it more evident than in the popular pro-Taylor election slogan, *You killed my ma, you killed my pa. I vote for you anyways.*

But there's a hint of insubordinate jesting attitude, isn't there? A shrug sense of fatalism that says, do what you need to, we'll go on living.

Morality suffocates, surrenders the high ground to the realist. No philosophy can outrun the bullet or dull the machete. When your president says he can murder someone on a public street and get away with it, people laugh.

Liberians shudder.

The people of Liberia have a low, low bar for how they expect to be treated by their rulers, whoever holds the most weapons at any given time. It's seated in their DNA, and it's what allows them to be taken advantage of. It's the way of their world, the guns get the resources of their country, the people get the spoils. There is a coup, a "rebellion" representing the will of the people, and the next despot steps up and changes nothing; Meet the new boss, same as the old boss. People go about the business of living. Makes it hard for Americans to understand them. The luxury of outrage, the reality of helplessness, the acceptance of a life imposed on you via impenetrable violence; that's the providence of many Africans.

. . . .

In West Africa, the major resources are universally valuable – diamonds, timber, minerals, and slaves to exploit.

In Liberia, it means all that, and it means rubber.

In 1926, the Liberian government leased to the Firestone Corporation of the United States a million acres of hevea brasiliensis for six cents an acre for ninety-nine years. Firestone's rubber farm became a share-cropping plantation in the sheep's cloth of a United States enterprise abroad. They claimed to be partners with Liberia in their commercial exertion to grab all the rubber possible from the country and sell it to the world.

Firestone propagandists worked hard to make sure that wasn't the global perception. They hired a thousand Liberians and gave them lives they probably couldn't have had otherwise – lives with food and homes, security, and consistent work. They shared a reasonable portion of their profits with their Liberian workers, promoted enough talented indigenous populace to demonstrate their entrepreneurial, philanthropic integrity.

Harvey Firestone, being one hundred percent capitalist, made sure the partnership was a one-way relationship. Firestone workers enjoyed their house-boys, their cleaning women, their butlers. Slavery isn't always service and life under the thumb of physical manacles and threat of physical punishment. As often, it's lording opportunity and resources. (Africa has no ground to stand on in the courts of morality when it comes to slavery. Governmental, tribal, cultural, and caste slavery is their bailiwick. They are very, very good at it.) With Firestone, they once again sold out their population, this time to a different and more benevolent master; but a master just the same.

This is evident to anyone who doesn't use capitalism to rationalize policy. The Liberian government vended the Firestone Corporation a license to appropriate resources and set up a haven of opportunistic semi-slavery, designed to profit a few and not the many. Instead of working to deliver a rubber product to the world, and ensure domestic financial security for generations of Liberians, they sold the trees, sold the labor, and kept a meager profit for themselves. Tolbert's and Doe's ambitious but lazy governments used those profits to advance their individual interests.

HARBEL was the name of the new plantation in Liberia – named after Harvey and (his wife) Belle Firestone; a planation built a few miles south of Monrovia, in a thick forest of rubber trees, centered between the ports in Monrovia and Buchannan on the Atlantic Ocean. Firestone owned access to a port for shipment, eight million rubber trees to harvest, and an oasis of tropical property to play in. American executives enjoyed an eighteen-hole golf course, some of the best fishing in the world, boat clubs, and ocean bay docks all within walking distance of their opulent homes.

12

Jehuu

"MAMA, I DON'T feel too good."

"You ate way too much Jehuu."

She's right, I ate so much it hurts. I ate for every day I went hungry. I ate for the kids in my country still starving. Mostly I ate because I could. Sugar, eggs, carbonated soda, more sugar, more eggs, more everything.

"But I'm really, really tummy sick. Gonna…"

Mum's eyes go wide, wide like the day she first sees us, wide like when she learns Grandpa got shot. Wide… "Jehuu, nooooo!"

Too late, there it goes.

The first hour I spent on US soil, landing in a gigantic airplane, I spent bent over a rubbish bin, tossing up all the food I ate on the flight.

I ate it all, everything in front of me, everything I could get my hands on. Kept waiting for someone to take it from me, ask me to share it with the rest of the people on the plane. The hardboiled eggs were especially tasty going down, awful coming back up. America! The land of hope, streets paved in gold. The first thing I do is throw up.

Ivory Coast to JFK in New York, five thousand miles. From JFK another plane to Pittsburgh. From there a car to Findley Lake. The I-79 corridor from middle Pennsylvania to southwestern New York is tree lined, country roads. I peer into the bush looking for soldier-signs, but there's only trees.

13

Liberia

TAYLOR'S NPFL CONTROLS the inner providences.

Prince Johnson's ULIMO forces in city suburbs, ECOMOG in Monrovia. Warlords divvied up the leftovers. Minor skirmishes, where armies pressed against the other, occurred daily. Big battles were rare.

The population mistook the lull for normalcy and not for the gathering storm that it was. People came back to Monrovia from hiding and outlying refugee camps. Approximately five to ten thousand refugees per week returned to the capital, protected then by ECOMOG forces representing the tenuous government of Thomas Sawyer. Some eighty-thousand refugees were repatriated to Liberia by boat and land between 1991 and 1992. Centers for displaced people outside Monrovia became vacant as the situation seemed to normalize.

This was the time the Caulcrick's were heading back to their home in Buchanan from their long walk. Bonita, having finally returned from the United States, was making her way in-country to find her children.

14

A Child Soldier

THE NPFL SPENT August and September of 1992 creating chaos in and around Monrovia.

The doorway explodes, bodies rush, strobes cast a dizzy fantasia of color and light into the night air. Two boys are by Ghost's side, Chaos and Bug, their dark magic names. They forget their weapons and gape into the maw created by the blast. So far no one escapes the front door of the nightclub where the Molotov cocktail was tossed.

Ghost looks away, eyes to the street. Targets will come from the street, not from inside the nightclub. Light from the fire reflects off dirty stucco buildings brightening the street. The show makes him sick, disoriented, disturbed, and angry. Flashes and sparks dance in his eyes, epileptic pulses massage his brain. The metallic smell of guns, blood, and fear grind his olfactory sensors, disorienting him, roiling his empty stomach. Nothing to throw up, that's good. He sculpts his nausea into anger.

Chaos rises, moves to the corner of the building, mesmerized by the bedlam. He grunts, "Ooh, ahh, oh man, oh."

"What's there?" Ghost asks.

"Lights, no peoples. They still inside."

Chaos and Bug have been with Ghost since Zero Week. They know to follow what he says. Both pull absently at their clothes, Bug in a white wedding dress over his street clothes, Chaos in khakis and a monster mask. They touch their talismans of the day, the ones that protect from death.

Ridiculous, Ghost thinks; *the bullet doesn't care what you wear, unless it's armor.* But the dresses and zombie masks are good disguise, good for terror. Ghost is irritated but patient. They're exposed out in the street, if ECOMOG patrols are in the area, it will be dangerous. His annoyance gets the better of him, "Why you always so stupid Wonlay?"

Wonlay is Chaos' given name, from his parents. He frowns, "Using my old name?" Then, puffing his chest, he pats Ghost with the flat part of his machete.

The raid in Monrovia makes Ghost nervous. He knows the bush. The streets are a different hunting ground. The boys get cleaned up for the incursion, disguised as locals, clothes that fit, hair cleaned and straightened, scars and open sores covered, teeth whitened. It's awkward and new. Ghost is country, a bush-boy, and a child soldier. He is not a playmaker and pretend city-Congo. Dark city streets don't suit him. He peers up and down Robertstown Street where there is still an improbable nightlife in the city, between tall buildings, broken shops and stores, looks hard for government troops. They must have heard the blasts. Low buildings, two-three-four story concrete foothills line his vision, box him in. Trash fills doorways along the street. A dog, two dogs, nose through the piles. Bug aims his AK at them, sights down the stock. "Pop pop," he says, "gone dog, gone ECO." The stock swings back to the club entrance, makes his weapon unsteady; he's too small to shoulder it and still reach the trigger, has to hold it on his hip, awkward in his small arms.

"Hold still!" Ghost seethes.

"Almost funny, you so small." Chaos grins, teeth flash in the lights and neon of the club, the only illumination in this hellish alley.

The nightclub is filled with teenagers and young adults dancing to pounding music. Everything else on this block is shuttered or destroyed. *Life dies harder than people*, Ghost thinks. It's a beacon of normalcy in the world of civil war, a place where people can just be people and do people things.

But these Small Boys are there to snuff it out, to soften up Monrovia for a siege. They are there to take lives, to take out buildings, to take away hope.

"When do we go?" Chaos.

"Not yet." Ghost pictures the inside of the club. They know there's only the one door, in and out. The explosion that blew up the front door was lethal enough to kill anyone standing nearby. The rest of the partiers will instinctively rush away from the blast; they'll have to gather in the back of the club, nowhere to go.

Bug flashes a crazed grin. He's wound up on heroin. "Call me 'little boy' I'll slit both you monkeys. *Eh?*"

The music from the club stops, screams from inside taper off, grow distant.

"How much longer?" Bug fidgets, pulls at his dress.

Ghost sighs. "Now." The two younger boys shoulder their machine guns, check their ammunition and walk to the destroyed entrance of the club. Ghost follows, searching the mysterious streets for enemies.

They step over bodies and cement detritus, through the dust cloud into the dark building.

They open fire.

15

Liberia

"When you're the big frog in the pond, you're sort of
wondering who is in charge of the pond."
—*Don Wiehe; Firestone Managing Director*

EIGHTEEN MILLION HIBISCUS trees say rubber is king in Liberia.

Latex accounts for sixty-five percent of the country's exports.
Gold, iron, and ore come in a distant second at seventeen percent.
Major imports are fuel and food.

As Firestone built a United States corporate empire on Liberian
rubber, native workers became experts at harvesting the black gold.
Some 6,500 Liberians farm over fifty hectares, four percent of the
land mass. Generations of families, mostly men, have spent their
working lives in Harbel nurturing the vast forests, overseeing harvesting and shipment to the United States, Ohio specifically, where
latex is made into everything rubber and sent around the world.

When farmed correctly, it takes twenty-five years to grow a
mature Hevea brasiliensis tree into a latex-producing fountain. The
patience, the attention span, to appreciate and nurture the process,
takes a special type of person. Liberians, with their casual, dedicated
personalities took to the profession admirably.

The seed of the rubber plant is germinated and sewn into the
ground, the soil in that part of Liberia is especially conducive. Once
a bud is grown, it's fused (taped) onto a wild rubber tree making a

hybrid plant. That hybrid is watched and watered for seven years. Then it's carefully tapped by workers skilled enough to extract latex without killing the plant (hundreds of trees were certainly created the day Jehuu was born and tapped for latex the day he became a refugee). If the tree-tapper is skilled enough, that tree can produce latex for up to eighteen years before it runs dry.

Natural latex is dried into wads of pre-rubber, colored to mark it as a Firestone product to keep it from being stolen and sold on a black market, processed at the Liberian plant into solid blocks, and shipped to the US, where it's melted and molded into your car's primary contact with an asphalt highway.

. . . .

In April 1990, Firestone executives hear rumors of Taylor's rebels making their way south. War is coming. Management makes contingency plans for evacuation, in case the rumors are true.

In May, the rumors persist, an undeniable movement is afoot in-country, different from other warnings. Women and children are sent back to the States. Local workers are excluded from evacuation plans.

In June, Taylor's rebels arrive at Harbel. Platoons camp along the eastern border of the Farmington River, four-hundred feet from the plantation. Firestone employees still on-site listen to the whoops of soldiers on the border of their two-hundred-twenty acre, supposedly sovereign, American corporate grounds. The rebels don't exactly represent a military operation, more like a gathering of crazy looking savages. The rebels dance, sing, show off, fire weapons into the sky. They parade, they preen for the white men staring at them across the short divide. They prepare primitive canoes for breaching the river and invading Firestone.

When they cross, they revisit the pattern the rest of the country has come to know. They present as liberators, the natives rejoice.

They promise freedom from Doe's oppressive regime; a new Liberian order is on the horizon.

Right up until it isn't.

• • • •

In Summer 1990, seven-thousand peacekeepers from Nigeria land in Monrovia, halting Taylor's advance on the capital city. Warlords fight for control of the country. The capital city is still considered the center of the Liberian government and Prince Johnson occupies a good part of it. Taylor's rebels rule the suburbs, his command set in the center of the country at Gbarna, his influence reaches south into Harbel and the Firestone plantation. While his troops, his beloved Small Boys Unit, terrorize the country-side, a hundred-thousand civilians flee into Monrovia where they hope to find protection from a toothless government.

Monrovia is overwhelmed. Ghettos and tent-camps spring into existence as the population doubles. A city capable of nourishing half a million swells to almost a million. No electricity, no water, no jobs, no hospitals, no money. With the intensity of the suburban fighting, supplies in and out of the city cease, an informal siege. If it isn't in the city when you arrive, it isn't coming. If you get sick, you die. If you're wounded, you die. Every animal is destroyed for food. People eat mysterious meat wheeled around the city on carts and do not ask its source. The city settles into misery. Day to day is finding a place to evacuate bacteria from your bowels, lose a tooth, a tuft of hair, tend a sore that refuses to heal, find food, drink dirty water, sleep, wake, and do it again.

Picture the accumulated waste of a million people in an infrastructure designed to handle half that. Picture the pestilence, disease, bacteria, insects. Picture desperate human beings and the things they do to stay alive.

Prince Johnson has no interest in coming to the aid of refugees. He is by all accounts a brutal drunk. The recognized government has no resources to lend, all their official energy tied up hanging on to Liberia as a recognizable nation by a frail thread.

The rest of the world looks on and yawns.

Taylor continues to consolidate power outside Monrovia, ravaging resources and people, effectively choking the city to death. Most of the warlords are bad, ruthless killers, one more dedicated to human suffering and self-interest than the next.

But Taylor's group is special. The Truth and Reconciliation Commission states; The National Patriotic Front of Liberia (NPFL) launched by rebel leader Charles Taylor in 1989, is responsible for more than three times the number of reported violations as the next closest perpetrator group, the Liberians United for Reconciliation and Democracy (LURD). While this is not necessarily the same distribution of murders attributable to groups, it is indicative of overall responsibility for violence.

Taylor's need to control Monrovia is his white whale. When the city refuses to yield, he ratchets up the war.

· · · ·

Within a day of Taylor invading Firestone, the hunting of humans begins, bodies pile up. Bloodlust, after all, is more exciting than liberation. Soldiers, mainly the Small Boys Unit, child soldiers, choose who to kill, who to torture, who to spare. Old scores are settled, real or manufactured. Revenge for revenge for revenge.

U.S. special forces come in and escort Firestone executives out of Harbel. Liberian employees, with nowhere to evacuate, are massacred, the giant luxurious homes of executives are commandeered by military officers and warlords. Resources are confiscated, including the ubiquitous white pick-up trucks used all over the country. Water, oil, gas, and equipment supply the NPFL army, and the Firestone advanced communication system allows Taylor to spread his message of false liberation throughout the country. Taylor's forces are in charge of the vast resources of a registered company of the United States of America.

It is here the idea of Operation Octopus is hatched.

The US Navy sits just off the shores of Liberia and does nothing.

. . . .

Liberia would have struggled to develop the commercial enterprise of making and selling processed latex left to its own. Firestone needed Liberia's hevea brasiliensis forests and cheap workforce to capture the world rubber market. The relationship between the two was symbiotic. It wasn't, however, equal and fair. One entity was definitely the shark, the other the minnow.

That changed when Taylor's rebels crossed the Farmington River and started killing. At his trial in Geneva years later he said, Once we captured Harbel, we made it very clear to the Firestone company that they could no longer be permitted to exercise allegiance to the government in Monrovia.

Firestone should have seen this coming.

16

A Child Soldier

GHOST LEADS.

The patrol parades up and down suburban streets, foraging, sweeping, looking for opportunity. Ghost's job is to go into houses first, clear them of bad juju and spirits. Alone in houses he looks for food, ammunition, knives, batteries, and food. He packs them into his clothes before he gives the all clear.

He has learned how to hide, like the cougar in the bush. He drinks jungle juice with the other boys, sits outside party-circles. When needle or blow is passed, he pretends to take it, leaves it in the dirt when nobody sees. He hoods his eyes, rubs them red, moves slow and lazy, a zombie. He laughs, cries to himself. He flashes his scars at anyone who looks, makes the white worms jump and squirm. Nobody looks his way twice. He's the Ghost, special, ruined. He's everywhere, he barely exists. You can't hurt, kill, or drug up a Ghost.

17

Jehuu

Jehuu in Clymer

It's OCTOBER 1992 in Clymer.

I swapped out African mangroves for American pine, rubber trees and mangoes for climbing elm and oak, the bush for the cut grass of a dark green lawn.

Mum gave me a JanSport backpack, replaced the one left on the roads of Liberia: Monrovia to Buchanan, down the coast to River Cess, Barclayville, and Harper. Then back north, across borders to Sierra Leone and The Ivory Coast. Crisscrossing a country the size of Pennsylvania on foot, me and hundreds of thousands of refugees.

I was vaguely aware that kids across an ocean were fighting in the heat of Liberia, neighborhoods and cities where I walked.

I was sent off to kindergarten, nine-years old now, two years of my life and education lost to the civil war in Liberia.

Grade school in Clymer is as strange to me as the roads of Liberia. A spoiled nine-year (a Liberian Jehuu) figuring out how to get from place to place, room to room, the gymnasium, there's a cafeteria full of food, playground, and library. There's nothing that here reminds me of the struggle to stay alive, of death. I watch leaves change from green to the colors of the rainbow. I smother my Liberian accent, learn to negotiate a world that's safe, without pressing danger, with plenty of food and water. I learn that the looks of strangers aren't likely to be fatal, I can meet eyes, keep my head up if I want, don't have to shuffle feet. Learn to appreciate the difference between a man who might kill me from someone who just sees me as different.

18

Liberia

"Do I think they have blood on their hands?
Yes. I believe they facilitated a warlord in his insurrection
and in the atrocities that he created".
—*Gerald Rose, former deputy chief of
mission for U.S. Embassy in Monrovia*

SPRING 1990.

The standing policy of the Firestone Corporation was to work with whoever governed Liberia. That control became a moving target starting in 1989 when Taylor moved south to the interior. The dynamics of The Firestone operations in Liberia stayed in flux for the entirety of the war.

After Taylor crosses into Liberia from Cote D'Ovre with his army of a hundred well-armed soldiers, he secured most of the Liberia countryside, aside from the major cities, declaring himself the ruler of Greater Liberia. He then set his sights on Monrovia. The timeline:

-June fifth, 1990. Taylor's NPLF pushes south and arrives at Harbel. His rebels cross the Farmington River on the west border in make-shift canoes and take over the plantation. U.S special forces escort Firestone executives to Monrovia for evacuation. Liberian workers are abandoned.

-August 1990. Seven-thousand peacekeepers arrive in Monrovia from Nigeria to halt Taylor's advance on the capital city. Taylor sets up command in Firestone. He tells Firestone that in order to make rubber, to be reinstated at Harbel, they must negotiate with Taylor alone.

-September 1990. Doe is assassinated. Monrovia is shared between Prince Johnson and the skeleton Liberian government propped up by ECOMOG forces.

-December 1991. Firestone management approves an agreement with Taylor, essentially recognizing his army as the government in Liberia.

-January 1992. Firestone resumes operations in Liberia. They pay Taylor in cash, checks, and food; $12.3 million US to fund his rebellion; money that turns to blood in the coming years.

-August 1992. Bonita, Jehuu and Mardea escape to the United States.

-October 1992. Operation Octopus begins.

19

A Child Soldier

"GHOST! DAMN GHOST, why are you here?"

Ghost says nothing, like always. His eyes penetrate something unseen just over the shoulder of his current commander called Mosquito.

Mosquito fights the urge to look away. "Answer me!"

Ghost and his platoon are camped in Firestone, preparing for the upcoming battle. Ghost shrugs under his large fatigues. "Just here." The AK slung across his back almost touches the ground, the machete hangs heavy by his side, leather belt pulled low on his hips.

"Someday you're shot, you creep around like dat, *eh*? Shoot you myself." Mosquito relaxes, drinks from a canteen, water mixed with cane juice. He slaps a large insect buzzing his neck, the irony lost on him. He eats a handful of dumboy snacks. He thinks, *This boy, skin and bones, small as the rest, smells like the bush.* "Go look at them boys, tell me who's ready, who's not."

Ghost nods, eyes never leave that spot just beyond Mosquito's eyes. He backs out of the room and is gone, into the sunlit yard. Mosquito sits in the big chair and watches the boy leave, wipes dribbled booze from the hair on his thin chin. Sometin about dat boy. I was smart, I'd kill him now. Mosquito doesn't like surprises, and Ghost was constantly in the wrong place. Or maybe the right place, that was part of the mystery. He rarely had to summon the kid, showed up when needed, and occasionally when he was unwelcome, overhearing plans, things he should not know.

Or was he? Mosquito could never tell. The first time the kid got underfoot, Mosquito took his blade and put it to his neck, ready to pull it through the arteries and watch him bleed onto a dirt road. As he tensed, he heard the kid speak, a whispered, Yes. Mosquito hesitated. Frowned. "What you say?"

Now, the kid hissed.

Mosquito pulled the knife back, confused. "You say now? What's your name?" Silence. "I said what's the name?" Mosquito spun him around, shook him. The kid had a soft smile on his face, eyes deep black pools of... nothing, emptiness that made Mosquito's eyes widen. That's empty, he thought. Nothing there but a black world. Very bad juju. Very bad magic. He pushed the kid away, wiped his mouth, sweat beading on his head. He looked around. Other boys standing in dull compliance, waiting, eyes watery and glazed, dumb looks, smiles pasted to dirty faces. "Not kill you just yet." Mosquito said. Something was wrong with this kid.

Now, it was too late to outright kill him. Somebody else mess with that juju, Mosquito thought. So he sent the Ghost to places where death was guaranteed. But Ghost always came back. And now the kid was someone he counted on, someone he could ask and have a thing done.

20

Clymer

KIDS CAME DAILY to see Jehuu, the new boy in town.

Mardea too, the new girl. The relative isolation of the Karr house, off the beaten path in Findlay Lake, meant coordinated meetings and playdates. It's hard to overwhelm children who spent two years surrounded by so many other people, refugees sharing everything, food, clothes, sleeping space, but this was indeed a new place, a unique experience.

The Clymer kids accepted the Caulcrick kids. Jehuu and Mardea's color, size, and cadence of speech were acute points for curiosity. Their differences were neat and interesting to rural white kids, rather than traits to cause suspicion and doubt.

But those doubts, that natural reticence, weren't completely stifled. There are reasons people live in Clymer, and it isn't usually to gain a greater sense of human diversity. Everyone looks almost the same there, to diverge is to call attention. The Caulcricks drew that attention, and if the judgement based on skin color wasn't always overt, it was still there.

21

A Child Soldier

THE HOUSE IN Firestone where Mosquito squats is luxurious.

Water runs through pipes into porcelain sinks, a kitchen painted bright white, ornate backsplashes fitted onto marble counters. The privy was gray tile, with a genuine toilet, not the ground-hole Mosquito grew up with in northern Liberia. Shitting indoors was a singularly unique experience for him, thrilling in a way he couldn't begin to understand. (He often shat on the floor instead of in the hole, making his troops clean it up.)

When he claimed the house as his own, as an officer in the NPFL, he took great pleasure in evicting the white owners. Firestone management was shocked at his audacity, his obvious blackness. The AK pointed at the chest of the white man with the big glasses, white tennis shorts, and drooping mustache, sealed the deal. A white man in my country, complaining about a Gia solider taking back what's his? Finally, justice for my people!

. . . .

Ghost walks from the house, through rubber trees lined like sentries. Azure sky above, purple on the horizon, looking west to the Atlantic Ocean. He passes boys squatting on skinny haunches, eyes vacant or closed in sleep, weapons slack but obvious. A few look and nod. He ignores them. *Not ready,* he thinks. No matter.

382

He climbs a small hill, away from the tree-lined paths. He brushes heavy black flies from his eyes and ears, his shoes pick up dust from the trail, his light shirt blows in a soft, hot wind the higher he climbs. Small birds chirp and hiss. He waves a hand at them and smiles. A week ago, no birds, chased away by the fire-fights. Now they are back to reclaim the treetops.

And the flies. So many flies come to feast on the decaying corpses still scattered across the plantation.

On the hill, there are more boys, his platoon. Morris and Zubin Cooper, brothers with thick lips and wide faces. Momo squats and draws in the dirt with a knife. Commando 2, 4, and 6 (boys who look alike and all want to be called Commando) kick at anthills, dance away, and kick again. Abel Moses stands against a tree, eyes closed, AK on his hip. Chaos and Bug sleep somewhere close by. All here, all eyes bright and active. *These boys here are ready, eh?*

In Monrovia, a hundred kids a day die of starvation. No dogs, no cats, no animals on the street, all turned into meals because of the siege. Vendors walk the streets with carts of human flesh for sale. One thousand Liberia dollars for a strip of human flesh hanging off poles, drying in the sun. The vendors call it dog, call it groundhog, or muskrat, but you can't hide the taste or smell of human flesh. People gotta eat.

Not here, not on the plantation. Here Firestone and Taylor provide. Shelter if you want. Rice, trucks, fuel, and weapons come in daily from roads, from the sea and the sky. Helios land and work crews unload crate after crate. Timber and diamonds and now rubber go out in fair trade. Boats and ships from the port in Buchanan sneak out into the night and bring back loads of ammunition.

Ghost knows all this. He also knows it will not be good if officers know he knows.

Top of his hill is staked out, Ghost's place, a clearing tucked behind thick brush, hidden from the path unless you know where to look. An alcove of thick trees in a rough square, leaning into a depression in the ground. Above ground is a place to sit, clean yourself and your weapons, covered in thick leaves and scraps of plastic confiscated from Firestone housing. Here Ghost can relax away from the world. There are covered buckets of water for drinking and washing. On a tree hangs a sizable mirror. Ghost admires his scars and searches daily for signs of Hope.

22

Liberia

THE NPFL USED Firestone to prepare for Operation Octopus.

The heavy machine gun mounted on house fifty-three in the Firestone Plantation was impressive. So were the Howitzers and 81mm mortars, capable of firing up to forty missiles at a time, placed around the plantation perimeter. The frequent military caravans passing through the streets of Harbel were also a sign that something was happening. The United States ambassador, stationed in Monrovia, noticed the brand-new AK47s on the streets. The monsoon season was over, things were drying out, sending a static charge around the capital city.

Liberia was electric.

. . . .

The world might have taken notice, but at the same time, the Gulf War was in full bloom, and Africa was a hotbed of genocide in The Congo and Rwanda. The United States military was distracted from Liberia, the stepchild status of the country long since abandoned. There's oil in Kuwait.

In Africa, there's mostly Africans.

When the world finally turned its attention to the Africa, it was to look upon the devastation in Rwanda and The Congo where the Tutsi and Hutu tribes went at it so hard. Liberia was an afterthought. The exhaustive massacre of almost a million Tutsi tribesmen in a hundred-day killing spree, dwarfed the ethnic/tribal killing of several hundred thousand Liberians. The Tutsi massacre was a genocidal industry that's hard to comprehend on a human or mathematical level; eight thousand murdered every day, fully seventy percent of the Tutsi tribe, generations extinguished in an extended summer of carnage. Movies were made of the large-scale of human suffering and tribal barbarism in those places. No Hollywood evidence of record was spent on Liberia.

. . . .

Where Jehuu's world was steeped in Christianity, for many child soldiers it was a brew of mysticism and the supernatural. Jehuu lived in the part of urbane Liberia where eighty-four percent of the population was guided by the lord Jesus Christ, none more so than his maternal grandparents. Jehuu's people stood on a cliff of redemption through worship, sin, and human nature ready to push you into the chasm of hell. Many of the children recruited into rebel armies came from families where bush-spirits could be gleaned in the shape of a rock or tree. Others in Liberia read tea-leaves, rationalizing outcomes in life by the whims of more than a single God they couldn't understand.

When Jehuu escaped Liberia to the United States, it was considered a miracle of deliverance by the one true God.

When Ghost was led into a life of murder and torture, it was bad juju, a bush God selling the soul of a hopeful life.

23

Jehuu

WHEN I STARTED school at Clymer unrefined physicality defined me.

Clymer kids are physical, farm workers, athletes, some toughened from family life. I was more visceral, hands-on, an African thing, a big-family thing. My life in a house full of cousins and friends made me that way. We touched and tugged. We wrestled and hugged. Human spaces are close in Africa, you're always around somebody, always sharing space and things. You don't step over dead bodies and wade through gun shells and see people bludgeoned, stabbed, and shot, without your idea of proper physical responses to every-day situations being skewed.

I was also made ready to run into a bush, climb a tree, and sleep there, ignore thirst and hunger, outpace a rebel patrol, hide from the bullet. Grandma and Grandpa kept me from becoming feral, but that instinctive physicality seeps in just the same. If Clymer kids are leather, I'm what you whet leather on, not necessarily an aggressive character, just the Africa in me.

The communal nature of Liberian life, my family specifically, made my adjustment to Clymer easier. I was born in a city of half a million people after all, raised in a plantation full of American businessmen, reared in a bustling suburban home. The United States, Clymer specifically, was similar enough to where I spent my childhood, just way quieter. I made friends right off the bat; our neighborhood had kids the same age as me. Plus, my mom spent two years paving the way for me and my sister.

School was the biggest adjustment, interacting with other kids, teachers, principals, coaches, adults who were looking out for me. Things as simple as tonality comes across as aggressive. The Africa roughhousing I was used to, I couldn't do in school. I had to learn to tone it down in the classroom and on the basketball court, even in playing backyard games with new friends.

But not on a football field. There I could use that rawness.

I wasn't able, at first, to fully appreciate my life in Clymer, a place where people didn't die for no reason. Clymer was embracing, easy. Liberia was the center of chaos and human agony. Where vile entropy was rampant in Africa, the center held in Clymer. Things flew apart in Liberia, you never knew where a meal would come from, or a bullet. You could expect to be safe in Clymer, you could reason with the people, you could count on law and order.

But Liberia followed me. To me and my sister, a loud noise, maybe thunder or a car backfiring, was the report of an automatic weapon. The smell of a dead animal on the roadside was the decay of humans. A white pickup truck passing by was a military transport, filled with guns.

Our dreams were of dead people, of ghosts.

24

A Child Soldier

GHOST WAKES IN the dirt curled next to his weapon.

Third straight night at Firestone, no more patrols into the city. He's in his perfect spot on the hill. A room and bed in the main house is his if he wants because of his rank, his presence, and because no one would argue if he took it. He chooses outdoors, the Wuteve mountain ranger is still in him.

Something feels wrong in his bones. It's the way the officers move around. The way command talks, a hushed expectancy, secrecy around the *SBU*, twitchy hands, darting eyes. Ghost looks for drugs and booze in the eyes of the officers and sees little. Most are sobering up. That's as strange as anything else. Commanders always take the blow, at least, but not the past three days. The boys get plenty, and jungle juice by the gallons. Something isn't right, so Ghost prefers his own company under the stars.

Patrols into Monrovian suburbs were halted after summer months of terrorizing neighborhoods, gutting every street, every house down to the ground, burning, raping, murdering. Missions into the city, slip in disguised, firefights, slaughter, then escape.

Then the boys were called back to Firestone for training. Weeks on end, march, fight, march, fight, sleep, wake, drink, take the needle, march, fight, march, fight.

And now a new regimen, three straight days at the plantation, eat, drink, take the needle. Brand new weapons, fresh from crates from the sea. The boys play with them.

389

He swaps out his torn shirt for a new one, throws the old one into his cooking fire. He prefers baggy, plain clothes, not the bright colors and crazy wardrobe of the other boys. They want to be seen and heard, photographed and feared. Ghost wants to melt, to turn to vapor, solid to gas. He keeps a stash of simple clothes where no one can find it. At night, he sews pockets inside pants and shirts, stuffs them with extra cloth to smooth out any edges or bulges that weapons and extra ammunition might make. Everyone in the platoon thinks he's twice his real size. He's hard to get a bead on.

"Where you get them clothes, Ghost?" They ask.

"Na mind ya." He grins, makes the question into a joke.

"Always you got dem slow clothes, so dull."

Ghost arches his eyebrows, makes his face-scars dance. "You want some my clothes, *eh*?"

"Nah." Eyes cast down. "I just lookin' dem."

"Look to your own clothes." Ghost squints over the hill. Trucks lined up, the Commander with a bullhorn. "C'mon, eh. Commander callin'."

"I don't hear no…"

Company! To me! Hup Two!

Boys jump beside cooking fires. One, two, cross themselves. Abel stamps in the cooking fire, Chaos yawns. The Cooper brothers scrape machetes against the nearest tree and haul AKs onto broad shoulders.

"Just come, *eh*?"

Something is very different. It smells bad. It's in the eyes of the officers. It's in their blood.

They're about to find out.

25

Jehuu

MY FIRST TWO or three years in the US I play summer soccer.

I ride bikes, I play kickball and some form of run-and-tackle with a football. Real American football – huddles, plays, blocking and passing – aren't on my radar. Men in padded uniforms, grabbing each other, bashing each other, using their hands, wrapping themselves around that brown, foreign ball. What a funny game. Big men, small men, throwing and catching, standing, crouching, facing off, waiting for that egg-shaped ball to move. I didn't know rugby, so I had no frame of reference for running with the ball in your hands. My football – God's football – has a rhythm and flow, a game of potential, runs at a goal tethered to discipline and timing, a coordinated dance for a Liberian boy who's fast and good with his feet.

26

A Child Soldier

THIS MORNING THEY pass the booze and the needle and the blow.

Palava is passed, bread, sweet meats. *Eat, eat! We going have a good day! Today we get ours, oh!* Commanders let soldiers gorge, dogs at a bowl of fresh meat. Daily discipline is ignored. Is this the end of war? the boys wonder. We done fighting? Most boys are happy by this idea. Some are not.

There is a reason for this morning greeting. Ghost has an idea. Officers want soldiers happy. They want boys seeing a future, who think life can be good, full of fun, drink, drugs, and sex.

Or maybe it's the opposite. Maybe they don't want to tell boys they have more trouble than they know. Maybe they are about to go into an impossible battle, to be returned to the Liberian soil.

27
Jehuu

"NO FOOTBALL? WHAT do you mean?"

"Just American football. There's no soccer at school, Jehuu."

"Soccer isn't a name. It's football mum!" Clenched fists by my side. This idea of my football not in this place is crazy talk. *Where do I go to score goals? To run, kick, chase.* I think back on my goals and my new ball in the backyard on Allison Street in Buchanan. I remember all the goals I scored on my cousins. Remember the fields of food, the mangrove forest where I ran and played.

The kitchen in Findley Lake smells nothing like grandma's kitchen in Liberia. No melting shea butter, no palava, no crawfish, no dumboy. Nothing boiling, nothing simmering on the stove. No potash fires for cooking gaygba. That kitchen was the nerve center of the neighborhood, people in and out, eating, cooking, a parade of cousins, step-siblings, neighbors.

Joseph.

My mother hums a beautiful African rhythm. She mixes a Gio folk song with a new version of Sweet Old Rose. I remember grandmum in her kitchen, on Allison Street. She hummed and sang like my mum. I miss her, but mum is enough like her that I feel her every day.

Here, it's different; everything tucked into cupboards, clean sink and marble counters, stove, oven, microwave, and a humming refrigerator. Spoons hidden in drawers, forks and dull knives. All you do here is ask for food, and it's there. No guns pop outside. No tanks in your yard. Nobody barges into this home, breaking down doors, smashing windows.

No ghosts, except at night, when it's too quiet.

Coming to America from Africa is nowhere near the jolt of moving the other way. Liberians aspire to travel abroad, yearning for the culture, media, and entertainment from the United States. A Liberian who's been abroad has been-to. They speak cull, western civilization accented English, to impress peers. Liberians study the United States, are acutely aware of it, emulate and take western culture like nourishment.

Americans do not study Liberia.

"Still, they don't play your football here, except in the summer."

"Yes, we play in summer! How are we having no football now? At school?"

My mum works the kitchen sink, plates and silver pass into the dish washer (water enough here to fill a machine just for washing dishes).

Mum gazes at me lazily, smiles, "You so big Jehuu. Look at you." Mum says stuff like this all the time. "Big like your daddy, and tall like me. Big head with lots of brains. Caulcrick lips!" She acts like I'm a miracle, like I'm not here every day. She smiles wider, and I blush.

September sun lights the room, outside the window is a green carpet of grass, not like the hot dirt of grandma's house in Liberia. That dusty, muddy field had no use for kids, except what we made of it, me, my cousins, Mardea, setting up football goals for a pitch. This yard is plush, like a carpet. It waits for me. So, I stomp my feet, legs raring to go go go, but first I am stubborn. *No football?* Makes no sense, doesn't register. I grew up a couple miles from Antoinette Tubman Stadium in Monrovia, the football center of the Liberian world.

"No football?"

"The boys play their football."

"I know." I did, but I didn't. "I know American football, Mum. I want to play my football."

She turns, hands on hips. "What you know about American football, *eh*?"

28

A Child Soldier

PILED INTO TRUCKS, no walking today, the boys whoop and holler.

They are kids on their way to a park, to a zoo, to see the ocean and maybe have a swim. Never mind they are loaded down with weapons and as much ammo as they can carry, enough to start a war)sadly not enough to finish one). Never mind that they are headed for the swamps on the southwest side of Monrovia. Never mind the ordnance soaring over their heads into that city.

They are fed and drugged and they are, after all, kids.

29

Liberia

SHAPED LIKE FLORIDA, at the size of Miami, Monrovia is a prime spot for port commerce, a resort city if it so chose.

These features also made it an attractive conduit for the slave trade for millennium as millions of natives were marched from the African interior to the coast to be bought and shipped around the white world. The city is naturally defensible from attack from the Atlantic, except by beachhead assault. Liberia has historically fielded no discernible navy. Rivers and swamps border the other points of the compass. Thick vegetation, molded by steam bordering miles of swamp, framing a man-made world of concrete and plaster. Southside of the capital is a vast arena of everything a tropical swamp has to offer, innocuous top layer of unassuming grass, underneath is watery detritus, a sucking morass of quicksand, lethal fauna, and bramble.

30

A Child Soldier

"A lot of child soldiers lost their minds."
—*Emmanuel Jal*

FROM BEHIND, A commander shouts, "The city is yours, *eh*. Go now and take it!"

Ghost frowns inside his smoking hot clothes, confused. That makes no sense. They know we're here. Nobody can cross a swamp in the day when they know you're coming. The morning is a blanket of humid fog. Vapor seeps from Mosquito's thin smile like smoke from a cooking pit.

"Suh." Ghost says. His voice dies in the mist. The boys gather around him. He takes note of the slack faces, over-cooked brains on the needle, others that are trigger-happy, the calm of his personal troops. He makes a mental picture of how he'll deploy them into the swamp. Slack faces first to go; they'll wake up fast when the first bullets hit. Let the crazies follow, throw some energy and fear at the other side. Then his trusted boys to clean up the mess.

Mosquito shouts, "Ghost goes in first. Head of the wave, arm of the Octopus!"

. . . .

"Give me six feet!"

During the second civil war, Liberians who heard that command had a better than average chance of being assassinated. Through long and lazy experimentation with violent death, it was discovered that the splatter of blood travels about six feet from a gunshot, in all directions, an arc of plasma. Soldiers not wanting to get blood or flesh on a uniform, moved their victims at least six feet away before murdering them. Six feet became the two-word death sentence of an entire country.

Ghost learned the six feet rule early, used it rarely, but not never.

He also learned to speak softly (None of the *Suh! Yes Suh!* bawls of the other boys), so people moved close to understand him. Soft, soft voice, calm but urgent. Officers lean in to hear, get close, maybe cup a hand to an ear. A hand by an ear isn't close to a weapon.

Today Ghost pauses before he speaks. Tired, so tired. Anger flares, enough to make him speak. He whispers, to hide his insolence, keep Mosquito close, "Just us, Suh? We clean the whole swamp? A swamp full of danger, a patrol on an entire city?" Ghost sweeps his hand at the high brush; eyes do not leave the Mosquito's.

Mosquito's smile fades, lips stretch into a grimace over yellow teeth. It doesn't go unnoticed that troops move to Ghost and not to him. He turns away, yells into the mist, "Today, we take the city. You win it; you keep it. You want food, you want water, you want power and women and riches. Go take it. Kill it, you own it. It is your power. It is your right."

The boys look at Ghost for the truth. Ghost knows it's a lie. He's been in the city, making raids, softening the people. The people don't need to be softened. They are beaten already. It's ECOMOG that have the weapons, and all they have to do is sit behind walls and squeeze a trigger.

· · · ·

High knees, protect your weapon.

This vast land is suddenly claustrophobic, a cave. It closes around his head, darkens his vision. The ground jumps, the swamp explodes. A whisper in his ear.

Hope.

Father? Is that you?

Run Hope. Run. He knows he's not Hope anymore. Hope would never be charging through a swamp to kill men.

From across the swamp, *Pop, crack, pop pop pop.* Water and weeds explode, like snakes thrown into a pit. Someone screams, *Ahhhhh. Hit!*

Run Hope. It's time to run. Daddy's voice in his ear. A whisper on the wind.

Where, Papa? Where should I run? He is calm. He has run before.

To the other side.

31

Jehuu

Before I go to the waiting yard, I pout right at her.

I'm the old spoiled Jehuu, full of insolence and puppy eyes. I almost forgot how; pouters don't get far in Liberia.

"Of course I know American football. Terrell Davis, he's my favorite. Number thirty."

"See, you know, Jehuu. So go play with your friends." Mum moves to the table to look at mail-bills, circulars, a newspaper. The Jamestown Post Journal spread out with pictures of white, smiling faces. The headline reads *Prendergast Library Donation Approved.*

"No football. I don't understand." This information isn't logical. I can't track from what I want to exist to what is real; that which should be, hits the stone wall of that which isn't.

Mum looks up from her newspaper. She's at the dining room table, still in her morning clothes, sweatshirt and bright pants, no shoes. "Jehuu, leave me be. No football. For true, *eh*?" Her singsong voice changes, gathers.

"Okay." I know better than to ask again.

My first full year in the United States, some of its familiar; Liberia has the same music, the same clothes, movies, some food the same, my favorite candy in both places – Skittles – and lots of the same holidays.

A lot of it's different. The weather isn't so hot all the time. Animals are different – birds, deer, fat beavers, and squirrels. Fewer

401

people crowded into houses. Mum had nine brothers and sisters, so many aunts and uncles and cousins, you can't count them.

Mum tells people, "We worked really hard as children for what we had. It was hard work, but we had all the fun things. We had a wonderful life."

I grew up in a nice house, plenty of new clothes and toys. Until the war. Then I had nothing except what was in my backpack.

People ask all the time, what was Liberia like? How do I answer? It was great. It was horrible. It was easy, then it was hard.

The United States, Findley Lake, is different, the house, the yard, the snow, the roads, the trees, the animals. The people are different, and they have better cars, better schools, hospitals, stores, places to eat, and places to play. A furnace to keep you warm in winter. Air conditioning to cool you in summer. In Liberia, it's heat, all the time hot, dust in the dry season, mud in monsoons. In America, grass everywhere, rolling fields, corn stalks, and hay as far as you can see, black roads climb distant hills and drop out of sight.

Liberia is still in my mind. Me and Mardea still flinch at a loud noise, a tractor, lightning, a hunting rifle in the woods.

But at least Liberia had my football.

And here, no football!? In this land of plenty? That's different on another level. *What kind of place is this?*

Oh, well. I grab a soccer ball off the back porch, boom it into the back corner, green grass of the back yard. *Game on!*

32

A Child Soldier

TROOPS SCATTER, ACROSS the narrow swamp, a race between the bush and the bullet, to the great capital city. The other side.

Ghost weaves in and out of the shallows. Bodies lie in his path through the churned-up earth, pits made by exploded mortar. Some bodies thrash in the teeth of dragons. Insects swarm to bleeding flesh. Thick red seeps into the swamp, covers grass thickets, pools, and makes scarlet mud, like after a rain.

Lift your knees, pump your arms, keep your head up. If you trip on a body, get up before the bullet finds you. Or something worse.

Run Ghost, run.

To the other side.

33

Jehuu

BE QUIET, JEHUU. Be small, so they don't find you.

In a ditch, lying on my back. Instincts scream stay still. I want to cry. Stay quiet you, Jehuu! Parts of me sting, parts bleed. I look at the sky, the bright sun. My clothes should be drenched in sweat by now, but this sun doesn't weigh me down; it wraps me in an embrace, doesn't smother me like a soggy blanket. This sun is only warm, strange. I listen for feet running, for the *pop pop pop* of weapons, for the command of an adult, for the shrill answer of a child soldier. For the screams of people of war. I smell for the telltale whiff of weapon discharge, the metallic hint of blood, the distinctive body odor of the soldier. The ditch is deep, too high to see out of, bordered by thick plants that pierce skin, grab at clothes, claw and dig. I reach down and feel a tear in my shorts, my shirt is shredded, sticky-wet blood comes back my fingers. I move an arm, then a leg. Every twist or turn is scraping pain. I flex hands, open, closed, open, closed. I'm suddenly thirsty.

Then I hear feet coming my way, the loud clapping of someone running. I close my eyes and listen.

34

Liberia

HEROIN IS A weapon, used by rebels in Libera as effectively as guns and mortar.

Heroin is made from opium, poppy, and morphine. It's particularly insidious, effective at producing painless euphoria, especially in a developing brain, one filled with young blood, fresh dendrites, and synapses. It takes ten seconds from the time of injection for heroin to reach the brain where it smashes unnaturally against normal receptors, a tidal wave of dreams, hijacking sensations of pain and pleasure. It targets naturally occurring opioid receptors in the brain and charges them like gasoline poured on a fire.

Take a garden hose, open it up, and let water flow. When the ground saturates and overflows, tributaries spill water away in rivers and streams. New low-points fill and the process is repeated, gravity works a water-solution.

The human brain does much the same when you wash it with heroin. It fills to capacity, binding with molecules (in the case of morphine and opium, these molecules happen to be the human receptors for pain and pleasure). When the brain's capacity of receptors are breached by this artificial wash, by the open garden hose, the brain is forced to create new receptors to bind up the washout. The wash overflows and tributaries gush into other parts of the brain.

Humans are wired for survival. We're built to last, either by God or evolution (you choose), or recently, science. From the very first iterations of a self-aware mankind, the mainframe brain was filled with software designed to seek out pleasure and avoid pain. The control switches for these regulators operate as an on-off switch, no volume control; we work to turn pleasure on and pain off, as much as possible. To crank up pleasure, we fire up more receptors.

In the beginning, when life was hard, this system kept mankind alive, well, and able to procreate a species. Pleasure is safe. Pain is dangerous.

But evolution hasn't been able to keep up with the exponential advancement of chemical science. Firing up brain receptors to control pain and pleasure is no longer a mortal imperative, but exterior manifestations of a lifestyle choice; what we do with the on-off switch.

When we can control pain and pleasure artificially with chemicals, then what?

. . . .

Wielding automatic weapons, machetes, and shielded in magic armor of pain-free exhilaration, lines of Liberian boys and girls race to Monrovia, oblivious of the swamp sucking at their legs, ignoring the animals who emerged from the soup to feast on them, and the bullets that kiss them on their way. Numb to the world, except for a maniacal need for instant gratification. How long can a boy run with a bullet in an appendage before he can run no more. How many animated steps can they take with lead in the heart or head. Very few of the ECOMOG ordinance stopped them at first strike, upon original impact. The crazed heroin vessels kept coming.

. . . .

Your first blast of heroin is the best you will ever have. Then you will spend the rest of your life trying to find that rabbit hole of ecstasy again. Life after that is a physiological, biological, and chemical journey to recreate that feeling. Except it's impossible. The brain, shocked at the usurping of its natural regulation, and eager to respond to the unnatural onslaught, rushes to make more opiate receptors. The next time you shoot up, those receptors are ready to regulate the high.

So, you shoot up more.

The brain responds.

This is why repeated blasts of heroin can't duplicate the initial, novel experience of the drug; there is no way for the user's brain to go back to the standard, original number of opiate receptors. The user is compelled to take more and more heroin because there are always more, new opiate receptors than there is heroin available, a thimble of gasoline poured on an inferno. Nothing in nature can compare to how powerfully heroin hijacks the brain's reward and pleasure pathways. Heroin erases the brain's ability to produce its own dopamine and instead takes over how the user perceives pleasure and satisfaction. There simply is no pleasure that can match heroin use. The body gives up trying and stops producing endorphins. The diabolical characteristics of heroin are contained in this self-repeating chemistry and the ability of God's creatures to adapt to abnormal stimulus.

The human brain overcomes and adapts.

35

A Child Soldier

THE MONROVIAN CITYSCAPE is silhouetted dark against the coming light.

The platoon pushes deeper into the swamp. Heroin has destroyed most of these boys. When they aren't crazed by the euphoria phase, they wear corpse-ridden masks of rapture and look like the dead. Their flesh rots, their eyes are heavy, unblinking even when raped by ever-present Liberian flies. Behind those young eyes, an empty slate, a brain like drying concrete behind a finger that pulls a trigger.

The heroin, the jungle juice, the violence and inhumanity, is insidious and penetrating, the cloud that never goes away, like the heat and the flies. Heroin, that started in a vial and syringe has ended in collapsed veins, infections in the blood vessels and heart valves, in tuberculosis that curls fingers in arthritis. AIDS invades soon after, naturally, from shared needles, along with hepatitis and then liver disease, everything you can catch from someone else. A young immune system tries to keep up; nasty teeth and gums, weakness, pustules on the face, children who didn't eat for days at a time, stupidity, and itching…constant itching.

On patrol, an addict might open up their weapon and hose every member of his squad in bullets, randomly, savagely. He simply itched, the poor child, delusional and confused. What he believed was one hand scratching was the other wrapped around the trigger of his weapon. He could not distinguish one hand from another. Often, officers had to shoot down one to protect the many.

Tracking the muzzles of a hundred AKs kept Ghost busy.

. . . .

Two miles of swamp is forever when you're slogging, cutting, and high-stepping to miss the snakes and poisonous frogs, gator, and beasts you don't yet recognize. The bottleneck for killing every child soldier is the rate at which government forces can reload their weapons. Death funnels you into your bullet-eating role in a war you don't understand because you're twelve or thirteen or fourteen, and don't know any other way out.

This operation, this arm of Operation Octopus, would be like trying to conquer New Orleans on foot against a garrison of armed soldiers. The swamps, lakes, and foliage are similar to those that surround that US city.

Ghost leads his Patrol into the mud. The going is slow, but the boys are lunatic-strong, pumped with drug-energy. Ghost gets a hundred meters into the shallows when there is a scream behind him. Bullets snap at his ears, metal insects he might swat if he didn't know better.

He looks back. Chaos is laughing, pulling at his foot. "Stuck! Mud," he shouts above the cacophony of war. "Help me loose."

Ghost turns back to help. Mud and water flash. Brown, green teeth wrap Chaos' leg. He's yanked backward in an explosion of blood. His mouth curls into a round O. The shock through Ghost is electric. He'd seen everything, thought he was incapable of surprise, but this was something new. Not the bullet, not the machete. Something else to worry about.

Even before ECOMOG troops have a chance to empty cartridge after cartridge of ammunition into the boy soldiers, it's the alligators that notice the boys traipsing in their swamp in rubber sandals. The primordial beasts don't see soldiers, they don't see children of Liberia, and they don't care if you're a drugged zombie fighting for Taylor.

They see food.

36

Jehuu

I'M A STATUE.

Breathe through my nose, and lie still. Freeze in place. The feet stomp my way. Is it a soldier? Is it grandmum?

"Jehuu! Oh my, Jehuu."

"Mum?" Mum is here? Watch for soldiers. If you yell, they'll come. Stay quiet. Don't look at them. They'll cut you open. I try to rise from the ditch, but I'm held down by the brush. I squirm and thrash, the prickers just dig deeper. "No mum, stay back."

"Jehuu, I'm here. I'm here. What did you do?"

A bike. I was riding the bike. I fell into the bushes. This isn't Liberia, it's not Africa. It's America. It's New York. I was riding a bike, and I fell. No roadblocks, no soldiers.

"I fell., Mum."

She reaches into the bushes and picks me out carefully. "Yes, you did. Let's go and get cleaned up." Her face is creased in concern, but she smiles into my sweaty face.

37

Liberia

"You could fire and fire at them. You'd get one down, and the
next one would come. They were more dangerous than beasts.
You really don't see them as children in the heat of battle,"
—*Innocent Nass; Nigerian Military Analyst.*

NIGERIAN SOLDIERS NGO and Sam stood side-by-side and reloaded. Aim wasn't imperative.

Days after the assault through the swamps by the Small Boys
Unit, both would need to be removed from Liberia and put into
some sort of primitive counseling.

For now, they reloaded and fired into the mass of banshee flesh.
Again and again.

The Small Boys weren't totally ineffective. They ran toward
peacekeepers, West African soldiers, firing and retreating, firing
and retreating. The children cut down adults guarding the city, the
sheer volume of ammunition being poured into the defensive line
was enough to poke holes in the fortified boundary at the edge of the
swamp. Some of the boys made it into the city, but without enough
force, they found themselves stranded behind the ECOMOG lines,
forced to either surrender, be assassinated, or hide in the city.

. . . .

The mangrove swamps around Monrovia are filled with Nile crocodiles and their food. That's it. There's no predator in between, nothing to threaten their existence. The brackish water makes for a perfect hunting ground, a home for them to grow and thrive. The average beast is fifteen feet nose to tail, can weigh half a ton. The largest weigh a ton and measure twenty feet.

They are the signature freshwater apex predator in Africa, called opportunistic, and very aggressive. They are frighteningly prehistoric in aspect and attitude. There is no reasoning with a Nile crocodile.

Nile crocs are considered generalists; they eat any prey they can. They mostly devour fish that swim in their vicinity, and animals they can catch. They have green eyes. They can wait for days to ambush a mammal. Their mouths have sixty-eight cone-shaped teeth. They can eat up to half their weight in one meal. They are communal, and hunt and eat in packs. A crocodile that grabs a prey will hold it in place while other crocs rush in and tear the prey to pieces. It's estimated they kill hundreds, if not thousands, of people each year.

On the morning of Operation Octopus, they fed on the Small Boys Unit of Charles Taylor's NPFL army.

38

A Child Soldier

THERE IS NOTHING to do but keep going, no longer a needle of survival he can thread that includes standing still.

Stagnancy is death in the swamp. Backwards isn't an option; that's where he came from. Forward means a fusillade of ECOMOG bullets. That is bad, but bullets don't occupy all the space. You can find places where rounds don't fly in your face. You can time the reloads, move and duck between barrages, hide deep in the grass, move behind other boys.

The bullet does not pick and choose.

Predators inundate all of the brackish water. They find you. You can maybe fight them, but there are so many. They pick and choose.

A small part of Ghost's mind registers that the men who ordered this assault, the officers, the Suhs, are on dry land, watching the boys take on the bullets and the swamp. They sit in a bunker at Firestone, feet up, maybe having a drink of cool water, directing mortar fire (in the wrong place). Or maybe they're in the northern suburbs tucked in tanks and trucks, firing weapons from behind heavy metal. The thought takes up very little space, holds very little emotional purchase aside from being a statement of fact, and that fact, that drilled-down reflection sparks a moment of pause, of disconcerted thought. *Why they there and we have to be here? Why they sit and smoke and drink, and us kids die horrible in this swamp?*

39

Jehuu

WEEKENDS I GET my allowance, five dollars.

A fortune.

In my driveway, I sit on my bike. (I mastered riding one after the bush incident.) I make revving noises, pretend it's a motorcycle, foot poised on the top pedal. One push and I'm off like a shot.

I live in a place where kids ride bikes up and down safe, whole roads. If there's a pothole, it's from traffic and ice-melt, not from a mortar or a pipe bomb. There's no destruction here from war. The eyes that track me from one place to another check to make sure I'm safe, the same as every kid in the neighborhood. If I fall, someone comes to pick me up, brush me off. If a tire goes flat, I take it to Mr. Skelly's, and he fixes it, no charge. If Mrs. Shade asks me to take her garbage out, I hustle over, take it out, and get a cookie in return. Someone needs their hay in the barn, that's what the football team does on a Saturday before practice. In winter, kids sled on my steep front yard; mom feeds every last one of them.

This is Clymer.

Today, like almost every weekend when the weather cooperates, Victor Gorden, Chris Petillo, and Brian Wholaver fly over to my house on bikes. They don't slow, just yell at me as they pass. "Let's go, Jehuu! Catch us. You got your money?"

Foot to pedals, I race to catch up. We stand and pump and swing handle-bars side to side, in and out of the country roads. At the top of Findlay hill, we bank-turn hard into town, skid in front of The Findlay Lake General Store.

Pockets empty on the front steps, my five dollars added to the loot, an impossible stash of riches. In the store, we turn all that cold hard cash into sugar, popsicles, soda, Swedish fish, my Skittles.

Pockets and mouths full of sweets, back on bikes, we head over to the tire-swing. Take turns flying over the bank of Lake Findlay, hover over the water, weightless, gravity takes a moment off, suspended in the air, weightless, free of the earth. Then swing back to terra-firma. That moment, suspended in time and space, when your ass leaves the tire, you let go of the rope and you just float.

40

Liberia

ON OCTOBER 15TH of 1992, Taylor launched his offensive on Monrovia,

It was called Operation Octopus, and the suffering in the capital city ratcheted up a hundred times. Sophisticated warfare, probably incongruent with your notion of Liberian warfare, peppered the city for hours on end – SAR's, mortars, 105mm machine guns.

It was a mad scheme, merciless, a manifestation of the rage Taylor felt when he was unable to take the city two years prior. The battle plan was an all-in effort by the entire NPFL army, every force that could be deployed, the entire arsenal, two years of stockpiles and planning. It was an attack on multiple fronts, meant to squeeze the life out of the city, the method of killing by the octopus.

Two attacks were staged from the Firestone plantation, one from the north and a second from the east while an allied rebel faction attacked from the west to destroy the base of the West African peacekeepers and seize the country's largest port. These arms of the octopus would envelope the city and drown it against the Atlantic Ocean.

Taylor's generals sat back and watched the action. Two weeks, they said. In two weeks, the airport, the merchant port, the government will be ours. The peacekeeping forces will go home or be food for the Octopus.

And waves of child soldiers, popping AK47s and slinging machetes, stormed the city through the swamps and marshes that bracket the city. They were mowed down by ECOMOG soldiers like a scythe through a soft wheat field. Then replaced by the next wave of drugged-up wild-eyed kids lined up to absorb a bullet, use up precious enemy metal, and die.

Kids don't understand politics. They don't care who runs their country. They do not line up to be massacred for a cause. They get manipulated, prodded, tortured, and filled with heroin to rush to a death they don't fully understand because they haven't yet really lived.

41
Jehuu

MY PART OF Western New York is hills and woods, deer and squirrels in your backyard.

The country stretches, relentless, dark hunter-green in summer, a kaleidoscope of foliage in the fall, a white blanket in winter. Different from coastal Africa where tropical heat, equatorial monsoons, saltwater, and sand-based soil dictates vegetation, fauna, topography, and geography. What thrives in my new world is not the same as what matured in my old. Deer, skunk, squirrel, garter snake, and frog here. Elephant, chimpanzee, pangolin, cobra, fruit bat there. Mango, rubber tree, thick bush in Africa. Pine, wheat, corn, and bramble in New York.

I was just another kid in another neighborhood. A Black kid, but just a kid. Clymer, Findley Lake, these places could have been stereotyped into the sketchy hole of racism, but they weren't. The people could have been suspicious, unwelcoming, stand-offish, but they weren't. The Johnsons, the Beninks, the Baileys, Mileckis. They could have looked at us Caulcricks, so different, so foreign, and they could have done a lot of things that would have made my life a challenge (not escape-Liberia-under-the-barrel-of-a-gun challenge, but a challenge just the same).

Instead, they embraced and welcomed a foreign family. I had my sister still, my mum and a stepdad, but I had another three or five mothers. I had a coach who acted like a father. I had teachers and principals and townies who were uncles and aunts. Teammates and neighbors were cousins. Clymer was very much Buchanan for me, as different as it was familiar. A big part of that was luck, where we landed. Another big part of that was my mum, me, and Mardea. The coincidence of people, of personalities, of community were too similar to be ignored.

42

Liberia

THE ATTACK DID not go as planned.

General John T. Richardson of the NPFL made the broadcast. Taylor's commander used the communications system at the Firestone plantation in Harbel. It was his voice that told Monrovia about the waves of mortars set to shower the city, to explode in their kitchens and bedrooms, to destroy their families. "Tomorrow I'm gonna rain hell on you guys", he told the capital city.

The NPFL stationed two aging missile launchers in the suburbs across from the capital that could fire up to forty rockets at a time. The rockets fired wildly, overshooting the city and landing in the ocean, as harmless as fireworks.

The artillery barrage was not hitting the intended targets. The 105mm Howitzer guns were old, their barrels locked in place by rust and disuse. The only way to change the trajectory of the shells was by moving the cannons back and forth.

. . . .

Ngo and Sam fired again, clips of 30-caliber bullets sweeping the swamp. Young men simply exploded in the field of fire, eruptions of red and white. The two Nigerian soldiers couldn't see much, waves of heat and smoke shimmered in front of their visual field. Sweat soaked into their clothes and flowed into their vision, nothing on them was near dry enough to wipe it away.

Reload, wait for another banshee wail behind the slaughtered file of humans, open fire, another wave of bodies. Occasionally, a bullet whips by their position as weapons pop in the distance, some of the boys, able to get off salvos.

"They are here to take bullets?" Ngo.

"Where are the men?" Sammy.

Ngo grunts and forces another clip into the breach. "Ready?" he asks.

Sammy nods.

"Fire." Another line of kids explodes.

43

A Child Soldier

FOR TWO DAYS Ghost held in a brush patch on the very edge of the swamp.

Crocodile, snake, and muskrat carcasses piled in a makeshift entry to his grass fort. This wall of kills kept most predators out. The animals, after trying to get at the young warrior, gave up, their kind piled high. Ghost harvested pelts and skins, providing a wall of smell and forbiddance that kept predators at bay. Insects, on the other hand, had no such reluctance. His hovel became a hive.

He soaked himself in alcohol to keep the bugs off, distilled grain he kept in a pouch from nights of revelry leading up to Operation Octopus. He lay still in his hidey-hole and willed bacteria to stay out of his open sores, scrubbed at every itch with booze-soaked cones, gnawed on raw gator and muskrat, sipped water distilled from swamp mud, and still threw up more than he took in.

The gators were the biggest challenge, primordial hunters of single purpose, all teeth and body armor. You had to stab them deep through the top of the head, one strike, otherwise you end up in a thrashing battle. If you couldn't get at the head or eyes, you had to gut them from throat to tail.

44

Jehuu

I CAN'T IMAGINE forgetting the first time I ran in a football game.

The feel of the ball shoved into my gut. The whoosh of air, the taste of my mouthguard, the bright white football pants, stuffed with pads, flashing in and out of my peripheral vision as I pumped legs, shoes churning grass and dirt. Didn't feel like it was really me. So different from kicking a rock down a dirt road in Liberia. I almost stopped to look down at my cleats grabbing grass, launching me forward, but I kept my head up looking for the defense, like Coach taught me. I won't forget the field opening up before me, a vast countryside of grass, so much grass. Running with a football, my mind became a quiet place of pleasure, exalting in the sheer ability to run free into bright daylight. My only limitations the white chalk boundaries of the field, out of bounds. The out of bounds in Liberia was a roadside ditch, the boundary of a mangrove forest, a line of soldiers.

Fifty-two yards later the goal line met me, and I stopped. I didn't want to stop; I wanted to run, but that's what you do when you arrive at the goal, you stop.

I couldn't get back into a huddle fast enough to do it again.

45

A Child Soldier

WHEN THE SLAUGHTER of Liberian lambs subsided, after three days of astounding carnage, Ghost peeks from his shelter.

The ubiquitous sound of weapons is far off, out of the swamp, toward the city. He doesn't wonder if Monrovia is in the hands of the NPFL. He knows a bloodbath route when he sees one, in the middle of it. The only tax on government ECOMOG forces from the swamp is ammunition. No boys made it through the fusillade into the city, and if they did it wasn't with force enough to make a difference. He pictured piles of bullet shells that lined the city defenses, an innate understanding that those piles were deep. If one of every ten bullets hits a mark, kills a child, that's a hundred-thousand shell casings piled somewhere.

That's a lot of bullets not picking and choosing.

He knew the number of kids marshaled for this assault, understood it was around ten-thousand children aimed at ECOMOG battle lines. He suspects that every one of those are dead, more or less – Chaos, Commando 2, 4, or 6, Bug, Mosquito even. All gone.

Especially Hope. There was none of him left.

He carves mud from his eyes, and peers over the top of the bush. He's a few hundred meters from the city limits. He waits until dark, then follows the shells into the capital city to see what's left.

46

Liberia

General John T. Richardson, that voice, that man.

He gives an interview after the war, sitting in his well-appointed house in central Monrovia, on the banks of the St. Paul River. He drinks beer with NPFL friends from the war days. He is clean, he is comfortable, he is rich, and he is well dressed in a light green chakra, clean-shaven, unblemished. He is unthreatened by repercussions, un-accountable.

He says into a microphone while he looks earnestly at an offscreen interviewer, *I saw skulls, I saw dogs eating bodies. I saw bloated bodies. I saw exploding bodies. I saw women dead. I saw children dead. I saw babies dead. I saw war. I hope to never see it again. I can't apologize for war.*

But you can apologize for the way you wage war, the use of children as cannon-fodder and bullet-eaters. Civilized people can ask that of men who wage war. Civilized people of the world notice that General John T. Richardson did not die in the Liberian Civil War. They notice he is a comfortable old man. They wonder if that old, comfortable man believes he is smarter, more talented, a better human being than every single one of the boys he sent to their deaths. Does he believe there is not one that could have grown to be a great man if given the chance? Does he not every day of his life believe that one of those children could have grown up to save Liberia. Can a man like John T. Richardson not believe there was not a better, more human boy than him, than Taylor? Not one who understood civilization and the value of life, the power of it, the potential for good?

Richardson did not die in his war. But his war did plunge the country into a place that, for the past five decades, on his watch, has become a very efficient place to die. It was his guns, his inhuman brutality, his arrogance that bred dysentery, starvation, AIDs, and Ebola that haunt Liberia to this day, the direct result of war.

The world does indeed notice that he did not die, but that maybe his war killed the next Biko, Mandela, or maybe it's Ghandi.

And all Liberia got was General John T. Richardson.

. . . .

When this part of the civil war ended a decade later, 200,000 Liberians would be dead or injured, half the population displaced, with no resolution to the rebellion; ten years and all that goes with that, death, disease, destroyed resources. In 1990, every person in Liberia was dependent on international food aid. Everyone. The country had essentially stopped producing a recognizable food supply, not considering eating all the domestic animals and widespread and well-documented cannibalism. Liberia went without electricity or running water from 1990-1997.

Fifty-thousand already dead with another 200,000 to follow, as many from disease and starvation as from bullets and mortar, random murder and tribal genocide.

47

Jehuu

YOU WALK INTO a dirty restroom and turn around, disgusted by the conditions.

Liberians shit where they stand, in front of you, on a sandy beach, a pristine coast turned into a litter box.

You see a teenager with dangerous eyes, pants slung low and the walk of a predator and you cross the street.

Liberians watch kids warily every day, not knowing the intent or lethality of the malnourished child with dead, drug-filled eyes, teenage hormones toggling between frenzied depression and hectic rage. They wonder if that kid will cross the street behind them and cut their throat. Demand, Give me six feet! You wonder who they are, how they became such different humans from you and me.

You drive into a rough part of town and roll up your windows and lock your doors.

Liberians like me walk for almost two years under constant gunfire, as steady as you might hear traffic in the city or crickets in the suburb. My family and I walk into a city, round a corner and bullets fly into buildings and space and people. Soldiers in camouflage, boys and girls in ridiculous clothes, tug at their own heavy weapons to fire back. We wade through spent ammo casings hot to the touch, ankle deep in streets riddled with corpses.

Here we drink water from a plastic bottle, careful to stay hydrated and healthy.

Liberians share a cup of water a day with the children walking to and from Red Cross refugee shelters. Adults don't drink that day.

You see a homeless person on the side of the road and turn away, refuse to make eye contact.

Everyone you see on the roads in Liberia is homeless. Thousands of thousands, day in day out, Liberians with no home, 1.4 million displaced during the civil wars. No place to put your stuff, everything you own on your back, your head, the only food you have is what you carry.

Look around your house, count the things you use every day, grab a spoon to stir your coffee or eat your cereal, fill a glass with tap water, open a door into your bedroom, turn on a light to read, look at your stove to cook, microwave to heat leftovers, fridge to keep food.

A million plus Liberians homeless, houseless.

Turn left in Liberia you might die. The mortality rate in Liberia during the civil war was one in four.

Turn left in the United States you're safe.

Turn right in Liberia, if you're a girl or a small boy, and you are almost assuredly raped. Seventy-five percent of them.

Turn left again in the United States, nobody waiting to cut off your head, light you on fire. Nobody will slice off the soles of your feet, eat your heart, take you or your child and hand them a rifle and point them in the direction of death. Run into one person who knows your father's tribe, and if it's wrong at that time and place, you are dead.

Just because they can.

. . . .

The vagaries of this existence, the randomness of life and death, are manifested in the world I inhabited the first seven years of my life. My family had some resources, contacts, friends. Their hospitality and philanthropy bought us some good will. That was a big factor in my survival. But I know lived where so many others didn't. I did little to make this happen. I was not braver or craftier, or more of anything really. My cousin Joseph was no different; a bullet fired blindly though a wall into a house occupied the same space as him, and he died by the whims of a random soldier with a mass-marketed AK47. The barrel of the weapon swept exactly wrong, the finger squeezed precisely in that fatal moment. Those moments were all over the place in Liberia.

And I sat one seat over, not where Joseph was murdered. I sat still (a rarity) and didn't rise and wrestle and play in that instant. Joseph died, and I moved on to the next thing. My life and death didn't overlap on that day.

Do I think I'm on borrowed time?

Do I think I owe the world something?

You're damn right I do.

The bullet doesn't pick and choose.

48

Liberia

THE COLOSSAL DAMAGE caused by the civil wars has kept Liberia staggering, even to this day.

Electricity in urban areas delivers around thirty-four percent of the daily need. In rural parts, it's zero. No electricity. Monrovia has a borough called West End that's eighty-thousand people crammed into a single square mile. That's living your life in a football stadium on game day. Imagine getting a drink of water, a meal, taking a shit. Traveling there is like going to the moon, just warmer, with more gravity and less math.

When Jehuu was a Liberian refugee, in the late 1980s to early 90s, it was the most dangerous place on Earth. It was Beirut on a steroid rage. Iraq, Libya, or Northern Ireland, only worse. Books say it was technically two civil wars, but that distinction is lost on the 1.4 million displaced Liberians and the quarter million that died over that period. It was ten-plus years of consistent turmoil and human suffering, an atrocity-filled decade. It was Armageddon. It begat AIDs and Ebola epidemics that torture the people today. The wars filled Liberia with unwanted children, seventy-five percent of Liberian women were raped in that decade. It transformed a peaceful, beautiful, resource-rich country into a petri dish of poverty and disease and human suffering.

The countryside was raided and burned in a scorched-Earth delirium that ravaged crops, livestock, chattel, and natural global-market resources, leaving a nation of hungry and poor to get hungrier and poorer. Bands of rebels, smelling blood, invaded from border countries, armed to the teeth with state-of-the-art killing munitions. Children as young as nine years old were recruited, stolen from murdered parents, handed automatic weapons and rocket launchers, and let loose on a docile and unassuming nation. Over 20,000 child-soldiers were weaponized, a combustion engine of innocence and killing potential, fueled with heroin and testosterone, forced into the service of evil adults unimpressed with humanitarian sensitivities. By the end of 1990, every single civilian in Liberia was dependent on international food aid.

Liberians were killed in ways you couldn't invent in your wildest, most vivid nightmares. People wrapped in mattresses and lit on fire. The souls of feet cut off. Babies carved out of pregnant women so men could bet on the gender. Little kids eaten (yes, eaten). Historically, the Liberia population increases at an average of almost three percent annually. At the height of the civil war in 1990, when the weapons were the best, it dropped almost a full percentage point. For that five-year stretch, Liberians were being killed exponentially faster than they could be replaced by birth rates. The country was dying.

What do civilized people do with that, the idea, the history, the presence of such possibility? How do they live in a place where people can remember such savagery, where echoes of those atrocities exist, where the real ghosts of bodies piled in ditches haunt the landscape? A place where words like massacre, murder, genocide, words like warlords and rape are used without exaggeration, with total certainty.

. . . .

In the United States, there are safe havens, people in uniform you can turn to, places where the mighty are moral and sane.

You can usually go to a police officer and find relief from danger (usually, not always). You can count on the military of your country for broader relief. Maybe the clergy or houses of worship for physical and emotional sanctuary.

In Liberia, during their civil wars, those havens had inherent fault lines, demons inside once-trusted institutions doing what demons do. The only relief from danger, death, mutilation, rape, and horror was luck and a reliance on the very people who could do the least about it. The general population, some two million, were reasonable, peaceable people. This is not a warring country overflowing with malice. It is a place of religion, all kinds, and the people who practice holy, dutiful, moral lives.

But the warriors, those responsible for the wars and the savagery, those people were all very bad, evil at their core no matter their excuses for the way they acted, not nearly enough noble actors wielded power. Charles Taylor, ECOMOG, Liberian military, one despot after another, lined up without a scorecard, words like patriot, national, liberating woven into their civil-war titles, meant to suggest righteousness, a jingoistic press to commit atrocities.

Woman and children first has always been a battle cry of the civilized. It's understood that the vulnerable need protection, deserve a chance at life surrounded by the honorable and the strong. In Africa, in Liberia, in those civil wars, the vulnerable were drooled over as prey, as easy targets, as a resource for brutality. The sick and elderly burned alive, women raped and enslaved as sex chattel, children weaponized and ruined, picked off from the herd as orphans, killed, starved, used as human sacrifice. Eaten alive by inhuman actors calling themselves men. Those not slaughtered were forced into hell, drugged, whipped, or confused into killing. The countryside was ravaged by pirates posing as liberators, a generation of animals and crops, and every renewable resource gone, sold off to the highest bidders. Devoured like a field of wheat before a biblical swarm of locusts. No offspring, no crops, and nobody to re-plant.

49

Jehuu

THE HAY HAS to be brought in and the Dueink's hired hands aren't available to sling the bales into the barn.

Winter is just around the corner; trees have gone from peeping season, to bare-branched minimalism.

When a Clymer family has a need, a series of things happen:

1. The family does not complain or ask for help. They work on the project without sleep, if need be, until the task is completed.
2. Someone discovers their need, rumors at the diner, church, or school.
3. The town lines up and finishes the needed task in record time.

This year it was the Dueink's who need help. My football team arrives at the farm at sun-up. We peel ourselves out of cars and trucks and we roll up sleeves. The hay won't wait, so we start slinging it into the barn.

We're barn-raisers in Clymer, we got each other's backs.

50

Bonita

BC: It was really scary.

There is finally a recognition of what the family had been through, what her family endured getting Jehuu and Mardea out of Liberia. Meeting her kids again after two years, very different human beings than the little children she left, was harrowing.

BC: People can try to understand that, but you never will until you're in that situation. If I could have found anybody to get them out of there, even if they wanted to adopt them, I would have given them to that person. I just wanted it to be over.

When Bonita talks about her kids and their time in Liberia, she is alternately nostalgic and emotional; a mother trapped in the memory of two years of exile from their existence in a place no mother would wish on any child.

BC: It [talking about my story] clears things up for me too. Last time, it really hit me, and I was really sad. When I was leaving them with my parents, I didn't feel like I was leaving them alone, but it hit me, how could I have done that? It really bothered me. I called Jehuu, and I was crying.

He said, you didn't do anything wrong. You did what was for the best. It was you making a better life for us.

It's really sad that the whole time they were down there and I was here. And the things they were going through. Whenever we talk about it, it really hurts me so bad.

Well, maybe now you can get past those feelings of sadness. Bonita, you wouldn't have survived that time in Liberia. The kids weren't noticed by the wrong people because they were so young and your parents were old enough. They would have not survived if you were there. You couldn't have done it any better than you did.

BC: It hits me...when the whole thing was going on, who could get them out. If anyone who wants a child can have a child, they can have them if they can go get them out. I thank God for looking ahead and making it work out.

You did as good as any mom could.

BC: I appreciate that. I'm very grateful for that. How do you come from all that and become the people they are now?

Epilogue

A Child Soldier

GHOST SURVIVES OPERATION Octopus.

One of only a handful of Small Boys who went into the swamp, he actually breaches the perimeter of the city. He sits at the Ducor Hotel and watches the shells pulverize that which has already been pulverized.

When he can no longer find food that isn't most probably human flesh, he returns to Harbel and Firestone, wandering a path through the suburbs of the capital city that he knows from previous patrols. At Firestone, he takes up his old residence, in the brush off the trail at the top of the hill.

He is completely alone.

Jehuu

Today, I'm a Liberian boy again.

I'm Jehuu, fussy, spoiled, sure, but mischievous too.

My family lives in a house in the country. There's a road in front of my house, but behind stretches into a New York forest, a place where a young boy can run and play, pretend to be the great football player from the Denver Broncos, Terrell Davis, number thirty. A boy can dodge and weave, outsmart the defense and *run run run*.

Today, I have another plan, another play. Our neighbors are Mr. and Mrs. Shade. The house we have now was once theirs; they moved next door. We share a bordered back yard. They have the best tree for climbing, like those Liberian mangroves.

When mum isn't looking, I sneak into the kitchen cupboard. (I don't fit inside this one, like the ones at the house on Allison Street in Buchanan. They must be smaller. I'm bigger.) Instead of crawling in and waiting for the war to pass, I pull out a pot and large metal spoon.

Along the edge of the woods, so nobody sees me, I pass from my yard to the Shades'. Then I scramble up the tree, not easy with a pot and spoon, but I can climb! Done it before in trees harder, in times harder. The beautiful leaves hide me; it's fall here. I settle my butt against a heavy branch and bang the pot and spoon together. Five times, *clang-ring, clang-ring, clang-ring, clang-ring, clang-ring.* The sound bounces off the back of the houses, dies in the thick trees.

Then I stop.

Mrs. Shade, Audrey, comes out the back door and stands on her porch. She puts her hands on her hip and frowns into the back yard. I'm quiet, cover my mouth with the back of my hand to stifle my giggle. I know how to be small, quiet, in a tree so people don't notice Jehuu. She shakes her head and goes back inside.

I wait. It's hard, waiting.

After what feels like an hour, I bang again, *clang-ring, clang-ring, clang-ring, clang-ring, clang-ring.*

I wait.

She comes back out. If I didn't know better, I could see the corners of her mouth tug upward. This time she says to the tree, "Now whatever could that racket be in my back yard?" She shakes her head, hair tosses in the light breeze. She goes back in the house, but this time I see her face in the backdoor window. She's spying me.

I fooled her; she doesn't know it's me.

I laugh, long and hard.

A Child Soldier

When the F14's start strafing and bombing HARBEL, Ghost's mirror shatters. He looks into the fragments scattered on the ground and sees himself, splinters of his face, his chest, his scars. *Which one you today? Which scars are yours, which ones belong to Ghost and which to Hope? Are you Hope with a dead mum, and a pa burnt alive? Or are you a Ghost who shoots at babies, burns people, stabs, cuts, eats hearts.*

Government forces have decided to put a stop to the unholy relationship between Firestone and Taylor. They do it in spectacularly clumsy fashion. Two Nigerian Alpha jets belonging to ECOMOG fly south to Harbel. The jets are officially aiming for arms depots and the plantation communication center. Instead, they strafe a soccer field killing thirty-eight Liberian employees having an afternoon match. Ninety-eight more wounded. None of the eighteen non-Liberian workers, including seven Americans, are harmed.

The attack played out as if ECOMOG targeted native Liberians, more propaganda fuel for Taylor.

We confirm that employees and relatives at the company's rubber plantation in Liberia were killed during a bombing raid on Nov. 2, says Trevor Hoskins, a spokesman at the company's Nashville office. *The wounded are being treated at the company's hospital in Harbel. We are very concerned about the situation. We are not operating our plantations at the moment.*

To this day, not one person has been brought to justice or held accountable for Operation Octopus.

Jehuu

"Only when the tree is big and strong
can you tether a cow to it."
—*Liberia saying*

The Caulcrick family

Lightening to the south.

A brilliant strobe bruises the sky above the home team press box, not a serrated electrical discharge heaven to Earth, but a blast of light, the signature of a late summer squall.

That's South, I think. It's raining somewhere. *Storm's coming.* I remember, when I was young, and the lights flashed behind my eyes, and I dreamed of Liberia.

Kickoff is seven o'clock, the weather is perfect for football; you could wear long sleeves or short, depending on your preference, that kind of temperature. Grass field, fresh cut, sharp white yard-lines vivid against a dark green field.

My team is up 7-0 early in the game. We scored on the first drive. They get the ball and they go down and score, now it's 7-6 we're still winning, but that's when I see the kids hang their heads because they have some adversity facing them.

Now we're losing in the second quarter. Trouble. But not real trouble, football trouble.

Coaching football, my first year, keeps me in the game I love, the one that brought me so much.

After I quit playing, I remember being at a Buffalo Bills game and realizing that I didn't miss being out there, the grind, the routine, the effort. But I did miss the game, the locker room, the camaraderie you get from physical battle. The first few years out of the game, I wanted nothing to do with High School football. I did some broadcasting with Time Warner Cable Sports locally a couple years. I did public speaking in California for a few years. Then I'm home golfing with some friends and someone says, *You should come to a practice at a local school.* I go, take the running backs through a few drills, next thing you know I'm there the whole season. Had a blast. Stayed the whole year.

I was never nervous as a player being bigger, stronger, faster. But I'm a nervous coach. I tried to install the basics I learned from Coach D at Michigan State. I call him every now and then when practices go sideways. Me and my staff at this school haven't been here long enough to form leaders, the ones that say *C'mon, let's go! We still got this!* Stuff I used to say when I played high school with my boys, Milecki, White, and Nickerson. It was so easy when I played, You give me five, and I'll give you five, and we'll never have to worry about a first down.

But now, at my first head job, my staff and I only had a month to practice with these kids. Did they really buy in? We have three captains, one yells and nobody listens to him. One who leads by example and only a few kids who can follow the lead. One who's just happy to be there.

Liberia

The fighting in Liberia continues, a constant phenomenon.

Liberia's seven basic fighting factions, the National Patriotic Front of Liberia (NPFL), the United Liberation Movement with two wings referred to as ULIMO-J and ULIMO-K, the Liberia Peace Council, NPFL-CRC, the Lofa Defense Force, and remnants of the Armed Forces of Liberia loyal to former president Samuel K. Doe, continued to fight throughout the later 1990s.

Operation Octopus turned the civil war into a bloodbath free-for-all, five years of an outlaw resource-grab for diamonds, timber, and power. Any warlord who could recruit or steal a dozen or more capable trigger-fingers had free reign on the country, a perverted army of reverse Robin Hoods was unleashed with Operation Octopus, a decade-long Purge movie series.

In 1997, Taylor was elected president of Liberia, a fact that left the rest of the world stunned, the population resigned to biting that bullet if it ended the bloodshed.

Sadly, it was too late, too many factions, too many weapons, too much anarchy. The atomic fallout from Operation Octopus was radiation released onto Liberia, death and misery from that cloud of horror that hasn't dissipated to this day.

Ghost disappeared back into the Wuteve Mountains.

Jehuu

The eyes of more than a few parents burn a hole in the back of my head as I coach their children through a football game.

And we struggle. A dropped pass, missed blocking assignment, whiffed tackle. The ball bounces to them more than us. The referees seem to hate us.

This has been my first game plan, first team bus ride, first warm-up, first everything. We aren't where we need to be as a team, I knew that, but didn't believe it until tonight. We had basically a short month of practice, no real pre-season. No time to build a culture through shared sacrifice. Both offense and defensive lines cobbled with kids who think they should be running, throwing, catching, and scoring touchdowns. They want their name in the paper. None of them want to block or tackle. It shows, not one of my linemen has reps from last year.

One month to install a program. One month to develop trust, rapport, system buy-in. It's a good group of kids, just not great football players. If you don't have great players, you have to out-program the other guys to win, and we only had six weeks to get ready.

I really believe I surrounded myself with the best coaching staff in the county. Still, at the end of the day, I'm the one who has to answer the questions. Going into this game, I never had a doubt we were going to win. Even when they put up thirty-eight points, I think, *Hey, we can do it too. Put up 39, 40.* That sense of belief, my competitive nature. It's never too deep of a hole, start digging!

A little over two minutes left before half and we're gaining on the game, down ten points driving in for a late score. From the sideline I call, *Trips hitch flag Y post. Look for the double, throw to the other side. Got it?* My quarterback squints through his facemask, nods. *Don't jump. No penalties.* Nods again.

A warm breeze brushes my face, the stadium lights show it blowing in the tree tops. It tugs silently at my clothes. It carries crowd noise, the sounds on the field of athletic labor from sincere kids. It carries a Western New York fall chill, the smell of leaves and grass, sweat and dirt.

You only see evidence of wind, not the wind itself. Same for things like trust, belief, courage.

Storm's coming.

Coaching these kids sends me back, back to when I was in their position. They haven't been there, fresh faces who don't really see what they're looking at, out of eyes that scan across the line of scrimmage and search for information, for openings, for opportunity.

443

They don't know yet that they will be doing this the rest of their lives, looking, finding, achieving or failing, and looking again. It's hard because I've looked and I've seen, more than them, definitely when it comes to football,

More of life. Much more of death.

I take a quick look into the stands, scan the crowd. They're sincere too, watching their kids win and lose, achieve and fail, play after play. Like my mum watched me years ago on the fields at Clymer, East Lansing, the NFL. Like my grandparents did on the streets of a war-shredded African country. Mom is here somewhere, watching me coach, pacing, fretting. She won't sit at games anymore, whether I'm playing or coaching, too nervous. It's a thing with her, I've noticed. She doesn't sit when I stand. She's the only one there who has a taste of what I've seen and done. And not even she knows all of it. She wasn't there when I paced and fretted all through Liberia.

These people, they don't know either. But that's not their fault, how could they? There isn't a person in the world, hell in the history of the world, who's walked the same convoluted path I've walked. To understand my life, from crib to coffin, isn't like anyone else's even in the broadest strokes imaginable. Nobody can really fathom walking over dead bodies in a street, wading through shell casings ankle deep, having a bullet graze your cheek and bury itself into your cousin sitting arm in arm with you on a couch; climbing in a private jet to go play football in a stadium in London, England in front of a hundred-thousand amused, confused football fans.

That won't happen again. To anyone.

I'm that one person in a million.

The sky flashes on, klieg-lights frame the football field, ghostly white remnants on the retina, reminiscent of my history. In a Buffalo Bills uniform, fireworks at Ralph Wilson Stadium, the Jumbotron in East Lansing flashing cheer-commands at the Spartan faithful, the flare of a camera at Clymer High School, sunlight glare off a rebel tank, the explosion of an AK47 by the side of the road outside Buchanan, Liberia.

My first game in the headset and there's trouble.
But not real trouble, just football trouble.

END

Jehuu and the Author

Acknowledgements

A Special Thank You to a Few Benefactors who made the publishing of this story possible.

James and Linda Sasone
Mary Kang
The Weatherby Clan (Whitey, Harriet, K-man, and Dana)
AB -Adam Barone
Bocko -Steph Boskin

Joanna Caulcrick
The Chautauqua County Hall of Fame

Tom Marra
Bald Timmy -Tim Beloat. Your financial faith in this project was above and beyond.

CROMEY! -Debbie Cromey. Your faith in my abilities far surpassed my own. Thank you for, quite literally, everything.

www.ingramcontent.com/pod-product-compliance
Lightning Source LLC
Chambersburg PA
CBHW020428130626
46549CB00001B/32